Stormy Petrel

TRICENTENNIAL STUDIES, NUMBER 8

This volume is part of a series of *Tricentennial Studies,* published by the University of South Carolina Press on behalf of the South Carolina Tricentennial Commission, to commemorate the founding of South Carolina in 1670.

STORMY
PETREL

N. G. Gonzales and His State

Lewis Pinckney Jones

Published for the
South Carolina Tricentennial Commission
by the
UNIVERSITY OF SOUTH CAROLINA PRESS
Columbia, South Carolina

FIRST EDITION

Published in Columbia, South Carolina, by the
University of South Carolina Press, 1973

Manufactured in the United States of America

Library of Congress Cataloging in Publication Data

Jones, Lewis P.
    Stormy petrel.

    (Tricentennial studies, no. 8)
    Bibliography: p.
    1. Gonzales, Narciso Gener, 1858–1903.
2. The State, Columbia, S. C. I. Title.
II. Series: South Carolina Tricentennial
Commission. Tricentennial studies, no. 8.
PN4874.G537J6   070.5′092′4 [B]   73-8792
ISBN 0-87249-253-2

DEDICATED TO a wife named Denny, who had the patience to tolerate this undertaking and the impatience adequate to prod the author to finish it; and

WRITTEN FOR Barney, Faris, Meng, and Charles, who had very little to do with it but who might like it in due season.

CONTENTS

PREFACE

THE BEST-KNOWN JOURNALIST YET PRODUCED IN SOUTH Carolina was N. G. Gonzales (1858–1903), a founder of *The State* newspaper of Columbia and its first editor. He was also perhaps the stormiest journalist in the state, as well as one who had as much influence on public affairs as any other editor. Naturally, judgments on such an intensely controversial person have conflicted, but few would question his significance. He was best known in his day as the leading voice in the opposition to the "Farmers' Revolt" (itself maybe a misnomer) headed by Benjamin Ryan Tillman.

This biography of N. G. Gonzales stems from a study of the Gonzales family which also examined the history of *The State* newspaper until 1937. That narrative, much over twice as long as this book, centered largely around the careers of William Elliott and the three Gonzales brothers of *The State:* N. G., Ambrose, and William E. Gonzales.

The present story is that of Narciso Gonzales, whose initials "N. G. G." at the end of his columns early became a hallmark in South Carolina journalism. The reader will note what may seem an inordinately long introductory section and much about the youthful Ambrose Gonzales. There are two reasons. First, one must perceive the background of a man with a Cuban name to understand why he was so intensely Carolinian and why he took the philosophical and political positions that he did. Second, his youth showed traits and characteristics which forecast the man with amazing accuracy. Another reason for the long introduction was the author's fondness for Ambrose Gonzales, whom N. G. so admired. I regret that space limitations practically rule him out of this story after his youth.

The title, *Stormy Petrel: N. G. Gonzales and His State,* may be misleading. If so, the ambiguity was intended. Whether the "State" of the title refers to the newspaper or to South Carolina is inconsequential. When writing of the career and the controversies of N. G. Gonzales, one is necessarily dealing with both. For those years, the story of *The State* is also the story of the state.

I am indebted to many: to the library staffs of the University of North Carolina, the South Caroliniana Library, and Duke University. I gained much from hours of talk and reminiscing with many people, especially Miss Harriett R. E. Gonzales and Editor "Billy" Ball. Whatever academic credit this work may have must go to Professor Fletcher M. Green of the University of North Carolina, who provided inspiration and guaranteed perspiration. No less important than his scholarship was the undergirding of a good wife named Denny.

LEWIS PINCKNEY JONES
Wofford College
June 1973

Stormy Petrel

CHAPTER I

A Cuban's Origins in Carolina

OPPOSITE THE STATE HOUSE IN COLUMBIA, SOUTH CARO-lina, on the sidewalk of the main intersection of the city (Main and Gervais) a man lay shot and dying. He was the best-known newspaper editor in the state, but famous also beyond its borders. Standing a few feet away, still holding his smoking pistol, was the wounded journalist's assailant, the lieutenant-governor of South Carolina.

Into this dramatic crucible had poured not just the personal antagonism of these two high-spirited personalities. The 1903 assassination was much more than the climax of a vendetta. It was the product of major historic forces which had dominated and determined the course of South Carolina history for a generation, forces which had roots that went back much earlier than that.

The slain editor was the stormy petrel of South Carolina journalism. He was an outspoken defender of the Bourbon regime and yet not a typical Bourbon Conservative. His assassin was a stormy petrel of Tillmanism, which as "the

1

Reform Movement" had led a revolt against Bourbonism. But the man with the gun was not a typical Reformer, nor was he noted for reforms.

The career of the high-spirited journalist is an intriguing one that cannot be divorced from the biography of his family, and especially from that of his brothers. Despite his name, which hardly sounds Carolinian, Narciso Gener Gonzales was as wholly South Carolinian as the palmetto tree, which is the symbol and trademark gracing the front page of the newspaper he founded, *The State*. The name was Cuban, but the man was a South Carolinian with an intense pride in his state, a fierce devotion to the mores of the past of which he was a product, and a burning determination to usher in a progressive present that would provide more genuine reforms than the Tillman Reformers against whom his career had become a crusade.

More than most men, Gonzales was a product of his background. Without a grasp of it, one finds it difficult to explain this controversial defender of the Bourbons, this man with the Cuban name who was so intensely South Carolinian. The tributary streams which converged in his intriguing personality help to explain the tragedy which marked the end of his career.

The killing itself cannot be separated, however, from many of the ingredients which had characterized much of the history of South Carolina: violence, caused by pride and heightened by the widespread habit of a population in which all classes were accustomed to carrying guns; political partisanship, too often furthered more by emotionalism than by judicious, tolerant reasoning; class lines, more emphasized than bridged; and pride itself, often built on justified self-respect but also often marked by petulance and arrogance. Maybe South Carolina truly deserved its nickname, the Hotspur State.

Particularly unfortunate perhaps was the fact that so

many South Carolinians actually prided themselves on the fact that South Carolina was called the Hotspur State. Too many preferred to be known as swashbucklers. Too often a politician preferred a reputation of being "one hell of a fellow" rather than that of a constructive statesman; obstructionism seemed to be the road to success regardless of what this stance did for South Carolina.

The man with the gun was one of those swashbucklers, Lieutenant-Governor James H. Tillman. In contrast, his victim, N. G. Gonzales, undoubtedly would have depicted himself as a devotee of progress, law and order, and decency. He was. And yet his own career in pursuit of these aims had been marked by harshness and intemperance of language which had made him famed afar as an ill-tempered firebrand. His judgments were sincere but often were compounded and stated with a note of self-righteousness that infuriated his opponents. His devotion to a better balanced economy and his acceptance of some progressive changes and reforms sometimes made this Bourbon spokesman not altogether orthodox in the Conservative hierarchy.

As a journalist, his fame rested on his position as the leading opponent of Benjamin R. Tillman—uncle to Jim Tillman—who, in 1890, had led the successful Farmers' Revolt, a part of the national agrarian crusade, which had unseated the Bourbon regime that had ruled the state since its "redemption" from Radical Reconstruction in 1876. Gonzales wrote pungently and incisively, striking his blows with a stiletto rather than with a meat cleaver. There were many in 1903 who were not surprised at the manner of his death after some of the tempestuous Gonzales-Tillman clashes— especially after the 1902 gubernatorial campaign in which Jim Tillman had been defeated.

The editor was the product of a unique marriage that had taken place in 1856 in the shade of the ancient, moss-

draped live oaks of an opulent, aristocratic coastal plantation, Oak Lawn. The bride was an Elliott, and her lineage
included names long revered in that part of the world—Barnwells, Rutledges, Pinckneys, Gibbeses, Rhetts, and others.
But to the surprise of many and undoubtedly to the horror
of a few, the groom was hardly a typical member of the
closed circle that was the low-country gentry: a dashing, impecunious soldier of fortune, a revolutionary, Ambrosio
José Gonzales, late of Cuba but now with no fixed abode or
occupation. From this union were to come six children,
including three brothers who made their mark as journalists: Ambrose Elliott Gonzales, N. G. Gonzales, and William Elliott Gonzales.

Perhaps their fire and ginger came from their father, but
much of their viewpoint came from their maternal grandfather, William Elliott (1788–1863), and from their rearing at Oak Lawn by the feminine members of the Elliott
family. Pride came from both lineages.

William Elliott, father of Harriett Elliott, the 1856 bride,
was one of the more prominent South Carolina planters.
Famed as a sportsman, political nonconformist (as befitted
a close friend of James L. Petigru), musician, writer (best
known for *Carolina Sports*), and widely traveled *bon vivant*,
he was basically a patriarch with a family empire of "fiefs"
scattered in the area between Charleston and Savannah, with
a town house in Beaufort, and the family capital at Oak
Lawn Plantation near the village of Adams Run.[1] (The
plantation there is still intact, its name coming from the
gigantic oaks planted early in the eighteenth century.)

Educated at Harvard, Elliott was steeped in classical
erudition. Most of his contemporaries knew him for his

---

[1] For a brief account of the "Old Sportsman," see Lewis P. Jones, "William Elliott, South Carolina Nonconformist," in *Journal of Southern History*, XVIII (August 1951), 361–81.

sportsman's book (which still sells!) or for his scientific agricultural articles in farm journals, where he became known for frequent attacks on wasteful practices and for demands for progressive reforms. His close associates and family knew his writing from his numerous letters—entertaining concoctions of wit, drollness, philosophy, sermonizing, and chiding, but letters always marked by obvious affection for his family. Rarely writing anything not entertaining, however trite the subject matter, Elliott penned letters far more charming than any of his published writing.[2]

Proud of his family and its heritage, determined to provide the advantages of society, travel, and education for his children, Elliott accepted a status quo which gave blessing to an aristocracy and to human slavery. This true and witty aristocrat nevertheless always stressed that with the privileges of class went responsibilities, humanitarianism, and generosity. As a slaveholder he was known as a kind master, "often imposed upon, chiefly by having Negro slaves, whom he didn't need, 'wished' upon him by widowed ladies, who, renouncing the responsibilities of planting, sought humane masters for the slaves they were forced to sell."[3] His attitude toward his state was almost a mystic love affair, his calling cards scattered during his numerous travels to the North and abroad simply noting "William Elliott of South Carolina."

Despite the hopes of a doting and conscientious father (whose most satisfying heir apparently seemed to be his son Ralph), the "Old Sportsman's" ideas and personality were

[2] His grandson, Ambrose Gonzales, said that his brother N. G. had inherited Elliott's gift as "a delightful letter writer." After reading many of their epistles, the present writer can testify that the compliment applies as much to Ambrose and also to his sister Harriett, who lived until 1957. See Ambrose Gonzales' comment in letter to Yates Snowden, May 24, 1926, in Yates Snowden Papers, South Caroliniana Library.

[3] A. E. Gonzales to Yates Snowden, May 24, 1926, in Snowden Papers.

not to be perpetuated with the Elliott name. William Elliott and his "Elliott world" were to be carried on by the three Gonzales boys, his grandsons. (A partial family tree is provided in the Appendix.)

The youngest of William Elliott's children was Harriett, who left home in January 1855, at the age of fifteen, for formal education at Madame Togno's private school in Charleston. Like all other family members separated from Elliott, "Hattie" was soon getting long epistles of advice, but her father was hopeful for her because he had "observed that your reason though not yet strong on the wing, makes short but successful flights to a sound conclusion."[4] Within months it had made a quick and astonishing flight to what the family must have thought an unsound conclusion. The schoolgirl, then aged sixteen, was engaged to a Cuban "filibuster," a "general" aged thirty-eight: Ambrosio José Gonzales.

This Cuban who so abruptly crashed into the Elliott world was the son of a teacher and journalist at Matanzas and had attended a New York boys' school where he had been a classmate of P. G. T. Beauregard, for whom he always had a striking resemblance. Completing his education at the University of Havana in 1839, he became a schoolteacher. In the 1840s he tied his fortunes to those of Narciso López, a colorful Venezuelan soldier of fortune who fled to the United States in 1848 after an unsuccessful plot to overturn Spanish control of the island.

After this, the plot leaders, wealthy planters and slaveholders, sought to promote annexation to the United States as a substitute for Spanish authority. They sent Gonzales

4 William Elliott to Harriett Elliott, January 22, 1855, in Elliott-Gonzales Papers, in Southern Historical Collection, University of North Carolina Library; hereinafter cited as E.G.P.

to the United States to renew contacts with López and to seek to hire an army of volunteers ("filibusters") to land in Cuba and liberate it from its masters. He was considered a good choice for this assignment because he was "an excellent mediator, an ardent patriot, very cultured, young, and one who spoke English perfectly."[5] Because of its proslavery overtones, the movement could look for support to the South, where some leaders were envisioning more slave states which might be created in the two-step process that had been followed by Texas—first, breaking from Mexico (1836) and second, subsequent annexation (1845).

The Cuban revolutionaries were busy in Washington and especially in the lower Mississippi Valley seeking aid and recruits, but stirring more interest than commitments. In late 1849, federal forces nipped a López expedition in the bud before it left from the Gulf Coast of Mississippi. Undaunted, the Cubans set forth from New Orleans in May 1850. Most of the adventurers were from Kentucky, Mississippi, and Louisiana (only 5 of the 610 were Cubans), but López was the leader, with "General" Gonzales, his second in command, described by one authority as "the very life and soul" of the venture.[6] Landing at Cárdenas (some 60 miles west of Havana) where the natives failed to rise to support them, the filibusters in a hair-raising race withdrew to Key West.

Undismayed, the Cuban patriots planned a third landing, with Gonzales establishing recruiting headquarters and assembling equipment at Savannah. Reports of a minor uprising in Cuba lured López into a premature departure from

[5] Herminio Portell Vilá, *Narciso López y Su Epoca*, 3 vols. (Havana: Cultural, S. A., 1930–1958), I, 239.
[6] Robert J. Caldwell, *López Expeditions to Cuba, 1848–1851* (Princeton: Princeton University Press, 1915), p. 72.

Louisiana in August 1851. At the time Gonzales, who had contracted fever on the Georgia coast, was recuperating at White Sulphur Springs, Virginia. He hurried back to take charge of his forces in Georgia, board their chartered steamer, and rendezvous with López in Cuba only to learn that the expedition had ended in utter failure and that López had been executed.

The remainder of the 1850s found Gonzales at loose ends but not diverted from his revolutionary efforts, but he and his Southern cohorts—especially John A. Quitman and John Slidell of Mississippi—became increasingly frustrated and disheartened, especially after the collapse of plans for a large "liberating expedition" in 1855.[7]

The decline of his revolutionary activity and plotting ended Gonzales' day of glory, but he was never to let this period or his efforts be forgotten or minimized. Records of him during this period are meager, but apparently he had a minor job with the State Department. It was then that he entered the Elliott circle, being on close terms with William Elliott's sons by 1852.[8] Perhaps his recruiting in the Savannah area had brought him to Oak Lawn; and definitely the family knew him at White Sulphur, saw him "frequently" in Washington, and were corresponding with him by 1854.[9]

Regardless of how it started, he visited the plantation in South Carolina and on December 11, 1855, became engaged

[7] A very condensed biographical sketch of General Gonzales is in Lewis P. Jones, "Ambrosio José Gonzales, a Cuban Patriot in Carolina," in *South Carolina Historical Magazine*, LVI (April 1955) , 67–76. Also, see Herminio Portell Vilá, *Vidas de la Unidad Americana* (Havana: Editorial Minerva, 1944) .

[8] Mrs. Mary W. Wayne to Mrs. William Elliott, August 11 and 18, 1852, in E.G.P.

[9] William Elliott, Jr., to Ralph Elliott, August 30, 1855; William Elliott to his wife, March 2, 1855; Mrs. Mary W. Wayne to Mrs. William Elliott, August 7, 1854, in E.G.P.

to the sixteen-year-old Harriett Elliott, who then had spent only a few months of her first formal schooling with Madame Togno in Charleston.[10] Returning to his clerk's job in Washington, he wrote frequently and passionately to his fiancée. Her friends meantime wrote to express amazement; one cousin delayed writing because she had thought the news a joke though she remembered "your General as an agreeable fellow . . . at Oak Lawn a year or two ago."[11] Schoolmates of the bride were astonished since she had expressed "resolutions to spend the next *two* years in hard study, at the North."[12]

After drawing up a marriage settlement with a bond of $10,000 to provide security for the bride, the Elliotts invited many prominent Carolinians to the wedding on April 17, 1856. The General and his young bride then went to Washington, where the State Department clerk moved in a social circle that included such notables as President and Mrs. Pierce and Secretary of War Jefferson Davis.[13] Letters to South Carolina during 1856 and 1857 do not reflect unusual activity, although the bride was pleased to hear the belief "that Gonzie would be Governor of Cuba."[14]

In 1857 Gonzales made efforts to secure a more important post under the new president. His failure evidently made his wife unhappy and critical, although he continued to be optimistic about his future.[15] His hopes seemed well founded since he was endorsed for a diplomatic post to Chile by

[10] A. J. Gonzales to Harriett Elliott, January 13, 1856; R. Acélio Togno to Emily Elliott, n.d., in E.G.P.
[11] Mrs. Mary E. Pinckney to Harriett Elliott, January 31, 1855, in E.G.P.
[12] "Marion" to Harriett Elliott, February 21, 1856, in E.G.P. There is a tradition that the family opposed the match at the time, but there is no evidence of this in the family papers.
[13] A. J. Gonzales to Harriett Elliott, January 27, 1856, and February 22, 1856, in E.G.P.
[14] Mrs. A. J. Gonzales to Mrs. William Elliott, October 23, (?), in E.G.P.
[15] A. J. Gonzales to his wife, September 7, 1857, in E.G.P.

prominent Democrats of nine Southern states.[16] Even his father-in-law called on Secretary of State Lewis Cass in his behalf; Elliott also learned from General Mirabeau Bonaparte Lamar that Gonzales could be made secretary of legation to Argentina, but the Carolinian did not think the General would be satisfied with that post.[17] The result of all this political maneuvering was that Gonzales received nothing and accepted William Elliott's suggestion in 1858 that he come to South Carolina and seek his Washington plums from a distance.[18] During this period he was in constant correspondence with other Cuban emigrés, never abandoning hope for a new revolution.[19]

On May 29, 1857, Ambrosio José Gonzales, Jr.—later to be known as Ambrose Elliott Gonzales—was born, and the following year on August 5 his brother first "sniffed the air of Edisto." The father wrote Ralph Elliott that he hoped that this second son, named Narciso Gener Gonzales, for two of his father's fellow patriots (Narciso López and Benigno Gener), would "give as much satisfaction and less trouble than his 'illustrious predecessor,' the 'little General' under your charge, and that your knees will be equal to the task when they both go to riding school upon them."[20]

Tense times soon provided the General with employment,

[16] Among others, they included Jefferson Davis, John Henderson, John A. Quitman, James H. Hammond, Robert Toombs, John Slidell, and Stephen R. Mallory. *The State,* August 2, 1893.

[17] William Elliott to his wife, n.d. (fragment), and A. J. Gonzales to his wife, October 27, 1857, in E.G.P.

[18] A. J. Gonzales to William Elliott, March 31, 1858, in E.G.P.

[19] Herminio Portell Vilá, *Vidas,* p. 376. This author says that Gonzales alienated South Carolinians by favoring abolition with compensation for slaveholders. No other evidence available to the present writer has substantiated this. It is also somewhat offset by a letter in which Gonzales invited James H. Hammond's attention to observations on slavery made by William Elliott. See A. J. Gonzales to James H. Hammond, May 9, 1858, in Hammond Papers, in Manuscripts Division, Library of Congress.

[20] A. J. Gonzales to Ralph Elliott, August 5, 1858, in E.G.P. N. G. Gonzales was born at Edingsville, seashore resort on Edisto Island.

for by 1860 he was active as a gun salesman to various Southern legislatures. In this pursuit he was associated with his old schoolmate, P. G. T. Beauregard. The Milledgeville *Recorder* reported how he demonstrated to the Georgia legislators his ability to hit the target nine out of ten times with his Maynard rifle.[21] To this group he also showed his grapeshot revolver—a terrifying machine with nine chambers and two barrels. Success marked his salesmanship, for Georgia bought a thousand rifles for which the salesman received a commission of $3,000. Meanwhile he was canvassing the South Carolina legislature through Ralph Elliott, his brother-in-law, who was serving his first term in that body.[22]

The Civil War restored briefly the glory that had once belonged to Gonzales and destroyed both the glory and the material foundations of the Elliotts' empire. The Cuban refugee entered Confederate service, his chief role being in coastal defense in South Carolina. He acquired some distinction for the "siege train" which he devised, a mobile coastal artillery unit which helped keep the Charleston-Savannah rail link intact during most of the war despite the large Union beachhead established in the nearby Port Royal area in November 1861. His greatest exertion seemed to be his war for rank; he was determined to be appointed a general and was acidulous in his condemnation of Jefferson Davis (whom he had known since his recruiting days) and the Confederacy for not showing proper appreciation for his ability. It was not his finest hour. The Confederacy did make him a colonel, but the title of 'general' which he used throughout his life had been bestowed on him by López in

---

[21] Clipping (n.d.) in letter of A. J. Gonzales to Ralph Elliott, November 28, 1860, in E.G.P.

[22] Ralph Elliott to Mrs. William Elliott, December 10, 1860, in E.G.P.

their 1850 expedition. During most of the war he was in the Charleston area.

Three of William Elliott's sons entered Confederate service. Two spent most of their military careers in South Carolina, constantly grousing about their fate. The third, Ralph (always pronounced "Rafe") seemed to "find himself" in the service and rose from the rank of private to that of captain.

In 1863 William Elliott, the old patriarch, died. One of the Elliott daughters died in 1862, and the husband of another was murdered in 1864 in his Flat Rock home by a band of Confederate deserters. The task of managing the family plantations now fell to Elliott's widow and her two surviving daughters. At least she did not have the whole task since some of the lands were occupied by Federal troops who held the sea islands around Port Royal and Hilton Head.

Toward the end of the war the women who had remained at Oak Lawn fled to Charleston, Darlington, Flat Rock, and Greenville. When they returned, they faced devastation: the old home at Oak Lawn burned by Sherman's troops, the plantation ruined, and other plantations on the sea islands confiscated. Later in 1865 the federal government granted clear title to Mrs. Elliott for four of them: Oak Lawn and three places on Cheeha Creek near the mouth of the Combahee River.

In early 1866 the remnants of the family began the sad trek back to the scenes of departed glory. William Elliott, Jr., the first to arrive, prepared the others with his description of the desolation which awaited them. The brick walls of the old English-style house still stood: "The skeleton that once encased the spirit (forever fled) of the Hospitality and Refinement of bygone days." He reported the trees, gardens, and shrubbery intact except those near the mansion, which were

as "blackened as the hearts of those who fired the house."
The china and crystal which had been buried were un-
touched, and the Negroes were working and "now civil."[23]
Like many ex-Confederates, Mrs. Elliott contemplated
emigration after the collapse of her fortunes, but in the end
she followed Bishop Stephen Elliott's advice and determined
to make the best of it. For a time she lived in her quite
dilapidated house at Adams Run. Later the family rebuilt
the old kitchen, and for several years lived in this cabin
which they called "The Ruins."[24]

In 1866 two Elliott sons, Ralph and William, were quite
unsuccessful in their attempts at farming at Oak Lawn and
at Social Hall (on Cheeha Creek). Their letters reflect total
frustration and resignation as the two aristocrats lived in
tents in the pines, ate terrapin "to break the monotony of
bacon," complained of lazy and undependable Negroes, and
longed for enough capital to acquire a sawmill.[25] After a long
and miserable illness, apparently tuberculosis, William died
on January 21, 1867. This left Ralph as the only male Elliott with his mother and sisters, and he determined "to
stick to the post—even though I die at it. . . . We are a
doomed people."[26]

If the war had seemingly wrecked the life of the Elliotts,
it had revised the future of the Gonzales wing of the family.
Actually, the postwar years were harder for them than they

[23] William Elliott, Jr., to Mrs. William Elliott, March 13, 1866, in E.G.P.
[24] Stephen Elliott to Mrs. William Elliott, August 2, 1865; M. W. Clement
to Mrs. William Elliott, January 16, 1866; Emily Elliott to Mrs. William
Elliott, "Saturday"; and Elliott Johnstone to [Emily Elliott], November 28,
1867, in E.G.P.
[25] William Elliott, Jr., to Mrs. Anne H. Elliott (Mrs. William Elliott),
May 25, 1865, in E.G.P. In contrast, they hardly sounded desperate as they
meandered from Darlington to Greenville, Flat Rock, Abbeville, and
Charleston.
[26] Ralph Elliott to T. R. S. Elliott, July 7, 1867, in T. R. S. Elliott
Papers, in Manuscripts Division, Duke University Library.

were for some of their more elderly relations, who certainly did not face their fate with stoicism, but rather bewailed their lot frequently and bitterly.

By the end of the war Mrs. Gonzales—Hattie Elliott— had four children: Ambrosio and Narciso, born before Fort Sumter; and during the war, Alfonso Beauregard—named for his father's friend the general—and Gertrude Rufini (also called Tulita), a daughter born in 1864. During much of the war Mrs. Gonzales and her brood lived at Oak Lawn with her mother and sisters, and in 1865 she "refugeed" with them. Peace found General Gonzales unemployed, unattached, and unadjusted—his normal state when divorced from military activity. Of material goods, only his horse remained.

Tracing his activities after the war is no easy task, for never did he take root. His biography resembles an itinerary. In late 1865 he made his first trip back to Cuba since his unconventional departure in 1848. His purpose was to find employment, but, finding none, he returned to South Carolina.[27]

In 1866 the Gonzales family set up housekeeping in Charleston—to the horror of the Elliotts.[28] As unreconstructed Ralph Elliott said, "This free nigger town is becoming very disgusting to me, and I pity poor Hattie having to live in it."[29] Nevertheless, her mother stayed there with her and "the chicks" while Gonzales made another quick trip to Cuba, this time returning in February 1866, again empty-handed.[30] Soon thereafter—April 24, 1866—a fourth

[27] Apparently he was gone by September and back by December. Cf. Elliott Johnstone to Mrs. Anne H. Elliott, September 5, 1865, and Richard DeTreville to Mrs. Anne H. Elliott, December 12, 1865, in E.G.P.
[28] Mrs. Mary E. Johnstone to Mrs. Anne H. Elliott, January 10, [1866] in E.G.P.
[29] Ralph Elliott to Emily Elliott, January 28, 1866, in E.G.P.
[30] Mrs. Anne H. Elliott to T. R. S. Elliott, January 20, [1866], in T. R. S. Elliott Papers.

son, Benigno (later called William Elliott), was born in Charleston. The father, however, was soon gone again, this time to New York where he became a teacher of Spanish and an interpreter, living frugally in order to send back to Charleston enough for the bare necessities of life.[31]

After abandoning this project, he undertook to follow in the steps of the Elliotts and become a Southern planter. In mid-1866 he initiated negotiations to buy two of the Elliott plantations from the estate of his father-in-law. Infested with loafing freedmen, the Cheeha lands had remained idle except for the little planting done there in 1866 by the two debilitated brothers, Ralph and William Elliott, Jr. Long and involved correspondence went on through 1866 about the sale, a transfer from one pauper to another. Desiring the pine trees of Social Hall and the grazing lands of The Bluff, the General offered Mrs. Elliott $17,000, giving his wife's discounted claims of $10,000 against the estate as part payment; his sister-in-law also lent him her credit in the form of a claim for $6,175 against the estate.[32] As a result of this intrafamily bookkeeping, the Cuban emigré and his family were installed by the fall of 1866 at Social Hall, part of the grandeur that had been the Elliott kingdom.[33]

Southern plantation life at Social Hall was no "big-white-house," "moonlight-and-roses" affair, but rather it was centered around the four one-room cabins that housed the family. In such a reduction in affluence, the adjustment was

[31] Portell Vilá, *Vidas*, p. 379.

[32] Both claims were for marriage bonds then provided for property that was then tied up in the estate of William Elliott. See A. J. Gonzales to Ralph Elliott, February 7, 1866; A. J. Gonzales' bond of May 15, 1866, to William C. Bee and Francis W. Johnstone, trustees for Mrs. Mary E. Johnstone; A. J. Gonzales to Ralph Elliott, May 31, 1866; and Richard DeTreville to Mrs. Anne H. Elliott, May 30, 1866, in E.G.P.

[33] Ralph Elliott, trustee for Mrs. Gonzales, took a dim view of these perplexing proceedings. See his memo to "My dear Brother," October 25, [1866], in E.G.P.

not to be made overnight. Despite their abject poverty, "Gonzie" and Hattie had two Irish maids and a Chinaman as servants—plus Negro helpers. Constant complaints about the Negroes' laziness filled family epistles, although Mrs. Gonzales admitted that her two Irish girls also "lack the refinements of language so striking in our former slaves."[34]

Despite the circumstances, one item was not neglected: the education of the Gonzales boys. This had been a family project during the war years when the boys had lived at Oak Lawn, where their training followed the best Elliott traditions. According to Ambrose, his brother N. G. learned to read at four, and both were trained by constant reading aloud from the two Charleston papers, the *Courier* and the *Mercury*.[35] Their Confederate enthusiasm did not wane when they "refugeed" to Darlington, where they sang patriotic songs in the woods and were wont "to sadden their hearts with Father Ryan's touching poetry."[36] Their grandmother praised their amazing intelligence and observed that "their fondness for girls is inherited as you know—their disobedience however may not be so certainly accounted for."[37] At Social Hall, their mother described traits that were to be frequently noted in the next few years: "Brosie" (Ambrose) was studious and also the most industrious of the children, doing everything to the utmost satisfaction of all his associates; "Nanno" (N. G.) often showed a warm temper and an all-pervading desire to curl up and read incessantly; and "Bory" (Alfonso Beauregard) preferred to do nothing, especially anything faintly re-

---

[34] Mrs. A. J. Gonzales to Emily Elliott, n.d. (fragment) , in E.G.P.

[35] A. E. Gonzales in foreword of N. G. Gonzales, *In Darkest Cuba* (Columbia: The State Company, 1922) , p. 10. This foreword includes a highly readable (but somewhat romanticized) sketch of their youth.

[36] *Ibid.*, p. 11.

[37] Mrs. Anne H. Elliott to Ralph Elliott, August 15, [1866], in E.G.P.

sembling study.[38] Their aunts aided by frequently sending
books to the omnivorous young readers—and by sometimes
upbraiding their mother for letting them do work which
they felt should be reserved for Negro labor.[39]

But grandeur was no more in vogue on the patrimony.
Various interests attracted the ever-hopeful Gonzales now
trying to start life anew in pursuits strange to him. His most
likely venture was the operation of a sawmill, much of the
output of which went to Cuba as railroad crossties. Mechanical difficulties, inept managers, and a scarcity of willing and
energetic labor handicapped his operations. A small store—
"Gonzales, Woodard & Co."—only demonstrated his lack of
business qualities.[40] Efforts were made to plant the land on
shares with both whites and Negroes, and though neither
showed the energy that the now-poor aristocrat thought
they should, Mrs. Gonzales was convinced that "the freedmen work better than the crackers. . . ."[41]

Few Southern planters met with much success during this
period, and the inexperienced Gonzales was even further
handicapped. After about two years' failure at this latest
stab at civilian unemployment he moved again, this time
back to his native Cuba.

Despite the misgivings and fears of the Elliotts, Gonzales
accepted the invitation of Benigno Gener and other Matanzas friends that he return and dedicate himself to teaching in that city.[42] Such employment would supply a living for

[38] Mrs. A. J. Gonzales to Mrs. Anne H. Elliott, June 7, [1867 or 1868], in
E.G.P.
[39] Mrs. A. J. Gonzales to Emily Elliott, n.d., probably in 1867 or 1868,
in E.G.P.
[40] Where this establishment was is not known, but evidence points to
either Green Pond or Jacksonboro.
[41] Mrs. A. J. Gonzales to Emily Elliott, March 9, (?), in E.G.P.
[42] Portell Vilá, Vidas, p. 379; Patria, December 31, 1892. (Patria was a
newspaper in Spanish published by a Cuban refugee group in New York,
1892–98.)

his family, and the schoolmaster had proved himself no Southern planter. One can only conjecture as to whether he planned to join the revolution that had begun in 1868, as some Cubans have felt.[43] In any case, the whole Gonzales family left Charleston on January 1, 1869, optimistic and cheerful about their bold venture, with Hattie "determined to be cheerful . . . , having been through one revolution, [and] . . . not . . . *at all timid* on the subject. . . ."[44] After a trip from Cedar Keys, Florida, marred, according to Mrs. Gonzales, by the fact that the captain of the ship had once been in the United States Navy and some of the crew were Radical Republicans, they arrived at Havana on January 20.[45] All political exiles having been pardoned at the time of the birth of Alfonso XII (1857), Gonzales was admitted after assuring authorities that he had come only to seek a means of supporting his family.[46]

For three months the family remained in Havana, much of the time with Gonzales' Aunt Lola. As a result of the current revolution, they were kept under close surveillance. The revolution also made it impossible for the General to succeed in finding a teaching job, but finally in April they moved to Matanzas where Gonzales was hired as a professor of English and French in a government institute.[47] Here the

[43] Emeterio S. Santovenia, *Huellas de Gloria: Frases Historicas Cubanas,* 2nd ed. (Havana: Editorial Tropico, 1944), p. 162, says that Gonzales believed he could join the revolutionary work begun at Yara.

[44] Mrs. Ebet Burnett to Emily Elliott, January 5, 1869, in E.G.P.

[45] Full accounts of this trip are in Mrs. A. J. Gonzales to Mrs. Anne H. Elliott, January 14 and 23, 1869, in E.G.P.

[46] A. E. Gonzales, in foreword to N. G. Gonzales, *In Darkest Cuba,* p. 11; Mrs. A. J. Gonzales to Mrs. Anne H. Elliott, February 27, 1869, in E.G.P.

[47] Mrs. A. J. Gonzales to Mrs. Anne H. Elliott, n.d. (fragment), and same to same, June 8, 1869, in E.G.P. In Havana the family was most hospitably received and feted by Gonzales' stepmother, brothers, and sisters; see Mrs. A. J. Gonzales to Mrs. Anne H. Elliott, March (?), 1869; and Mrs. A. J. Gonzales to Mrs. Mary E. Johnstone, April 14, 1869, in E.G.P.

family enjoyed briefly the only normal existence it was ever to know. The General taught not only at this school but also at another institution; besides holding these two jobs, he was also giving private lessons. His popularity and hard work were rumored to be bringing an income of $3,000 a year, his greatest financial success in years.[48] This new stability and the pleasantness of their new life made Mrs. Gonzales hope that they would never again have to begin life anew.[49]

The old friends of Gonzales were more than hospitable to his Carolina family, and life ran smoothly. During vacations, he stayed with them and continued his private lessons.[50] Conflicting stories reached the Elliotts about their welfare, but Hattie's optimistic reports were confirmed by a friend who said they were "getting on *very comfortably* and had every *luxury* and *necessary*. . . ."[51]

The three older boys—Ambrosio, Narciso, and Alfonso— attended public school and studied geography, grammar, history, religion, sacred history, catechism, reading, writing, and arithmetic. Of course, all of their classes were conducted in Spanish, and their father instructed them in French.[52]

The last Gonzales child was born in Cuba on May 21. Vital Gonzales statistics then included, in order of age, Ambrosio José, Jr., Narciso Gener, Alfonso Beauregard, Gertrude Rufini, Benigno, and Anita Rosita.[53] The new baby, who showed "good taste in resembling her mother," im-

[48] Mrs. Ebet Burnett to Emily Elliott, "Sunday," in E.G.P.
[49] Mrs. A. J. Gonzales to Mrs. Anne H. Elliott, June 8, 1869, in E.G.P.
[50] Same to same, August 14, 1869, in E.G.P.
[51] Mrs. Ebet Burnett to Emily Elliott, "Sunday," in E.G.P. Mrs. Gonzales wrote in similar vein to Mrs. Anne H. Elliott, August 1, 1869, in E.G.P.
[52] A. E. Gonzales to Mrs. Anne H. Elliott, August 12, 1869, in E.G.P.
[53] Later several were renamed; the Gonzales children became, respectively, Ambrose Elliott, Narciso Gener, Alfonso Beauregard, Gertrude, William Elliott, and Harriett Rutledge Elliott Gonzales. Some of them frustrated the researcher by going through intermediate stages.

mediately became the pet of the happy family, and glowing
reports of her were sent to South Carolina.[54]

If the reports were true, the Elliotts back at Oak Lawn
may have been envious. That once-opulent family now was
reduced to welcoming many gifts charitably bestowed on
them, often by old acquaintances in the North. (Their al-
most-annual trips before the war had taken them to such
places as Saratoga Springs and Newport.) A typical letter
might enclose "to your sisters a small sum as my testimony
of remembrance to them in their adversity."[55] Chief bene-
factor apparently was William Amory, old Boston friend of
William Elliott, whose frequent letters might on occasion
contain money from an unidentified Yankee lady "to yr.
mother with . . . kindest regards as an old friend of yr.
Father—and as a very inadequate evidence of her friendly
interest."[56] The Elliotts sent preserves to such friends, who
sometimes sold them for the former Confederates. Through
a friend in England they also managed to get issued in 1867
a third edition of William Elliott's *Carolina Sports*, which
brought in some small royalties. In 1868 Ralph Elliott
toured the North in search of a loan among old friends;
one New Yorker "succumbed to my eloquence," he reported, and advanced him $5,000 for two years, secured by a
mortgage on Oak Lawn.[57]

That same year, one of the Elliott girls reported that
Ralph had begun selling shad at nearby Jacksonborough,
that she herself was selling hundreds of pounds of preserves

[54] A. E. Gonzales to Mrs. Anne H. Elliott, May 29, 1869, in possession (in
1951) of Miss Harriett R. E. Gonzales; also, Mrs. Mary Pinckney to [Mrs.
Anne H. Elliott], September 20, 1869, in E.G.P.

[55] Mrs. E. Henderson Otis to Ralph Elliott, May 14, 1867, in E.G.P.

[56] W. Amory to "Miss Elliott," March 26, 1867, in E.G.P.

[57] Ralph Elliott to T. R. S. Elliott, March 13, 1867, in T. R. S. Elliott
Papers. Mortgage to George H. Hoppock is in E.G.P.

which she prepared at "The Ruins," and that much of the family silver was finding its way to market through Northern friends serving as agents.[58] The copious family correspondence of this early Reconstruction era consists largely of jeremiads—letters both bitter and sad, lambasting freedmen who were not disposed to work supinely for them and lamenting that Ralph was reduced to doing the kind of work hardly suitable for one to the manor born. Their pluck and strength are evident in these letters, but so is their failure to adjust to circumstances. Flexibility was not one of their more notable characteristics.

In the midst of these burdens, typical of the postwar plantation areas, another tragedy befell the Elliotts. In the fall of 1869 Hattie contracted yellow fever in Cuba. Three of her children also suffered from this disease about which the Elliott family had repeatedly warned, and although the children recovered, she was dead within two days after the initial attack. The Elliotts contacted the grief-stricken father at once concerning the welfare of the six orphans, although they were dubious about what their war-wrecked means could provide for them.[59]

Leaving two sons—Narciso and Alfonso—in the care of friends, General Gonzales made the sad return to the United States, arriving with his brood in Savannah in November 1869. Evidently the Oak Lawn community had no advance notice of the trek, but many friends reported the General

[58] [Miss Anne Elliott] to A. E. Gonzales, January 27, 1868; Lambert Gettings to Miss Anne Elliott, March 2, 1867; Anne Johnstone to Mrs. Mary E. Johnstone, April 10, 1867; Elliott Johnstone to Emma F. Johnstone, June 15, 1867, in E.G.P. These and other letters indicate that they received hundreds of dollars this way.

[59] Mrs. Mary E. Johnstone to Mrs. Anne H. Elliott, October 30 and November 7, 1869; J. M. Drayton to Mrs. Johnstone, November 9, 1869, in E.G.P.

as being thoroughly overcome with grief and frustration.[60] The two boys left behind in Cuba lived on a sugar plantation with Theodore Dalcour, a friend of their father. He gave them wise training, took them fishing with "parties of gentlemen," and introduced Narciso to libraries which fascinated him. Both boys continued there to show traits that proved lasting: "Nanno" reveled in wide reading in American and English history, attained a remarkable knowledge of world affairs, and led his classes in the Cuban school. Although he was only twelve, his letters to South Carolinians showed the literary and intellectual qualities of a superior adult. He could pen a dramatic word picture of a West Indian hurricane, demonstrate keen insight into the background of the Franco-Prussian War, or write a scholarly treatise on the flora and fauna of the neighborhood.[61] As for "Bory," he also showed his permanent pattern: "He hates his books . . . and would do nothing but worry and won't learn a thing." His studious brother said he himself had given up when he found he was no longer big enough to spank Bory. Nanno reported that the intransigent Bory could read and write—but would not. He suggested that his relatives "put him in a school where he'll have to learn or get whipped."[62] After over a year in Cuba, their father reunited them with their two sisters and two other brothers at Oak Lawn. The General himself then moved on.

[60] Mrs. Leila Habersham to Emily Elliott, November 19, 1869; W. P. Mannigault to Emily Elliott, November 19, 1869, in E.G.P. Full details of the return trip are in A. E. Gonzales to N. G. Gonzales, December 3, 1869, in E.G.P.

[61] For samples, see N. G. Gonzales to Mrs. Anne H. Elliott, March 28, October 22, and November 19, 1870; N. G. Gonzales to Emily Elliott, July 29 and August 22, 1870; N. G. Gonzales to A. E. Gonzales, February 10 and August 26, 1870, in E.G.P.

[62] N. G. Gonzales to Emily Elliott, August 22, 1870, in E.G.P.

CHAPTER II

School and Telegraphy

RETURNING TO THEIR MATERNAL HOME IN LATE 1871, NANNO and Bory Gonzales were only two more charges on the overburdened resources of the Elliotts. The old Oak Lawn plantation now was a community of paupers: Mrs. Anne H. Elliott, the matriarch; her two unmarried daughters, Misses Anne and Emily Elliott; her son, Captain Ralph E. Elliott ("Uncle Rafe"), who came and went; and the six Gonzales children, the oldest of whom was fourteen. Feeding and educating this group of impoverished aristocrats was no mean task.

A crude cabin had been built around the old kitchen that had been spared from the flames by the pleading of an old caretaker. Years later, Nanno wrote that he had been a "man of all work" from the time he was twelve, doing everything from wood-chopping to hoeing corn under a Colleton summer sun.[1] All the family considered Ambrose as the

[1] N. G. Gonzales in *The State*, April 15, 1892.

most industrious of the boys, but Nanno seemed to be
emulating him in 1873 when, at the age of fifteen, he became
the "man of the house" and reported that he brought water,
ground coffee, cut wood, built fences, hoed and planted in
both vegetable and flower gardens, churned, and cut crossties for sale.[2]

Poverty did not beget ignorance, for Aunt Anne conducted
a rigid school for the Gonzales group of her nephews and
nieces. Studying from a few antiquated texts and newer
books supplied by sympathetic friends, they dipped into
everything from arithmetic to Plutarch's *Lives*. Although
most of the Oak Lawn library had been destroyed, the family
had taken a few books with them when they "refugeed,"
and now the boys reveled in the plays of Shakespeare, the
poetry of Burns and other English authors, and the novels of
Scott. In such pursuits, Nanno was the leader; the only
coercion necessary in his education was that used to get
him to stop reading.[3] Noting that he constantly went "from
history to water, and from Arithmetic to hoeing," Nanno
was determined not to grow up in ignorance; one who
claimed to enjoy Hume's *History of England* at the age of
fourteen was hardly likely to do so.[4]

In the early 1870s the Gonzaleses showed traits which were
to be relatively constant throughout their lives. It was early
noticed that Nanno "had an excellent mind and a good
start in writing" but also a "desponding view . . . of everything."[5] Even his brother complained that Nanno was "very

[2] N. G. Gonzales to A. E. Gonzales, August 1, 1873, in E.G.P.

[3] A. E. Gonzales in foreword to N. G. Gonzales, *In Darkest Cuba*, pp. 15-17.

[4] N. G. Gonzales to A. E. Gonzales, March 2 and February 23, 1873, in
E.G.P. When he was eight, he reported on a biography of Alexander the
Great. The boys also evidently read their grandfather's *Carolina Sports*
many times.

[5] Mrs. Mary E. Johnstone to Mrs. Anne H. Elliott, March 18, 1874, in
E.G.P.

unruly and quarrelsome" and all members of the family observed he had a quick temper.[6]

As for young Bory, his determination not to study plagued both his aunts and brothers. A conscientious objector to routine chores as well as things literary, he rapidly became classed as a problem child. Actually he did have some interests: hunting, fishing, and animals. Despite Bory's easygoing amiable ways, the three Elliott ladies continued their persistent but futile efforts to induce him to imitate his older brothers.

The baby of the family also expressed an early independence. Her grandmother noted that "Hattie when she is good is very good indeed—& when she is bad—she is horrid."[7] In one respect she resembled Bory who said that "she reads . . . very well but she is an awful lazy girl she would wrather [sic] put the dogs on a rabbit track than learn a geography lesson anyday."[8] And Bory undoubtedly would have been disposed to go along.

Favorite of all Oak Lawn generations was "Brosie"—or Ambrose Gonzales, the oldest of the six. Serious but full of humor, scholarly but laboring incessantly, practical but always a plunger—here was a man, regardless of his age. By the time he was fifteen, he was admired by his elders and respected by the younger Gonzaleses, for whom in many respects he was to serve as father into the twentieth century. Utterly unselfish, he did a man's full work from his youth. Never passing through a normal adolescence with its flights, fancies, and freedoms, his character crystallized into manhood without any brittle edges or rocky surfaces. Always sentimental and emotional, he could slip instantly from

[6] A. E. Gonzales to Emily Elliott, June 15, 1872, in E.G.P.

[7] Mrs. Anne H. Elliott to A. E. Gonzales, February 15, 1873, in E.G.P.

[8] A. B. Gonzales to Gertrude Gonzales, n.d., in E.G.P. Bory's unique letters are so rare that they might almost be considered collector's items.

laughter to tears. With a capacity for the work of two and the demands of many resting on his huge shoulders, he never experienced a slack period or a real vacation. Nearly everything produced by this human dynamo went either to others or to some enterprise from which he demanded principles but not necessarily profits. By 1880 he had developed a delightful combination of the best traits of William Elliott and A. J. Gonzales.

On the other hand the story of General A. J. Gonzales after 1865 is not a pleasant one. Here was a man who had tasted military glory; a chieftain who felt himself a soldier and a patriot; a Cuban transplanted to the South in its darkest hour when even its best-adjusted natives, including his relatives, could not find a secure foundation or even find reason to hope for one; a widower whose children lived with proud and aristocratic relatives who now blamed him for the death of his wife; a man who had arrived at the starting place of life when he was fifty-two years old. Under these circumstances, ease and success would have been miracles.

In 1870 the unemployed soldier took his namesake, Brosie, to Charleston where he placed him in school. His plans included early entry in Washington College, but President Robert E. Lee advised that Ambrose had "neither the age nor the preparation to enter his institution."[9] Boarding the boy with Mrs. Ebet Burnett, a friend of the Elliotts, he settled down temporarily in Charleston.

Family trouble broke out in 1870. In 1869 Mrs. Elliott praised the "accustomed energy" of her son-in-law, but in 1870 she and her three daughters began a vicious campaign to sow dissension between him and his children.[10] Fulminat-

<hr>

[9] A. J. Gonzales to Mrs. Anne H. Elliott, May 16, 1870, in E.G.P. Mrs. C. P. Mitchell to Emily Elliott, May 8, 1870, in E.G.P., indicates that the Elliotts had other plans for the boy, but the father had interfered.

[10] Mrs. Anne H. Elliott to Mrs. A. J. Gonzales, May 28, 1869, in E.G.P.

ing against him in nearly every letter they wrote, they blamed him for taking his wife to "that death hole, Matanzas," and for not properly caring for his children and their education. Since the family papers contain only one side of the story, it is impossible to assess the validity of their scores of vituperative charges during the postwar years. Certainly the General never prospered, and evidently he never settled down; on the other hand, he succeeded as well and stayed with a job as long as any of the Elliott brothers, whom the ladies idolized and whose misfortunes they ascribed solely to Reconstruction and Yankees. Occasionally, he sent pitifully small sums of money to the children, money which the aunts disdainfully returned as tainted, while they merrily continued to accuse him of nonsupport. On the other hand, the aunts, sorely beset with utter ruin by postwar troubles, did add to their many difficulties the task of rearing and educating all six of his children.

Soon after Ambrose, age fourteen, had reached his Charleston school, the poison against his father began to flow. The boy's aunt wrote him, "His meaness [sic] my dear boy, is marvelous." She alleged that the General had denied him necessities while splurging on himself and that although the father had a new teaching job, "You won't get much of the proceeds—I fancy."[11] When the General defended himself to his son, one aunt wrote and warned the schoolboy not to believe one "so false to every duty." When he contemplated moving the boy to Savannah, she angrily wrote, "May God frustrate his plans."[12] Eventually the aunts at Oak Lawn succeeded in their effort to turn the whole brood against "the mean ungrateful contemptible creature. . . ."

In Charleston by 1870, the former filibuster had lost the glamour which once had surrounded him. As one of the

[11] Emily Elliott to A. E. Gonzales, June 4, 1870, in E.G.P.
[12] Same to same, June 14, 1870, in E.G.P.

friends of the Elliotts wrote, "I hesitated about addressing
him before the Pinckneys, he looked so rowdy—attired in
his usual hunting costume—great coat, slouched hat & that
hideous old scarf wound around his delicate throat. . . . I
do dislike that man more than I can express. . . ."[13] The
General claimed, "To know that my children are well is
the only comfort that I have." He wrote that despite his
"strained position," he hoped soon to be able to care for
them all.[14] Constantly penning pathetic letters of his troubles,
he went to Savannah in March 1870 where he soon had a
teaching sinecure and was made a guest by an old friend,
A. B. Luce, who owned the Marshall House. In the fall,
his travels began again, and after a brief and probably unhappy stopover in South Carolina, he arrived in New York.

In that city López's lieutenant became a businessman,
"obtaining the agency for the Southern States for three large
concerns. . . ." He immediately made arrangements for
little Brosie to go to school again and promised to send Mrs.
Elliott the arrears for servants and other expenses.[15]

The New York job proved transitory, and General Gonzales next turned up in Baltimore, where his sister-in-law,
Mrs. Mary Elliott Johnstone, was living. She refused to
see him when he called "because I do not wish to be rude
(something that I cannot reconcile with a lady) . . . ."[16]
She did report that he had a job in an Episcopal choir where
"he is very erect—although quite grey and bald—a black
moustache and a closely shaven head . . . an odd appearance."[17] For his singing, he received $300 a year, out of

---

[13] Fragment, n.d., apparently c. 1870, in E.G.P.
[14] A. J. Gonzales to N. G. Gonzales, August 7, 1870; A. J. Gonzales to
Ralph E. Elliott, April 20, 1870, in E.G.P.
[15] A. J. Gonzales to A. E. Gonzales, March 27, 1871, in E.G.P.
[16] Mrs. Mary E. Johnstone to Mrs. Anne H. Elliott, January 3, 1872, in
E.G.P.
[17] Same to same, "Sunday," in E.G.P.

which he soon sent $25 to South Carolina, saying "it is little, but it is *the very first* money that I have made. . . ."[18] Finally seeing Mrs. Johnstone, he eagerly asked if she had any news of his children, assuring her of his desire to help them. But she discouraged him from even calling.[19] In Baltimore he eventually eked out an existence by giving lessons—whether in music or languages, the records do not say.

Besides giving studied affronts to the General, Mrs. Johnstone soon admitted she had also been intentionally rude to a Miss Martha Custis Williams, who was frequently seen with Gonzales. About her, the irritated sister-in-law said, "I don't know who or what she is—an old tabby—probably in want of a beau." Worse still, she was "ugly & about 50—I should judge & poor besides. . . ." Miss Williams was pointedly advised to show no attention to Gertrude Gonzales, the General's daughter then in school in Baltimore, and—*mirabile dictu*—was told that no money from Gonzales was expected by the Elliotts. Said Mrs. Johnstone, "I was just as cold as an icicle to the woman" and convinced "the old lady that her attentions must cease."[20]

The unsettled Cuban now toyed with another idea, namely, that of colonizing "good, honest industrious hands or laborers from Denmark or Norway" on Social Hall plantation, which he still owned. Failing to launch that scheme, he wrote his son Ambrose that he was going to seek a Northern farmer to "go shares with me . . . at Social Hall and thus . . . gradually reclaim the place in order that it may become hereafter of some value to yourselves."[21]

[18] A. J. Gonzales to W. C. Bee, February 25, 1872, in E.G.P.
[19] Mrs. Mary E. Johnstone to Mrs. Anne H. Elliott, "Sunday night," in E.G.P.
[20] Emily Elliott to A. E. and N. G. Gonzales, June 21, 1872; Mrs. Mary E. Johnstone to Emily Elliott, February 14, 20, and July 10, 1872, in E.G.P.
[21] A. J. Gonzales to A. E. Gonzales, August 28, 1872; on colonization scheme, see A. J. Gonzales to "Mr. Hammerick," June 15, 1872, in E.G.P.

In early 1873 General Gonzales reported that he had at
long last been rewarded with permanent employment in
New York, and he promptly sent money to his children and
promised more. At the time, he averred he would have
starved earlier had he not been helped by his aunt in
Havana.[22] There is some evidence that his new bonanza was
a minor job on Wall Street, but during the decade of the
seventies he also did some private teaching and served as an
interpreter. Meanwhile, his children were admonished by
the Elliotts to tell him nothing.[23]

While this family feud was smoldering, the Gonzales boys
were beginning their limited formal schooling. In February
1872 Ambrose undertook his second educational venture
away from home, this time going to a school run by Barnwell Fuller in Beaufort. Despite having spent only a few
months in the Charleston school in 1870, he found that he
was "not at all backward." He did well under Fuller but
rebelled at "the Yankey school marm" who was "the dread
of all the small boys."[24]

Nanno disliked being left behind and sought Brosie's
advice. His reply reveals something of Narciso's personality
as well as Brosie's trials:

You ask me if you can get on in Beaufort in lessons you can but
you will have to curb your temper Nanno and not behave as you
do at Oak Lawn all people are not as forbearing as our old folks.
. . . there are a good many low & bad boys who will provoke
you in every way "as they do me." . . . the only way I do is to
have nothing to say to them it is a very hard thing to keep my

22 A. J. Gonzales to Mrs. Anne H. Elliott, January 30, 1873, in E.G.P.
23 N. G. Gonzales to A. E. Gonzales, February 10, 1873, in E.G.P. More
prepared "hate letters" were supplied to Ambrose while he was in school
in Virginia with suggestions that he confuse "the Pater" by getting them
mailed and postmarked in Baltimore by his aunt there.
24 A. E. Gonzales to N. G. Gonzales, March 2, 1872, in E.G.P.

hands off them some times I never go into the streets but I hear
"Gonzales! Gonzales! calling me Spanyard & trying to provoke me." . . .[25]

Brosie was soon determined to leave school, having become thoroughly rebellious about living in the home of
Mrs. C. A. Hamilton, an overly pious cousin, and feeling
that he should go to work to support himself. Instead of
leaving, he was soon chaperoning Nanno who joined him
in Beaufort at Mrs. Hamilton's. The newcomer reported to
Bory their daily routine, as follows: at 5:30 A.M. they got
up and studied till 8:00; prayers and breakfast from 8:00 to
9:00; school from 9:00 to 3:00 P.M.; after supper, prayers and
study till bedtime at 10:00 P.M.[26] Bory probably resolved
never to get in that vicinity.

School did not accomplish miracles for Nanno, for his
older brother sadly related that he still had "fits of badness
now & then & on those occasions he abuses me before any
body who happens to be present."[27] Nevertheless, Nanno
consistently was the top student in the small school, as he
had been in Matanzas.

In Beaufort, Brosie early showed a tendency to be a business man, buying and selling poultry for a profit and tending
to plantation matters for his aunts at Oak Lawn. All was not
work, however; the boys took frequent fishing and swim-
ming excursions, but this did not remove the cross they
had to bear: Mrs. Hamilton, their landlady. Her soul
grieved that Nanno refused to go to Sunday school, although Brosie assured her that both had "graduated." Undaunted, she warned their guardians that " 'Fear of the
Lord, is the beginning of Wisdom,' " and she was gravely

[25] Ibid. At this period, A. E. Gonzales might write one letter which was a
model of composition and in his next letter omit all punctuation.

[26] N. G. Gonzales to A. B. Gonzales, June 6, 1872, in E.G.P.

[27] A. E. Gonzales to Emily Elliott, May 31, 1872, in E.G.P.

upset because Brosie went out "to play cards, even if it be
at my Nephews house."[28] Ambrose had his own opinion, as
his letters show: "Mrs. Hamilton is now in her glory as she
is never so happy as when going to see a sick or dying person
telling every body that he has given his soul to Jesus. . . ."[29]
And Nanno was quite in agreement when he said, "My
greatest trial is Mrs. Hamilton, and it takes a large stock of
patience to deal with her."[30]

Their trials were short-lived, however, as this part of
their education lasted only a few months. Their landlady
would probably have been in her glory if she had read
Brosie's declaration that he would be "heartily glad to quit
Beaufort & Mrs. H. whose christianity I do not appreciate
although strange to say, I am becoming a little religious
much to Nanno's wonderment."[31]

Back at Oak Lawn in 1872 the boys' home education continued amid the depressing poverty which precluded formal
education for a time. Mrs. Elliott confessed that she would
sacrifice almost anything to advance the education of her
grandsons, Ambrose and Narciso Gonzales. Accordingly she
frankly solicited money from old friends and was successful.[32] Then she made arrangements with a schoolmaster,
J. Peyton Clark, to take Ambrose first at his private school in
Virginia. This young teacher severely forewarned her that
his circular *"means what it says"* and that he would take the
boy only if he wishes *"really to study* and will respond to my
efforts."[33]

[28] Mrs. C. A. Hamilton to [Mrs. Anne H. Elliott], May 1, 1872, in E.G.P.
[29] A. E. Gonzales to Emily Elliott, May 31, 1872, in E.G.P.
[30] N. G. Gonzales to A. B. Gonzales, June 6, 1872, in E.G.P.
[31] A. E. Gonzales to Miss Anne Elliott, "June 6," in E.G.P.
[32] Mrs. Anne H. Elliott to W. W. Corcoran, n.d. [1873?] He had paid for
the education of A. E. Gonzales, and she was again seeking aid, this time
for N. G. Gonzales.
[33] J. Peyton Clark to Mrs. Anne H. Elliott, August 8 and September 16,
1872, in E.G.P.

In September, Brosie left Nanno. The little school was located on a farm, "Buffalo Marsh," near Middletown, a village about thirteen miles south of Winchester, Virginia. Obviously homesick and also embarrassed by not being as advanced as the other boys of his age, Brosie sent some gloomy reports home. He noted that Clark was "quite religious but is very different from Mrs. Hamilton and feeds his boys well."[34] Virginia also seemed a dull place to the Carolinian who lamented that he did not see much of the society which Clark had mentioned in his prospectus. Gloom increased: "I don't think any more of the boys now than I did at first one or two are gentlemanly but the rest are a set of scamps."[35] He conceded that Clark was "a nice old gentleman" but his charges were "the most disgusting rowdy & unmannerly set of boys that I have ever seen" and "go about the country robbing orchards shooting peoples hogs & turkeys & getting into all manner of scrapes. They provoke me. . . ."[36] This mood continued all fall as Brosie complained of "this disgusting country." Nevertheless, before long, while Clark was away, he joined other "scamps" and "illuminated the old School house until 11 oclock" and made music on "the tin pan and tambourine."[37] A new scamp had been born.

By December contentment displaced homesickness. Indeed, Brosie's feeling of inadequacy was replaced rapidly by confidence as he found that by constant work he could keep up with his companions, whom he increasingly liked. Clark said Brosie was several years behind in his work but rapidly was overcoming the deficiency. One problem still burdened the boy: his name. Convinced by his aunts that his "noble progenitor" was the source of all evil, he changed his name

[34] A. E. Gonzales to Mrs. Anne H. Elliott, October 6, 1872, in E.G.P.
[35] Same to same, September 29, 1872, ibid.
[36] Same to same, September 22, [1872], ibid.
[37] A. E. Gonzales to N. G. Gonzales, October 19, [1872]. in E.G.P.

from A. J. Gonzales, Jr., and insisted that he henceforth be called "H. Hutchinson Elliott."

The Virginia Christmas in 1872 rekindled his homesickness. He reported it the dullest holiday in his memory, for "although there has been plenty to eat I have not tasted eggnog or even wine as the folks here are strictly temperate. We have no fun or frolic but have had to sit in the house & listen to these lazy girls playing on the piano."[38]

Here Brosie demonstrated his remarkable capacity for work. He used all of his play time for study since he realized that this might be his only chance for an education. His normal routine called for studying from five in the morning until breakfast; classes until two; and then studying until eleven, "when I retire to my downy couch where I am soon locked if not 'in the arms of Morpheus' in those of Bed bugs which have begun to bite. . . ."[39] Such work produced monthly reports that bordered on perfection, and Clark noted that "H. H. Elliott" easily had the best record in the school.[40]

Despite such work, Brosie kept up a constant correspondence with the family but complained mightily that he did not get enough mail. He confessed that his letters did not please certain cousins. "I am too matter of fact & can't write *gas*."[41] One might question the latter statement upon reading the following sample of his epistles:

The moan of an expiring "Northeaster" is faintly heard among the branches of the cedars carrying upon its whistling wings the humming of Mosquitoes and the melodious notes of the Bull

---

[38] A. E. Gonzales to Emily Elliott, January 1, 1873, in E.G.P.

[39] A. E. Gonzales to "Dear Aunt," May 14, 1873, in E.G.P.

[40] Reports in E.G.P. The highest grade given was a "10"; out of sixty-three grades on one typical report, his lowest was "9¼." Courses included reading, spelling, chemistry, Latin, geometry, algebra, English composition, history, surveying, and natural philosophy.

[41] A. E. Gonzales to Emily Elliott, February 8, 1873, in E.G.P.

frog. The Governor [Clark] is sitting out on the porch minus his coat and vest and maybe his britches, with his feet above his head making a disturbance with his flute.

Mr. Clark is so lazy and his daughter who is to be confirmed on Monday is upstairs praying as if the devil was at her door . . . , but this place is not the "Eden" you imagine it to be. I have made several friends in Winchester, particularly among the ladies.[42]

This interest in the fairer sex was new, because his aunt had recently upbraided him for his shyness with the girls— "*not* like Your Grandpapa." She gave him sage advice:

The Virginia girls always enjoyed the reputation of being able to put shy diffident youth much at their ease and I pray you in all seriousness to take advantage of this aimable [*sic*] feminine quality and learn to talk nonsense agreeably and dance the Round dances.[43]

He did so, and he soon gave frequent reports on the ladies of Winchester. Handicapped by poverty, he said he often went to town with fifty cents, spent forty of it for fare and ten cents for beer, which left him "little to spend" on hiring a buggy to call on the pleasant girls.[44] Years later, he reminisced about "the Marshall girls" who "came over to our school to visit their kindred, the Dominies family. Worthy young women, doubtless, and as virtuous as plain women find it so easy to be. But, oh God, they were bow-legged!"[45]

The Virginia experience also showed that Mrs. Hamilton's exuberant piety in Beaufort had made little headway with Brosie. He announced:

[42] A. E. Gonzales to N. G. Gonzales, May 24, 1873, in E.G.P.
[43] Emily Elliott to A. E. Gonzales, n.d. [late 1872], in E.G.P.
[44] A. E. Gonzales to N. G. Gonzales, May 24, 1873, in E.G.P.
[45] A. E. Gonzales to Yates Snowden, "Oct. 9," (?), in Snowden Papers.

We go to a little church in Middletown & our Minister is a Mr. Ambler whose only fault is that he measures his sermons by his legs which as he is six feet three are very tiresome. . . . I am a member of the choir . . . [but] I am afraid I will never make the churcher.[46]

This interest in music was a new and permanent one, however, and he expressed a hope that Clark would also teach him to play the violin.

Despite his work, Brosie kept in close touch with Nanno, who wrote him animated records of Oak Lawn life. The latter, then fifteen, revealed in these letters the vocabulary of an adult, a keen interest in nature, a love of the land, and an insatiable thirst for more education. He admitted that staying on the plantation was "a bitter pill" for him and that he preferred to get a job where he could save enough money to go to school.[47] At the time, he still faced the insuperable task of trying to teach Bory. His letters varied from the gay to the formal, the following being an excerpt from one of the latter:

Although I have not had the honor to receive an answer to a letter I wrote you 2 weeks since, my dear Brother, & though I feel belligerent about it, still at your request I will endeavor to indite a scrawl & hope to receive better treatment in the future.[48]

By the end of the school year, Brosie wanted to stay on with Clark, whom he had come to admire, but his aunt decreed that "we can not dream of it—we will *require you to help us.*"[49] The schoolmaster at least provided for him to

46 A. E. Gonzales to Mrs. Anne H. Elliott, March 9, 1873, in E.G.P.
47 N. G. Gonzales to A. E. Gonzales, February 4, 1873, in E.G.P.
48 Same to same, July 28, 1873, in E.G.P. The writer was then fifteen years old.
49 Emily Elliott to A. E. Gonzales, June 18, [1873], in E.G.P.

spend the summer there, working on a farm for twenty dollars a month. During his last months, his relatives were active in negotiations for a job for him, but none was in sight when regretfully he left Virginia for South Carolina in July 1873. One reason that Ambrose could have only one year of school was that his grandmother was determined that scholarly Narciso should also get his chance. Ambrose had warned that Clark's school was not the place for the younger brother because the other boys would torment him when he wanted to study; Ambrose said his own system had been to knock them down, "and you know Nanno is neither very strong nor very patient."[50] Mrs. Elliott made contact with Professor David S. S. Johnston who conducted St. Timothy's Home School for Boys at the village of Herndon in Fairfax County, Virginia, not far west from Alexandria. After deciding that the Episcopal school in Alexandria was too expensive, she sent Nanno to Johnston, who limited the number of his students to twelve.[51]

Here was one scholar who went his way eagerly in the fall of 1873. The unreconstructed rebel stopped en route in Washington where he "looked at the dingy & dirty old capital, saw crowds of niggers who seemed to enjoy such social equality with the whites that the sight was sickening."[52] Arriving at Herndon, Nanno and Johnston at once developed a mutual admiration, the schoolmaster considering the new boy "modest, amiable, and *well-bred.*"[53] Of the teacher, Nanno said: "Mr. Johnston is very kind, as are his family. . . . [He] is religious in the extreme & is peculiar

[50] A. E. Gonzales to Emily Elliott, July 27, 1873, in E.G.P.

[51] David S. S. Johnston to Mrs. Anne H. Elliott, September 10 and 15, 1873; Rev. John H. Elliott to Mrs. Anne H. Elliott, September 29 and October 8, 1873, in E.G.P.

[52] N. G. Gonzales to Mrs. Anne H. Elliott, November 4, 1873, in E.G.P.

[53] David S. S. Johnston to Mrs. Anne H. Elliott, November 3, 1873, in E.G.P.

in some things. He is not very strict as to study but is very particular as to manners, general deportment, & tidiness." Mrs. Johnston was indelicately described as "fair, fat & forty."[54]

In one respect, Nanno did not have one worry that had plagued Ambrose in school, for he wrote, "Fortunately, the Pater is not known here, 'tis a source of thankfulness."[55] Like Ambrose, he also masqueraded under a new name he adopted: "N. Elliott Gonzales." Going to Washington for Christmas, the fifteen-year-old Carolinian wrote, "I hope no one will take me for my venerable progenitor."[56] No one did.

The Carolinian soon found that leaving Mrs. Hamilton in Beaufort had not removed him from religious influences. Nevertheless, Johnston did not affect him as his former land-lady had. Nanno observed that his schoolmaster "is enthusiastic on religion, fasts frequently, & is very High Church. Is a very kind man, & easy to get on with, except when he gets in temper, & then he is the Old Nick himself."[57]

Nanno continued his studious ways, and his pious teacher considered his the best first-month report he had seen, adding "if it betoken the succeeding months & their reports, all interested . . . have great & just cause for thankfulness to Almighty God whom we pray that this may be the case."[58] The precocious boy even regretted that his Christmas holidays were so long and spent part of the time studying arithmetic.

Although he studied almost constantly, Nanno read the *New York Times* and maintained a keen and constant alertness about current affairs. In this field, the admired school-

---

[54] N. G. Gonzales to A. E. Gonzales, November 8, 1873; N. G. Gonzales to Mrs. Anne H. Elliott, November 4, 1873, in E.G.P.

[55] N. G. Gonzales to A. E. Gonzales, November 8, 1873, in E.G.P.

[56] N. G. Gonzales to Mrs. Anne H. Elliott, December 23, 1873, in E.G.P.

[57] N. G. Gonzales to Emily Elliott, April 18, 1874, in E.G.P.

[58] Report of "Master N. Elliott Gonzales." November 28, 1873, in E.G.P.

master was a disappointment, for "Mr. J. doesn't take other than religious papers, & is no politician & so are pretty nearly all around here, so you can imagine yr. brother is out of his element."[59] His comments on current news were frequent and not always reverent: "By the way, old 'nigger loving [Charles] Sumner' has just gone up the spout. It took a long time for that horse whipping to send him below."[60]

Despite his eagerness for study, Nanno's lively letters do not reveal a dull bookworm. Soon after he arrived, he commented on the pleasant company, "some pretty girls, & especially, a pretty Post-Mistress. Therefore I will be & *am,* prompt in getting the mail."[61] But his social activities were not confined to the post office, and even the fasting school-master was no impediment to the boys: "He has given up festivals 'as they encourage flirting,' but has invited all the girls to the 'Lodge' Thursday evening's, to learn sacred music which answers the same 'sacred' purpose."[62] Unusual was his braggadocio as the young Lochinvar reported to his brother: "I am amusing myself . . . with a very pretty girl of 19 . . . much to the derangement of her rustic admirers, to whom she has given the cold shoulder, since my memorable advent. (N. B. I find 'brass' succeeds very well here) ."[63] So successful was Nanno that he soon reported "considerable experience" at "encircling waists."[64]

After a trip to a picnic on the Potomac, Nanno wrote at mellow length to his aunt. The letter fairly glows with romance and is worth citing as an example of the flowing phrases of this fifteen-year-old. He had been

---

[59] N. G. Gonzales to A. E. Gonzales, November 8, 1873, in E.G.P.
[60] N. G. Gonzales to Emily Elliott, n.d. [probably March 1874], in E.G.P.
[61] N. G. Gonzales to A. E. Gonzales, November 8, 1873, in E.G.P.
[62] Same to same, November 22, 1873, in E.G.P.
[63] Same to same, December 16, 1873, in E.G.P.
[64] Same to same, February 21, 1874, in E.G.P.

invited into the wagon which contained all the eligible girls, and so had a gay time. . . . We were packed in as tight as herrings, but agreeable company alleviated it. . . . The more juvenile excursionists followed in another wagon . . . & indulged in psalm singing all the way, an infliction we "elders" escaped.

After a "sylvan repast," he returned at night "to my virtuous couch," and before retiring concluded his idyllic account.

The melodious & elegant frog, "is discoursing sweet music," without the mission, in which I am scribbling; the moon has risen, red & "dry" above the roofs of Herndon, the lively candle bug is cracking his mailed pate against the glass that encircles the dying flame of my lamp; the "whipoorwill" is crying mournfully in the distance; and an occasional cur is yelping in . . . the streets at some belated pedestrian; . . . clock points to 9.45 & I must "git up & git." . . .[65]

Devotion to school did not weaken Nanno's interest in things agricultural, and he cultivated his own flower garden while at school. This horticultural interest was a common one among the Elliotts and always evident in the correspondence of William Elliott and all the rest of the family. Seeds and plants traveled in both directions between Oak Lawn and Herndon.

Still Nanno was undetermined as to his future. Johnston said he was qualified to keep books, teach school, study drafting, or perhaps even to be a reporter; Nanno himself preferred bookkeeping, provided the family would approve.[66]

At the end of the term, he—like Ambrose before him—stayed on a Virginia farm, "Whitehall," during the summer. The owner was an aristocrat, Nathaniel Fitzhugh, and John-

[65] N. G. Gonzales to "Dear Aunt," "Sunday," in E.G.P.
[66] N. G. Gonzales to Emily Elliott, February 17, 1874; N. G. Gonzales to A. E. Gonzales, February 21, 1874, in E.G.P.

ston arranged that Nanno should pay his board by teaching the two small Fitzhugh boys. The schoolmaster observed, "Elliott was made to teach, & he may as well find it out," but the young tutor said teaching was "a profession which I abhor (perhaps on account of my early experiences with Bory) ."[67] Johnston had obviously never met Bory.

On the farm Nanno lived with the family: Mr. and Mrs. Fitzhugh, Mr. Fitzhugh's father, "his sister (a maiden lady past the meridian vulgarly called 'an old maid') ," and the children. His chief duty involved teaching "a couple of the boy brats." This proved to be a task, even for Bory's ex-pedagogue: "One of my 'pupils' is very sick, the other is a small sized Satan, & all my spare time is taken up spanking him."[68] Even so, despite fruit picking, hoeing, wheat stacking, and teaching, he complained that he had too much spare time on his hands for the experience to be profitable, even though his leisure time was utilized for further study.

With the Elliotts unable to keep him in school a second year, Nanno returned to South Carolina in the early fall of 1874. His regret was rivaled only by that of Johnston, who for a number of years was to keep in contact with a pupil for whom he had developed considerable admiration and hope. Nanno came home penniless and jobless after his eight months of education. He was confronted by the same problem that Ambrose had faced when he returned from Virginia the year before. On that occasion, the older brother held some hope of utilizing the knowledge of surveying which he had acquired, and his aunts made successful overtures in his behalf to Christopher S. Gadsden, of the Charleston & Savannah Railroad.[69] By the end of the year (1874) , he was

[67] David S. S. Johnston to Mrs. Anne H. Elliott, June 30, 1874; N. G. Gonzales to "Dear Aunt," July 6, 1874, in E.G.P.

[68] N. G. Gonzales to an aunt, July 6, 1874, in E.G.P.

[69] Emily Elliott to A. E. Gonzales, June 17 and July 10, 1873, in E.G.P.

settled in the depot of the small low-country village of Grahamville (on the modern Seaboard Coast Line in Jasper County) where he began learning telegraphy from the railroad agent, his cousin Arthur Elliott. As an apprentice, Ambrose had little or no income. Nevertheless, he refused to operate Arthur's saloon for him, since he considered it "demoralizing to retail bad liquor to Nigs."[70] His duties during this period consisted of doing office work, running the freight and express departments, and keeping books. His ambition, however, was to become an agent as soon as he finished learning telegraphy.

Ambrose's chance came in 1874, when at the age of seventeen he was left in charge at Grahamville while Arthur Elliott went to New York. Signing his letters,

> "Your Affectionate Nephew,
> Brosio
> Agt. & Opr. pro Tem indefinio,"

he won the place permanently in October 1874, when Arthur stayed in New York.[71]

Being an agent-operator at a small station in the Reconstruction Era was no easy task. Generally, the Western Union furnished the wires and equipment, and the railroad paid the operators. In small stations, like Grahamville, the operator was also the railroad agent and received only a little or no extra compensation for his work in telegraphy; in some cases, an operator was hired by the railroad as "clerk of the agent," received a clerk's salary, and did all the railroad and commercial telegraph business without any extra pay.[72] Ambrose eventually kept hours at Grahamville of 7 A.M. to

[70] A. E. Gonzales to Ralph Elliott, March 8, 1874, in E.G.P.
[71] A. E. Gonzales to Ralph Elliott, August 3, 1874; A. E. Gonzales to Emily Elliott, October 9, 1874, in E.G.P.
[72] N. G. Gonzales, Charleston News and Courier, July 30, 1883.

9:30 P.M., and often had to return to the office during the night.[73]

Despite his demanding duties as a railroad agent, the young telegrapher found time and energy to branch out. In 1875 his uncle Ralph joined him, and for a time the two maintained a small store in the hamlet. This went the way of all of Ralph's ventures, and he warned the plantation ladies, "Brosie will [soon] dispense with my cheerful society, when you will once again be bored by having a horrid male creature in your domestic circle."[74] Nevertheless, the energetic agent was simultaneously serving as telegrapher; selling crossties; buying and selling animals, seed, and produce; managing the lands at Cheeha; and working a profitable vegetable garden. His admiring brother Nanno wrote, "That same Brosie is already a selfmade man. Heaven knows how many joint enterprises he is going in."[75]

Life in Grahamville offered little to Ambrose. Enlivening his days with a guitar, he spent all of his spare moments reading. Only rarely did he complain of his lot, and then in a rather whimsical mood: "Grahamville is dead, and the dry spell has left nary a frog to chant its requiem."[76] Frequently he had unenergetic Beauregard to visit him. After one sojourn he could make a report: "Was much pleased with Bory's behavior. . . . He was gentlemanly in the extreme and did not give me cause to be ashamed of him. Made friends with all the owners of fine horses around and gave them his opinion as to their good and bad qualities. . . ."[77]

Claiming that his loneliness gave him a chance to "realize to their fullest extent, the 'blessings' of bachelorhood," he

[73] A. E. Gonzales to Emily Elliott, January 3 and 10, 1878, in E.G.P.
[74] Ralph Elliott to Mrs. Anne H. Elliott, "Thursday," in E.G.P.
[75] N. G. Gonzales to Emily Elliott, March 6, 1878, in E.G.P.
[76] A. E. Gonzales to Emily Elliott, May 19, 1876, in E.G.P.
[77] Same to same, March 9, 1875, in E.G.P.

told his sister that he usually spent his autumn Sundays in the woods with a book. Such was unsatisfactory, however.

This weather makes me feel young again [he was then twenty], & I crave after a hunt, or a race of some kind, but those pleasures are not for an orthodox Railroad Agent, who is supposed to have no other wish than that his trains arrive on time & no other thought than to keep his switch gate locked.[78]

During one period, however, there were distractions to provide thoughts on things other than the switch gate when his brother Narciso came to town. Having ended his Virginia experience in the summer of 1874, N. G. followed Ambrose's tracks. His Beaufort cousin, William Elliott, had been unable to get him a job. So he went to Grahamville where his brother began teaching him telegraphy. By February 1875 his tutor could report good progress,[79] and on September 15, 1875, N. G. went to a job of his own at the rough little backwoods town of Varnville, a way station on the Port Royal Railroad.

As soon as he arrived, N. G. "fairly 'biled over' with wrath" as he "went to work to restore order out of chaos."[80] Although descended from Rutledges, Pinckneys, and Barnwells, this victim of war and Reconstruction now lived in a rough railroad shanty, had a counterpane over pine trash as a mattress, and slept with the money of the express company pinned inside his jacket. At night, he had to keep handy his matches and light wood splinters for "vagabond and irresponsible freight trains."[81]

[78] A. E. Gonzales to Gertrude Gonzales, October 21, 1877, in E.G.P.

[79] William Elliott to Emily Elliott, September 16, 1874; Ralph Elliott to Mrs. Anne H. Elliott, December 31, 1874; A. E. Gonzales to Miss Anne Elliott, January 31, 1875, in E.G.P.

[80] N. G. Gonzales to Mrs. Anne H. Elliott, September 26, 1875, in E.G.P.

[81] *Ibid.*; also, A. E. Gonzales in foreword to N. G. Gonzales, *In Darkest Cuba*, p. 18.

From the beginning he detested the town, but he tried to ignore it, noting, "The more occupation the better, for I won't have time to think of the confounded place."[82] Although he commented on the place as "sterile . . . would almost prefer the Sahara," he soon learned that a roaring wood fire in the depot stove "makes the V. population very sociable, and we have a levee every P.M."[83] He soon wrote, "It takes a week or two of Varnville to deaden a fellow's feeling to a point of don't-care-a-damitiveness, and that point I am glad to have reached. . . ."[84] Actually, he never quite reached it, for after a residence of five months he vowed that he had not spent a single pleasant day. After a trip down to Grahamville, he complained, "Brosie is very sensitive when I go with him shabbily dressed. Poor fellow! he needs 6 months in Varnville to teach him humility."[85]

Among his lamentations was the fact that the Port Royal Railroad carried so much guano; hence he longed for a huge supply of cologne to apply to his depot, and, "Oh! for a pen like Byron's to do justice to these spring perfumes!"[86] Actually, life in his wilderness was not uneventful, for he could announce, "Varnsville [sic] is (excuse me) infernal, all agog over a stabbing affray this A.M. What a villainous hole!"[87] Or Again:

Things are as usual here, dull but worrying, the only excitement being occasioned by the every day fights, which do something toward keeping our enterprising population from stagnating. We have had a full line of them, more or less destructive . . . , men

[82] N. G. Gonzales to the family (at Oak Lawn), September 29, 1875, in E.G.P.
[83] Same to same, October 15, [1875], in E.G.P.
[84] N. G. Gonzales to ———, n.d. (fragment), in E.G.P. In the 1880s, Gonzales always spelled it "Varnsville," although today it is Varnville.
[85] N. G. Gonzales to Emily Elliott, March 13, 1876, in E.G.P.
[86] Ibid.
[87] Same to same, January 1, 1876, in E.G.P.

& women, both drunk, having Billingsgate matches in the street, ending with a free fight.[88]

For this life, N. G. received twenty-five dollars a month, payable in railroad scrip worth fifty cents on the dollar when he could get it.[89] Frequently he asked his relatives to send him newspapers, magazines, and books with which to pass his spare time because "it's distressing to have to *think* in this place."[90] From his letters, one judges that he was thus able to keep up his remarkable knowledge of current affairs.

Soon after his arrival, he was vainly seeking a place on the Charleston & Savannah Railroad, and Ambrose was overly optimistic to think that N. G. would eventually become reconciled to Varnville. Instead, during the summer of 1876, N. G. visited his brother again in Grahamville and made it headquarters until November 1877.[91] Such an arrangement did not spell dull inactivity for the brothers; indeed, few South Carolinians were calm and inactive during 1876–1877. This was the period of one of South Carolina's greater political upheavals.

During his second stay in Grahamville, N. G. assisted his brother in his railroad work, but both of them devoted a great deal of time to the intense political activities which ended Radical Reconstruction in South Carolina and ushered in white rule under Wade Hampton in 1877. Both were active in forming Democratic clubs at Grahamville and elsewhere, and in 1876 they took the Grahamville Democratic club to a Hampton rally in Beaufort where the Gon-

88 N. G. Gonzales to Emily and Anne Elliott, October 5, 1875, in E.G.P.

89 *Ibid.*; N. G. Gonzales, *The State,* April 15, 1892.

90 N. G. Gonzales to Emily and Anne Elliott, November 20, 1875, in E.G.P. His favorite magazine at the time was *The Nation.*

91 C. S. Gadsden to N. G. Gonzales, November 20, 1875; A. E. Gonzales to Emily Elliott, April 3, 1876, in E.G.P. His last letter in the E.G.P. from Varnville is dated August 19, 1876. Also see *The State,* February 18, 1916.

zales brothers wore the first red shirts ever seen in that town.[92]

Their telegraph office added to their political significance since it was the only one between Yemassee and Savannah and served an area of 2,500 square miles. Eager Democrats rode in from all over the neighborhood to glean what they could of the latest news. The brothers even "printed" with pen a small newspaper of the latest news, "The Palmetto," which first used the palmetto tree and state seal today appearing in the familiar colophon of *The State*. This journal had a "run" of two copies which were passed throughout the village where the inhabitants could read the general and local news and find quotations on the cotton, rice, and naval stores markets; even a literary department and a poet's corner graced "The Palmetto."

A leading factor in the political fight of 1876 was the "Straightout" Democratic paper, the Charleston *Journal of Commerce,* which first appeared May 1, 1876. The staid Charleston *News and Courier* for some time had been a "fusionist paper," urging that the white people could best redeem the state from Radical Republican rule by uniting with the most able of the Radical governors, Daniel H. Chamberlain. Although the paper finally went along with the "Straightouts" to abandon fusion and to make a stand under Hampton, the *News and Courier* never became as unrestrained as the flaming *Journal of Commerce,* edited by Robert Barnwell Rhett, Jr. As its Grahamville correspondent, it enjoyed the services of N. G. Gonzales.

Another reporter on this Straightout sheet was a brilliant Virginian, Alfred B. Williams, a descendant of John Marshall.[93] This able writer, later the founder of the *Greenville*

[92] A. E. Gonzales in foreword to N. G. Gonzales, *In Darkest Cuba,* p. 19.
[93] Yates Snowden to P. S. Barry, July 5, 1931, in F. W. Dawson Papers, in Manuscripts Division, Duke University Library.

News, first met his Grahamville colleague at a Hampton rally in Colleton County in 1876 where he read a poem on D. H. Chamberlain "with a proper pride in the wealth of its anathema."[94]

In May 1876 journalistic opportunity knocked at Grahamville. Six to seven hundred Negroes in the rice fields along the Combahee went on strike on May 16 when their wages were cut from fifty to forty cents a day. Although many of the workers seemed reluctant to join, their leaders were severe and uncompromising, and violence threatened when a Red-Shirt company under Captain Henry D. Elliott was beleaguered. After a few days of tension around Whitehall and after some violence against nonstrikers the novelty of marching over the country with drums and horns wore off, and by the end of the month most of the Negroes were back at work at the old rates. Nevertheless, it was a potentially dangerous situation and attracted widespread interest at the time. N. G. was nearby and received frequent telegraph reports from the operator at Green Pond, near the center of the troubles. He then sent in full telegraphic reports to his paper, which had been in business less than a month, thereby winning a clear "scoop" over the established *News and Courier,* which contained no news on the "Combahee riots" until a week after they had started. Years later B. R. Riordan and Francis W. Dawson, owners of the older paper, admitted they had become interested then in acquiring the services of this young reporter who had beaten them on the story.[95]

N. G. continued to mingle journalism with his telegraphic

---

[94] N. G. Gonzales in *The State,* October 27, 1899.

[95] Charleston *News and Courier,* May 23–June 1, 1876; *The State,* February 18, 1894; A. E. Gonzales in foreword to N. G. Gonzales, *In Darkest Cuba,* pp. 19–20; and A. E. Gonzales to Emily Elliott, May 26, 1876, and A. E. Gonzales to Ralph Elliott, May 31, 1876, in E.G.P.

and political activities.[96] In March 1877 he almost had a chance to report another Negro riot from Green Pond, but Hampton authorized a posse to go "in pursuit of the fleeing champions of 'five years more good stealing.' " His report is the oldest surviving Gonzales news story; it is a good example of the verbose, personal, opinionated journalism of that day.

> If I in this recital unconsciously assume a tragic tone, attribute it to the difficulty experienced in endeavoring to keep out of the track "blazed" out for me by my predecessor in these reportorial woods.

He stated that the pursued Negroes, "being ephemeral, fled precipitately," and a threatened revolt against white rule was thereby squelched. The neophyte newsman concluded: "Justice under Hampton is somewhat prompter and more complete, than it was under a government whose existence depended upon the continuance of just such anarchy and defiance of law."[97]

The uncompromising *Journal of Commerce* soon had served its purpose and could not survive the competition of the stronger *News and Courier;* its last issue appeared July 24, 1878.[98] By then, Gonzales was no longer with it, having gone off to conquer new railroad fields. Nevertheless, he always kept a soft spot in his heart for the paper. At the time of its demise, he even wrote a poem about it, adding: "Very

[96] Too many years later to be very dependable (as was indicated by some obvious errors), General Milledge L. Bonham recollected that Gonzales "covered" a bloody political meeting at Edgefield, scooping the other papers by walking seven miles to a telegraph office to send his story. See S. C. Press Association *Proceedings* (1915), p. 21.

[97] Charleston *Journal of Commerce,* March 3, 1877. Also, see A. E. Gonzales to Ralph Elliott, March 3, 1877, in E.G.P.

[98] Clipping of Charleston *News and Courier,* July 25, 1878, in Dawson Papers.

sorry, but I . . . wanted it to 'do something or bust'! It has chosen to 'bust'. . . .'"[99]

N. G.'s political and journalistic career in Grahamville was terminated November 10, 1877, when he was able to end his enforced idleness by taking a job in Savannah. There he was the night telegraph operator for the Atlantic & Gulf Railroad, his first real work on his own in a year.[100] Sending fifty to seventy-five messages a night and worrying about the wrecks (which averaged one a week), N. G. found that his new job was a hard one. By 1878 he was working eighteen hours a day and making sixty dollars a month. "By restraining extravagance," he hoped to save money, but when he failed in this effort, he feared that his aunt would reinforce her "principle . . . that the country scrub released in the city is 'deceitful and desperately wicked.' "[101] In his economy efforts, he finally had to move to a less desirable but cheaper boardinghouse where "seasons may come and go, but the grub is as fixed as the laws of the Medes and Persians."[102]

Although he complained in Savannah as he had in Varnville, N. G.'s letters back to the ladies of Oak Lawn plantation now began to take on a new spark, showing the vigor and easy flow which were to characterize his writings. Certainly he was a gem among correspondents who have no news, as the following samples show. Writing to his aunt during his all-night shift, he said:

Life flows a cussed sight too smoothly over me; in fact, it approaches stagnation. . . . The monotony of silence is now broken

[99] N. G. Gonzales to Emily Elliott, July 25, 1878, in E.G.P.

[100] Naturally he received little, if any, money as local newspaper correspondent in a small village, and indications are that he was not on the railroad payrolls at Grahamville, although he did assist Ambrose in his duties as agent.

[101] N. G. Gonzales to Emily Elliott, February 12, 1878, in E.G.P.

[102] Same to same, April 20, 1878, in E.G.P.

by the invigorating notes of the mosquito, the bullfrog and the
chuck-wills-willow as they luxuriate in the lowlands of this in-
terminable [railroad] yard, when the toot of the engine is no
more. . . .[103]

Even his nocturnal grumbles had charm:

Then the genial weather has brought a host of new visitors, who,
with the best intentions in the world make my nights a period of
sackcloth and ashes. Candlebugs and fleas!

The former [are] of "assorted sizes" and warranted to more
than suit all tastes. You see I have quite a menagerie of men eating creatures—denizens of the heavens above, the earth below,
and the waters under the earth. (These last . . . are the
'skeeters.') Even the bug ariseth as a Phoenix from the (lamp)
flames to vex my soul. . . .

Today, it had been somewhat better, and the thunder is even
now beginning to "cuss" "sotto voce"—perhaps at its inability to
"raise the wind" as it were.[104]

By September 1878 he had moved again, this time becoming the telegraph operator in Valdosta, Georgia, although
technically he was only clerk to the agent.[105] At first, he liked
the town very much and was hospitably welcomed by the
citizens. Noting that there were many beauties among the
girls, he explained, "This country was settled by S. C. emi-
grants, which accounts for its superior pleasantness."[106]

For some time this honeymoon continued. Although he
worked from breakfast until nine at night, he thought he was
well paid at fifty dollars a month. With his board costing
fifteen dollars a month, he anticipated saving a great deal in

[103] *Ibid.*
[104] Same to same, May 27, 1878, in E.G.P.
[105] This was the Atlantic & Gulf Railroad, which in 1879 became a part
of the Savannah, Florida & Western Railroad.
[106] N. G. Gonzales to Emily Elliott, September 29, 1878, in E.G.P.

Valdosta. All he asked for was more mail, especially "from such of my numerous and interesting relatives adept at . . . 'wiggling a mean quill.' "[107]

Within a few months he was no longer impressed by the Valdosta populace and again avowed that reading was his only pleasure; after all, "one page of Thackeray was more to me than all the narrow brains of Valdosta."[108] Even his salary now seemed inadequate, as he wrote, "I'm ill at ease now and careful how I turn my back on a man because I have a chasm in the seat of my only pair of pants. But I'll be darned if I get another just to please modest Valdosta."[109] Many letters reflected a petulance and an increasing unhappiness, which were augmented by what he considered the inordinate prosperity of the Georgians.

His moroseness and misery steadily grew as he complained that he did three-fourths of the work of the lazy agent.

I don't mind the *work,* but I do mind the utter *subserviency.* . . . And all the time there is not one man or woman whom I can talk intelligently to in the place. I am as morally isolated as if I were among the intellects of Dahomey. . . . If I can shake off this self-repression I have worn so long to cover my disgust and anger, I will be glad indeed.[110]

His thoughts now turned to grandiose plans for returning to South Carolina and following his grandfather's advice for a wide diversification of farm products. He was particularly optimistic about sheep-raising at Oak Lawn and also began to make great plans for having bees and grapes. Diversifica-

107 *Ibid.* He also hoped to make something extra as reporter for the *Valdosta Times* as his predecessor had, but there is no concrete evidence that he did. N. G. Gonzales to A. E. Gonzales, September 7, 1878, in E.G.P.
108 N. G. Gonzales to Emily Elliott, December 21, 1879, in E.G.P.
109 N. G. Gonzales to A. E. Gonzales, December 30, 1879, in E.G.P.
110 N. G. Gonzales to Emily Elliott, July 26, 1879, in E.G.P.

tion and self-sufficiency seemed to him to explain the prosperity of his Georgia neighbors. Having learned that, he wrote that "my ambition is to save up now, so that I can take sufficient Georgia money over the Savannah to restore the financial equilibrium of the two states."[111]

While in Valdosta, N. G. became involved in a controversy which brought out the acrimony that many people later considered to be his chief characteristic. The telegrapher had a garden and became victimized by a super-salesman from Alabama who sold him a preparation that was supposed to preserve fruits. It failed miserably, and N. G.'s threats evoked warnings of a libel suit. The tone of his reply to this warning is characteristic of his later journalistic work:

You have been pleased to write me twelve pages of explanation and declamation and hallucination, which would require the fullest capacity of twelve ostriches to digest. I haven't any ostriches . . . and very little time. . . .

Even *Jews*, Dr. Jeter, do that [offer refunds]! And even *thieves*, have, in remorse, made restitution! But *you*, Dr. Jeter do not!

You need not answer this if you have nothing to say beyond platitudes and protestations.[112]

In late 1879 N. G. tried to escape from the purgatory of Valdosta. B. R. Riordan offered him encouragement about a place on the *News and Courier;* the Combahee riots had stood him in good stead. When he was finally put off with an indefinite promise that something might eventually turn up, N. G. wrote two letters typical of his voluminous correspondence. They read in part as follows:

[111] Same to same, December 8, 1878, in E.G.P.
[112] N. G. Gonzales to H. M. Jeter, October 5, 1879. Also, see H. M. Jeter to N. G. Gonzales, September 15, 1879, replying to Gonzales' letter of September 12, 1879, in E.G.P.

Exit Hope. . . . If this had occurred a week ago when I was confident, I would have done something dreadful—committed suicide or fled to weep in the bosom of my family. . . . But, as . . . I have had the delights of that "hope long deferred which maketh the heart sick," . . . and perhaps considering that the bosom of my particular family isn't the pleasantest place to shower brine upon in misfortune, I have done neither. . . . I wrote R & D [Riordan and Dawson] . . . a letter in my most captivating and airy style. . . .

Well, Don Quixote is unhorsed in his passage with the "News & Courier" windmill. His worship, however, has no Sancho to annoint his bruised shanks. Neither has he a Dulcinea at hand to soothe him. Poor Don Quixote! Let us leave him.

It does look now as if, perhaps, with a great effort, the world and the "News and Courier" might manage to get along without me! This is a sad thought.

I am not "buoyant," my dear Aunt, and I can't make the pretense long, of being so. It is a dead march in dry prose, this life here. There isn't an hour of the day that I don't writhe and gnash my intellectual teeth at my confounded destiny. The most fun I can have, is to ridicule my own misery and be sarcastic to myself. . . . Having consumed my accustomed two pages of anathema, which I know you would miss unpleasantly, I proceed to other subjects.[113]

Actually, correspondence concerning the longed-for newspaper job continued, but N. G. sadly determined to stay in Valdosta until he could save enough money to begin farming. Besides working at telegraphy, he hoped to speculate in eggs, poultry, hides, and wool. The prospect was not pleasant: "Valdosta life is as waveless as Coleridge's 'silent sea'. . . . Twenty-six months of Valdosta will expiate a good many of

113 N. G. Gonzales to Emily Elliott, November 30 and December 14, 1879, in E.G.P.

my sins, I'm thinking."[114] And thus he began 1880—with the supreme hope of saving at least $400.

While N. G. had been shifting from one telegraph key to another, his father had likewise resumed his travels. As has been seen, General Gonzales spent much of the 1870s in New York and gave some indication that at last he might have a permanent abode. But in early 1879 trouble again visited the former "filibuster," and he left New York for Havana. Stopping en route in Charleston, he repeatedly and pathetically asked his son Ambrose to call on him; the latter was then at Grahamville nearby, but adamantly he spurned the invitation.[115] Pausing briefly at Oak Lawn, he went on to Cuba—with the express wish of the Elliotts that he never return. Mrs. Mary Johnstone wrote her sister, Miss Emily Elliott, that she was relieved to learn "that your 'bête noir' has departed and trust that his position in Havana will be sufficiently lucrative and comfortable to keep him there. . . . His indolence will be your security."[116]

In Havana, Cuba, the General worked for a railroad, but eventually he moved to his native Matanzas. Wanderlust seemed to accompany his lack of application, however, for late in 1881 he reappeared at Saratoga—"Occupation unknown, but appearance 'youthful.' "[117] Suddenly in 1882 his financial fortunes changed when his Aunt Lola in Cuba died and left him $10,000. Simultaneously, there was also an abrupt change in the Elliott animosity. His son N. G. even wrote his Aunt Emily that he "wouldn't be surprised if the old gentleman were to send you an Easter card with a pretty

[114] Same to same, February 8, 1880. Also, see N. G. Gonzales to Emily Elliott, December 21, 1879, and January 25, 1880; N. G. Gonzales to A. E. Gonzales, December 30, 1879, in E.G.P.

[115] A. J. Gonzales to A. E. Gonzales, December 27, 1878, and January 6, 1879, in E.G.P.

[116] Mrs. Mary E. Johnstone to Emily Elliott, April 23, [1879,] in E.G.P.

[117] N. G. Gonzales to Ralph Elliott, September 18, 1881, in E.G.P.

angel on it. Wouldn't that be nice!"[118] The son also defended "the Pater" for the first time in years: "And as you say he expects to live forever, he will not spend the principal. Be easy. He is *not* a nabob. But I hope he will receive all the benefit it can give him. He has had a pretty hard time, whether deservedly or not, and he is an old man."[119] But Aunt Emily would have no truce, and thus Ambrose also became blunt in telling her that he would accept his father's money in order that his sister Hattie should get the "schooling which *I intend that she shall have.*"[120] The General also supplied part of his inheritance to his son to pay the taxes necessary to redeem the plantation and to help build a small wooden house at Oak Lawn to replace the rough cabin which had housed the family since the war.[121] Even Mrs. Johnstone tried to spread a little oil on the waters by noting that "he has done nothing *dis*honorable."[122]

Part of Gonzales' new wealth was spent on a trip to Paris late in 1882 where for six months he underwent medical treatment for nasal difficulties.[123] With his health somewhat improved, he returned to New York in 1883, and later in the year moved to Charleston for an indefinite stay. There his son William, then a student at The Citadel, avoided contact with him and refused to accept any financial help from him. At the time, the father was employed as a translator for a South American newspaper and hoped to get more work of that nature; meanwhile, he was underwriting about half of

[118] N. G. Gonzales to Emily Elliott, March 27, 1882, in E.G.P.

[119] Same to same, April 9, 1882, in E.G.P.

[120] A. E. Gonzales to Emily Elliott, October 9, 1882, in E.G.P.

[121] A. J. Gonzales to Ignacio Gonzales Gauffreau (his half brother in Cuba), August 5 and 19, 1883, in possession of Major R. K. McMaster. In 1882 General Gonzales had let Ambrose Gonzales have $2,000 as a loan.

[122] Mrs. Mary E. Johnstone to Mrs. Anne H. Elliott, February 16, [1882], in E.G.P.

[123] A. J. Gonzales to Ignacio Gonzales Gauffreau, August 19, 1883, in possession of Major R. K. McMaster.

the school expenses of his youngest daughter, Hattie.[124] At the same time, he also supplied money to Bory and the other children.

Despite the General's new solvency and Ralph Elliott's seniority, Ambrose Gonzales emerged as the *paterfamilias* of the Elliott-Gonzales clan—a position he was to occupy for half a century—especially after the death of his grandmother, Mrs. William Elliott, in 1877. He undertook the responsibility for the education of his younger brothers and sisters. (He gave up on Bory, whose energies were monopolized by fishing, hunting, and holding soirées at the Adams Run depot.)

In the late 1870s Ambrose again tried farming at Social Hall plantation on Cheeha Creek, but then after a time at Oak Lawn migrated to New York where he worked two shifts a day—eighteen hours—as a telegrapher, making $140 a month thereby and sending as much as he could back to South Carolina.

Although the Elliotts and the Gonzaleses by the 1880s had not recovered the affluence once so familiar to William Elliott's empire, they had at least recovered their footing, and the two older Gonzales boys had definitely matured—before either was twenty-five years old.

[124] A. J. Gonzales to Emily Elliott, November 29, 1883, and W. E. Gonzales to Emily Elliott, November 27, 1883, in E.G.P.

CHAPTER III

Journalist for
"Old Lady of Broad Street"

I N 1879 THE NATIVES OF VALDOSTA, GEORGIA, PERHAPS WERE not impressed by the fact that their local railroad telegrapher was simultaneously serving as writer for the *Valdosta Times*. Alfred B. Williams, however, still thought of his young 1876 colleague on the defunct *Journal of Commerce* as a potential journalist, not as a telegrapher. Thus it was that Williams was instrumental in ending the not-too-happy telegraphing career of N. G. Gonzales.

After covering the Wade Hampton campaign of 1876, Williams had gone as a Charleston *News and Courier* correspondent aboard the *Azor* which carried a shipload of freedmen to Liberia in a tragic colonizing effort in 1878.[1] In May

[1] His articles on the trip appeared in the *News and Courier* July 6, 1878, *et seq*. See also George B. Tindall, *South Carolina Negroes, 1877–1900* (Columbia: University of South Carolina Press, 1952), chap. 8. For a biographical sketch of Williams, see the *Greenville News*, September 25, 1949. For a human history of the short-lived *Journal of Commerce*, see A. B. Williams, "The Press of South Carolina in the Revolution of 1876," *News and Courier*, June 16, 1907.

1880, he arrived in Greenville, soon became editor and one of the proprietors of the new *Greenville News,* and in June summoned his old acquaintance Gonzales to join him in Greenville, then a booming raw up-country town of 6,160 (up 123 percent in the previous decade).

Thus Gonzales began a career of newspapering that was to last until his death. The South Carolina that he came to "cover" was then well into "the Bourbon era," led by a regime of Conservatives with whom a grandson of William Elliott could feel both congenial and comfortable. Because of N. G.'s close association with this post-Reconstruction regime, a brief analysis of it may be in order here.

Led by Wade Hampton and Matthew C. Butler, the white Democrats—who preferred to be called Conservatives since the term made sharper the distinction between them and the Radicals and attracted former Whigs more easily—were in complete political control. The leading historian of this era of the South prefers to stress the label of "Redeemers" for this group, a quite proper term since they unceasingly kept reminding all that they had "redeemed" the state from Radical Reconstruction in the counterrevolution of 1876.

Many, both then and since, have felt that the Conservatives had returned the South to the "old regime" and restored the ante-bellum rulership. But the coming of the Bourbons was not quite so simple. One of the major goals of Radicals had been to break forever the aristocrats' control of the South by using pressure, force, and outsiders; once that was done, with the Carpetbaggers (not the Negroes) supplying the leadership, internal social and economic revolutions would be implemented. But by 1877 the outsiders were gone or going, and the South turned to the "Redeemers" to lead the region now in a return to "home rule."

Since all that had happened under Radicalism seemed to white Southerners as an abrupt nightmare, they now stam-

peded for the opposite pole of "Conservatism." Since all that
had happened since the Old South had ended at Appomattox
now seemed corrupt or stifling, Southerners looked nostal-
gically back at the Old Regime of the Old South and the
dominance of aristocratic planters as "the good old days"—a
classical golden age. One searched for Utopia only in a rear-
view mirror.

By no means were all of those who had redeemed the region from Reconstruction rule traditional aristocrats. But
sensing what Southerners seemed to hunger for, they
promptly posed as such and as participants in a Restoration
—welcoming the label Bourbons, so called because they were
likened to that French royal line who after their return in
1814 had "forgotten nothing and learned nothing" from the
experience of exile. To superficial observers, this new Conservative class appeared a reincarnation of the old oligarchy,
and it was this appearance which they sought to give. After
its trials and tribulations the old oligarchy was so respected
and revered as to be almost sacrosanct; naturally the new
would-be oligarchy embraced that image for themselves.

Much of this was a false appearance because in most Southern states the new oligarchy was not identical with the old
one. It was a new cast of characters posturing and posing with
the courtly manners of the old, making oblations and sacri-
ficial burnt offerings to the mores and ideals of the ante-
bellum mystique, and almost daily conducting rituals in the
new religion, the "cult of the Lost Cause." The old oligarchy
came from plantation families. The new Conservatives, however, often did not. In 1880 not a single dominant ante-
bellum figure of Georgia occupied a place of high prestige
and power; only 38 percent of the legislators there had any
agricultural interest; Mississippi was in the hands of a tri-
umvirate of lawyers; Florida was run by a department store

owner and lumber interests.[2] To a degree, South Carolina was an exception: many of the leaders of the "Wade Hampton–M. C. Butler party" did come from planter families, but they were now spokesmen for the new business interests of a region that was seeking to undergo an economic transformation. Many of them were primarily commercial men and lawyers.

In all states the Bourbon spokesmen seemed to look both forward and backward. Bourbon phrasemaker Henry W. Grady of the *Atlanta Constitution* set the target: a reconciliation with the North which might provide economic salvation through industrialization and Yankee capital. In pursuing this goal, Bourbons were willing to sacrifice Southern agrarianism for a Southern share in the new boom and the industrial wealth of the Gilded Age. This alone seemed the way to participate in the "Big Barbecue." But this new economic order, this "New South," must be built on the foundations of the Old South and accompanied by its manners and mores. The orthodox "Southern way of life" was somehow to be preserved intact.

One factor helped make it possible for the Bourbons to fasten their control firmly. In the Old South class lines had been supinely accepted: certain leaders were almost blindly acknowledged, and opposition to their policy could be made to appear as a threat to the whole system in that already-achieved Utopia—a threat that would undermine the "Southern way of life." This blind loyalty was now continued and fortified by two new factors: If the Conservatives were those who had led the children of Israel out of the Wilderness of Reconstruction into the Promised Land of a restored "White Rule" (or "Home Rule," as they more delicately phrased it) ,

[2] John S. Ezell, *The South Since 1865* (New York: Macmillan Company, 1963) , p. 102.

then one who dared to oppose this self-annointed leadership would be obviously threatening a return to the Dark Ages, to evil days. One hardly defies Moses. The rank-and-file were kept in line with a ritualism that could brand a rebel against Bourbonism as automatically a traitor to the white race. If the whites divided, the blacks would rise again, or so ran the orthodoxy of the times.

Opposition did arise, nevertheless. The "wool hat boys," largely small farmers, often were restless against what their disaffected leader Martin W. ("Mart") Gary of Edgefield called "those elegant, smooth mannered, oily tongued bond-holders, bond speculators, bankers and members of financial boards" and all "the lowly minions" of the "Duke of Charleston" or the "Earl of Columbia." Colonel E. B. C. Cash expressed his independence also of the *"thieves, tyrants and cowardly murderers"* led by Wade Hampton.[3] But the "red necks" were kept in line over a decade until Gary's young friend and disciple, Ben Tillman, gave them the nerve to defy the Bourbon leaders even at the risk of splitting the white vote in the face of a black majority.

A second factor guaranteed the almost blind acceptance of the Bourbon oligarchy: Nearly all of the Redeemers had been Confederate leaders. This was the "reign of the brigadiers." The "cult of the Lost Cause" firmly undergirded the 1876 leadership in South Carolina. As one scholar put it, any man who could claim to have held the bridle for "Traveler," Lee's horse, "was assured of political tenure."[4] If one had a wooden leg traceable to Shiloh, having a wooden head was no political liability whatsoever. If one could dress in gray and wave an empty sleeve at a county Democratic convention, he could assure himself of nomination and lifetime

[3] C. Vann Woodward, *Origins of the New South, 1877–1913* (Baton Rouge: Louisiana State University Press, 1951), p. 76.
[4] Ezell, *South Since 1865*, p. 105.

service as county treasurer even if he were also utterly empty of financial knowledge. Such was the *quid pro quo* for political leadership, and once in power these Bourbon Confederates were safe from defiance.

Worse, they were even safe from close scrutiny, and until recently most Southerners have thought of this era as being one of honest, well-mannered, polite regimes—the "Good Old Days," Part II. Historians have begun to discover it was not all quite so nice. Since officials were those who redeemed the South, served the Confederacy, and were now "the very best people," citizens assumed their total integrity and no more questioned it than they would their own mothers' virtue. With this freedom from scrutiny, their fiscal record in some states was filled with defaulting treasurers, vanishing embezzlers, and unethical officials. Their well-smothered scandals were reminiscent of the well-aired scandals of Reconstruction. Confederate gray could cloak many a hidden sin, although South Carolina Bourbons set a better record than certain other states. W. J. Cash, part-time South Carolinian, explains the hypnotic power of ex-Confederate Bourbons well:

During these thirty years the South was nothing so much as like a veteran army. The people—crackers and farmers—stood to their captains in very much the same way that, say, the troopers of Austerlitz and Marengo stood to Bonaparte and his marshals; gave them the same idolatry, the same high faith, the same quick and sure response to suggestion; waited upon their word with the same respectful attention; were cast down by their frowns, elevated by their smiles, and, in a word, were scarcely less dependent upon the favor of their commanders for a good opinion of themselves than the most zealous trooper.[5]

[5] W. J. Cash, *Mind of the South* (New York: Alfred A. Knopf, 1941), p. 112.

In this strict one-party system, the Southern states were each ruled by one faction (known in South Carolina as "the ring") which was normally the state Democratic Executive Committee. In South Carolina, they were actually more rooted in the pre-1860 era than were the rulers of other states and just as wedded to the Confederacy. Nearly all members of this inner circle were either "General this" or "Colonel that," wartime comrades. There was little rotation of officers, the state party being a closed circle with positions being passed around among a group who now (unlike the antebellum period) made political officeholding a permanent professional career.

Dissenters and rebels like Mart Gary usually failed to crack the system. Loyalty was rewarded by long apprenticeships in lower positions, and hence the origin of "the courthouse gang." With the general election being but a rubber-stamping of Democratic nominations, average citizens were hardly active participants in state elections. Nominees were selected by party conventions that were dominated by the political leaders and political hacks. The danger of party division was reiterated again and again; bolting the party or defying its leadership was the cardinal sin of the times since it conceivably could lead to undoing "the Redemption" and might lead to "Africanizing the state" again.[6]

The Conservatives hardly had a program or a platform unless it was governmental inactivity, economy—even niggardliness—in spending, low taxes, respectability among officeholders, and as few state-supported services as possible. William Cooper correctly notes that this ideology—or absence of it—ultimately brought the Bourbons' undoing be-

---

[6] On the political system, see Dewey W. Grantham, *The Democratic South* (Athens: University of Georgia Press, 1963); and William J. Cooper, Jr., *The Conservative Regime: South Carolina, 1877–1890* (Baltimore: The Johns Hopkins University Press, 1968).

cause they built everything simply "on the influence and prominence of men in their communities and counties," resting their fortunes "on public respect for individuals," who were supposed to be respected and venerated simply because of their service to the Confederacy.[7] This was not a program, and certainly not government "for the people."

The Bourbon leaders of South Carolina—Generals Wade Hampton, Matthew Butler, James Connor, Samuel McGowan, John B. Kershaw, John Bratton, John D. Kennedy—were quite respectable men.[8] They were affable "gentlemen," usually well mannered or downright courtly. Most were good speakers, and could pour forth oratory for two hours at a time with ease, usually in a speech glorifying the heroism of the Confederacy and romanticizing the "glorious victory of 1876." This flowery oratory was devoured with relish by South Carolinians, who were constantly extending fawning invitations to the Conservative leaders to attend various public events (many of really minor or local importance) and "deliver the oration for the occasion." Times do change.

It is not surprising that N. G. Gonzales defended this Bourbon order. He was descended from the Elliotts of the ante-bellum aristocracy, reared at Oak Lawn amid ruins from Sherman's devastation, frustrated by poverty during Reconstruction, partially trained by his unreconstructed uncle, Ralph Elliott (always to go under his Confederate rank as "Captain Elliott"), and influenced by the excitement of the 1876 counterrevolution in which the boyish telegrapher had participated with the enthusiasm of a partisan and the excitement of youth.

[7] Cooper, *Conservative Regime*, pp. 19–20.
[8] Cooper has an interesting analysis of the background of forty-three Bourbon leaders; *ibid.*, pp. 208–13. Of these, 67.4 percent were lawyers; 79 percent had been in Confederate service (88.2 percent of these being officers) ; 88.4 percent had attended college.

But Gonzales was also like his grandfather, a nonconformist even with his own class. Acceptance of the Hampton-
Butler regime did not mean blind acceptance of it. Their
power and position he accepted as being in the best interest
of society and the future of South Carolina, but this end did
not justify the use of any means. He did not automatically
distribute a halo to a man because of his Conservative label.
Perhaps some people could blindly follow the Bourbons and
assume universal righteousness among them, but not N. G.
Maybe it was his cynicism, his inherent aloofness, his superciliousness, but the Gonzales who returned to South Carolina
in 1880 was destined to be loyal but critical. He had an abid-
ing devotion, a keen feeling of patriotism, for South Carolina.
Yet he was not one of those who insist one must "love" his
native land or else "leave it." He felt that love reflected concern that would not only permit recognition of its faults and
shortcomings but also would demand unceasing effort to
eliminate its faults and to make progressive changes. Rooted
in the Old South, he sought to usher in the New South.

Hence in this Bourbon era of conformity, Gonzales was
destined to be a not-always-conforming Bourbon. He was a
"progressive conservative" who glorified much of the past
but was aware that it could not be restored and who worked
unceasingly to introduce a more prosperous future.

Alfred B. Williams, the twenty-four-year-old editor of the
Greenville News, lured his twenty-two-year-old reporter
(Gonzales) away from railroading in Georgia into this Bourbon South Carolina for ten dollars a week. Within two
months, however, the Charleston *News and Courier* had
gathered in the Greenville reporter "on the condition that
'if he should turn out a failure he would not feel aggrieved
at a discharge after two months trial.' "[9]

---

[9] *The State,* January 30, 1899. N. G. admitted that he soon would have
had to leave the *News* because of an economy drive. As late as 1881 Williams and one other helper did all of the writing for that daily which

In 1880 the Charleston *News and Courier* was easily the apogee of Carolina journalism. Founded in 1803, the *Courier* was combined with the *Charleston News* in 1873 by B. R. Riordan and Francis W. Dawson, expatriots from Virginia and England, respectively. Drifting into Charleston after Appomattox, they had acquired the *News* in 1867 and by dint of hard work and ability had become able to buy out their rival. When Gonzales joined the staid "Old Lady of Broad Street,"[10] these two unique and able gentlemen were the sole owners of an influential paper running on a budget of about $75,000 a year.[11] Going into all corners of the state, it had no serious competition. It permeated the home areas of such regional papers as the *Columbia Daily Register,* the *Greenville News,* and others in somewhat the same fashion as do the national papers of London.

The Charleston editor, Francis W. Dawson, had a fabulous career. Born in England in 1840, he became infatuated with the Confederate cause and came here in 1861 to serve in both the navy and army, ending as a captain (and hence in Bourbon South Carolina was always addressed as "Captain Dawson"). At the end of the war, he drifted into newspaper offices at Richmond and became a friend of B. R. Riordan (pronounced RIDÉ-EN), then a veteran journalist on the staff of the *Richmond Examiner.* Having once been managing editor of the *Charleston Mercury,* Riordan succeeded in getting Dawson a post on it, where in November 1866 he began eleven months' service under Robert Barnwell Rhett, Jr., the editor of this old flaming voice of Charleston. By October

---

was then running on a budget of $325 a week. See A. B. Williams to J. C. Hemphill, October 18, 1888, in Hemphill Family Papers in Manuscripts Division, Duke University Library; N. G. Gonzales to A. E. Gonzales, March 22, 1881, and to Emily Elliott, December 12, 1880, in E.G.P.

[10] Then located at 19 Broad Street. For a history of the paper and some of its personalities, see Henry Ravenel Sass, *Outspoken: 150 Years of the* News and Courier (Columbia: University of South Carolina Press, 1953).

[11] *News and Courier,* July 25, 1878; May 1, 1928; *The State,* March 22, 1897.

1867 Riordan and Dawson joined forces in Charleston and, with the secret backing of Benjamin Wood, editor and owner of the New York *Daily News,* acquired control of the little *Charleston News.* The *Mercury* folded up the next month, with a final salvo in behalf of the Lost Cause, one that was answered by Dawson in a more hopeful note: "Respect for ourselves and our fathers requires us to reverence the past; but we cannot rebuild the fallen structure, and it would be simply foolish in our people to spend the fleeting years of opportunity in lamentation; let us help rear it, and make it better if we can."[12]

When the *Courier* fell on evil days during Reconstruction, Riordan and Dawson also acquired that property for $7,100 and began the new combination, *The News and Courier,* on April 7, 1873. In opposing Radical Reconstruction, Dawson was "the ablest, most fearless and relentless of all the editorial critics of the Republican regime." As a leading authority of that period saw it, "never in South Carolina's turbulent history has a single paper so dominated the thought of the state."[13] In 1875–1876 Dawson formed a close relationship with Governor Daniel H. Chamberlain, advocated a coalition of Conservatives with this reform-minded Carpetbagger Republican, and only belatedly switched over to the movement of "Straightouts" to elect a Straightout Democratic (white) slate, from coroner to governor, in the tempestuous contest of 1876.[14] In the course of the campaign, the *News and*

[12] *Charleston News,* February 24, 1869, as cited in S. Frank Logan, "Francis Warrington Dawson, 1840–1889," in S. C. Historical Association *Proceedings* (1952), p. 20; Sass, *Outspoken,* pp. 39–40.

[13] Robert H. Woody, *Republican Newspapers of South Carolina* (Charlottesville: Historical Publishing Co., 1936), p. 52.

[14] Dawson's enemies later charged him with being in collusion with Radicals in order to get printing contracts. It was never proved, and there is no clear proof of it in Dawson's private papers. These do include much interesting and frequent correspondence between the governor and Dawson, with apparently sincere mutual respect.

Courier had tremendous influence and became thereafter the major newspaper voice for the Conservative regime, with the astute English editor becoming a major power in inner Democratic circles.

In some respects, the *News and Courier* was Bourbonism in microcosm. Not disavowing agriculture, it nevertheless stressed business interests and commercial opportunities. It often lectured farmers for their failures to change, coining the phrase "bring the mills to the cotton." The paper exploited every success major or minor that indicated modernization or industrialization. While continuing to cherish "our heroes in gray," the news columns, features, and editorials kept looking to a future New South that would reveal the cultural traditions of the Old South but not its economic traditions and emphases.

In 1880 Editor Dawson gave his new reporter, N. G. Gonzales, a significant assignment as Columbia correspondent. Here the budding journalist faced a heavy load. Not only did he have to report the state government activities for the state's largest newspaper but also a large volume of local news since so many Columbians at the time took only the Charleston paper. Although his first day of work involved a buggy ride of twenty-six miles, an interview with a participant in a duel, and the dispatching of a whole column of news by telegraph at ten that night, Gonzales reported that he liked his new duties and considered it "a relief to have no one present to order me around, as I have had plenty of that for three years."[15]

Instead of filing many separate stories daily, Gonzales submitted usually a hodgepodge of various items gathered without separate headlines or captions into "the Columbia column." Each paragraph might deal with a different topic, or

[15] N. G. Gonzales to Emily Elliott, August 6, 1880, in E.G.P.

certain items might be given several paragraphs with a one-line caption setting them apart. A typical daily Gonzales dispatch might include notes on round-trip rates to New Orleans; a list of the latest arrivals at the state penitentiary; a description of services at Easter in Columbia churches; and, invariably, a cryptic closing comment on the weather: "The weather today is charming", or "Enough rain fell today to lay the dust." Usually these heterogeneous columns extended one column, but if the legislature and criminal court were both in session, Gonzales' gleanings might utilize three or four columns.

Although most country correspondents signed their literary efforts with "Veritas," "Brutus," "Psi," "Rusticus," "Carolina," or such names, the unvarying initials "N. G. G." soon became a daily feature and eventually a hallmark in the *News and Courier*. In this day of personal journalism, the name of the Columbia correspondent was quickly becoming a household word throughout South Carolina.

The Columbia column appeared under varying heads, such as "The City on the Congaree," "News from the Capital," "Columbia Notes," or "Chitchat of the Capital." It was always a mixture of everything from gory murder details to "Senator Hampton has gone fishing at the famous Waccamaw Lake" (the story in its entirety). Readers could not tell from the head what events they would encounter in this jumble of one-sentence or one-paragraph items that ranged over cockfights, new immigrants, temperance meetings, crop conditions, funerals ("The service was touchingly read"), health reports ("Col. Butler is better tonight"), sales of current books, firemen's tournaments, and assorted acts of violence. Not limited strictly to Columbia events, N. G.'s prolific pen even reported hearsay from elsewhere: "It is rumored that an affray has occurred in Chesterfield County between Franklin Rollins and Joseph and James Griffin. The former is probably cut and shot." The "Columbia Chitchat" had everything but unity.

During all of his years as Columbia correspondent, N. G. G. showed a marked affinity for certain types of stories. He gave copious details to the testimony of criminal trials, and he spared no feelings or sensibilities in his sanguinary descriptions of violence. Perhaps because of his earlier work, he showed an unflagging devotion to news of the railroad world. He evidently daily visited the penitentiary and the office of the state commissioner of agriculture. Nothing if not versatile, he included highly opinionated reviews of all stage attractions appearing in Columbia; in 1881 he quite lost his heart to Eleanor Calhoun, "the new Juliet," who prompted the Columbia Silver Cornet Band to serenade her before the Grand Central Hotel.

The Columbia to which N. G. Gonzales reported was still a town rather than a city, with an 1880 population of 10,036. It was not booming with growth. In the decade of the 1870s, Spartanburg surged ahead 201 percent, Greenville 123 percent, and Columbia only 15.5 percent (which was at least more impressive growth than that of Charleston, a city which in 1880 contained 49,984 souls). The State House was still domeless; the streets were not paved; the first street cars were still in the near future and then to be drawn by horses; the college was limited to "the horseshoe"; a bridge had crossed the Congaree at Gervais Street since 1827, and another across the Broad since 1829, both toll bridges; and the town did not extend far north of the present Elmwood Avenue. Main Street was still Richardson Street, and Plain Street had not yet been renamed for Hampton (nor did many know that Lady Street was named for the wife of the man who gave the next thoroughfare its tag—Washington). A few roads connected the capital with other towns, but railroads had a monopoly on transportation (although neither the Seaboard

nor the Columbia, Newberry & Laurens existed in 1880).
The railroads held a fascination for newspaper reporters,
who almost daily included railroad news items. (For example, news of a special train for a famous personage would always include such pertinent facts as the engine number and
names of engineer and conductor.) The big event of the year
was the State Fair held at the fairgrounds on Elmwood Avenue (originally called Upper Street, being the upper bound-
ary of the town).

In his writing as the Columbia correspondent, Gonzales
adopted the informal and personal note that is so popular
with newspaper columnists today. Not only did his writing
include much use of the first personal pronoun, but it also
often revealed his very decided opinions. Such journalism
soon made N. G. G. one of the better known personalities in
South Carolina. His opinions and his candor often involved
him not only in controversy but often in personal clashes
and vendettas.

In 1881 the last famous duel in South Carolina took place,
the Cash-Shannon affray. Already F. W. Dawson had boldly
opposed violence in general and dueling in particular, both
of which had long been strikingly evident in the Palmetto
State. Colonel E. B. C. Cash became so annoyed with Dawson
that he read disreputable implications into the fact that Dawson's original name was Austin John Reeks and charged that
he had been a Union spy during the Civil War.[16] Gonzales
likewise incurred the Cash wrath because his reporting reflected Dawson's opposition to dueling.[17]

The opinionated Gonzales' writing also soon won for him
denunciation from a prohibitionist, John F. Hobbes, who

[16] S. Frank Logan, "Francis Dawson," p. 14.

[17] *News and Courier*, February 25 and 28, 1881. On the duel, see D. D.
Wallace, *History of South Carolina*, 4 vols. (New York: American Historical
Society, 1934), III, 330–32.

denied the veracity of the Columbia column which had noted "his effort to run the gamut of three political parties in one year." In reply, the "City on the Congaree" showed some of the venomous style later considered by many to be characteristic of N. G.: "An insect when in process of vivisection is given to squirming. I am sorry for the squirmer, but the vivisection is for the good of mankind."[18] Thus did he concisely express his permanent conception of the role of an honest journalist.

He also attracted readers with some of his own bold exploits. In 1881 the Charleston paper received a letter from an escaped prisoner charged with murder who agreed to "tell all" if a lone reporter would meet him at midnight of August 10 at the mouth of the abandoned Blue Ridge Tunnel in the mountainous west corner of the state. Nobody appeared except N. G., but his two-column report was a model ghost story replete with both suspense and satire.[19] He felt that the soreness from the horseback trip was worth the effort, for if the hoaxer had appeared, the reporter "would have made a 'ten strike' in reputation and notoriety."[20]

In a state so deeply immersed in politics marked by passionate partisanship, naturally the Columbia correspondent wrote many political and election stories. Modern readers of late nineteenth-century Carolina newspapers might come to conclude that impending elections had as much drama and significance as an impending hurricane and to suspect that most citizens felt that they were always facing doom but were being saved only by sterling knights (of Bourbon persuasion)

[18] *News and Courier*, August 1, 1881.

[19] *Ibid.*, August 13, 1881.

[20] N. G. Gonzales to A. E. Gonzales, August 14, 1881, in E.G.P. N. G. Gonzales was irked by a cartoon of himself posted in the office of the *Greenville News* in which he was shown at the tunnel, "dodging behind a tree very much scared, with a bottle of whiskey handy, labeled 'Courage,' and other appropriate surroundings." N. G. Gonzales to A. E. Gonzales, August 21, 1881, in E.G.P.

who stood at Armageddon and tilted manfully with assorted monsters. When one recalls that the Republican party was moribund and its voting strength shrinking steadily in each election and that South Carolina was basically a one-party state in the 1880s,[21] one wonders what all of the commotion was about and why so many awesome spectres were raised. Actually, precinct meetings and conventions dominated the political life of the state. Once the county Democratic convention made its nominations, in most cases the issue was closed. The nominees would be elected in the general election without Republican opposition or with very slight opposition from a shrinking, apathetic group of Negro Republicans. The same process was used to select state officials; the real choice of governor was made by the state Democratic convention.

Obviously, rank-and-file Democrats were tempted to become lethargic and apathetic. Their participation in general elections shrank as these elections ceased to be real contests. Hence the party machine—and the Democratic press—kept "whooping things up" with constant activities and functions which most nearly resembled modern college "pep rallies" during football season. (The latter ritual presumably helps guarantee a respectable turnout on Saturday.) Obviously there was much county "politiking" to determine whose partisans would be selected by the county convention to attend the state convention. Once the state slate was chosen there, "the ticket" would proceed to "stump the state," going to the scheduled "speakings" all over the state just as if they faced real Republican opposition. If "the Democracy" (as the members of the Democratic Party were regularly called) showed sufficient enthusiasm and support, presumably they

[21] James W. Patton, "Republican Party in South Carolina, 1876–1910," in Fletcher M. Green, ed., *Essays in Southern History* (Chapel Hill: University of North Carolina Press, 1947), pp. 91–111.

would later vote in the general election, thereby preventing any Republican renaissance. The demonstrations of devotion and sheer noisy enthusiasm were supposed to so cow the black Republicans that they would feel any scheme of revival would be too hopeless to contemplate or attempt. Hence the Bourbon candidates regularly made their exhausting tour of the commonwealth, showing to the faithful the Redeemers in the flesh, intoning all the Confederate shibboleths, and bringing shivers of delight to partisans who probably had no entertainment ever available to them quite so exciting as this one-ring circus.

Reporting such campaigns frequently took Gonzales away from Columbia. As reporter for the leading newspaper in South Carolina, he traveled with the "campaign party" and got to know nearly all the leading political figures in the state. On these canvasses, he gave a realistic flavor to his reports by portraying the background of the scene, describing the country towns and their rustic people, and giving the details of the campaigners' accommodations and arduous schedules which he shared. In these accounts one can almost smell the horses, the audiences, and the barbecues as the campaign caravan arrived in a county seat: "twisting like a fiery serpent through and around the town, the head of the column reached the hotel, while its rear was Heaven knows where."[22] When the florid orators arrived at the inevitable grove for "the speaking," N. G. was always on hand to report almost verbatim their thunderings and to record all banter and audience reactions.

The Republicans were still alive but only as a feeble shell of their old Reconstruction selves. A few party hacks kept the organization intact for personal and patronage reasons with the rank-and-file participation still being mostly Negroes.

[22] *News and Courier,* September 18, 1880.

N. G. G. covered them in his vivid style too. His record of
a Republican convention was as colorful as it was biased:

Columbia, November 1.—A melancholy procession wound
through the streets . . . today. It was very black, very dirty, and
very shabby. It is needless to state that it belonged to the Union
Republican party of the city aforesaid. . . .

Reaching the scene shortly before the speaking began, I found
Stolbrand, the ex-Penitentiarian and candidate for Congress and
defeat, struggling desperately with the English idiom and getting
worsted at it. . . . The close proximity of . . . picaninnies at
his feet may have accounted for his nervousness. His discourse
was tame, although he touched on "Aitchfield," "der Rade-shuts,"
and "der tarff." . . .[23]

In opposite mood did he report rallies of the Democrats:

The symbolic Swamp Fox of Marion did not cower today
among the solitudes of the Pee-Dee swamps . . . but showed his
teeth and came out boldly, lending his spirit to the day, his
effigy to the banners and his plume to the men. . . . The fields
might be snow-flecked, the labors of the farmer imperative, the
foe invincible . . . but the men of Marion did not plead excuses
for their lethargy—they *came,* not in a hurrahing mood either;
not drunkenly nor recklessly, but quietly . . . with the determination to clinch, to rivet the gallant reputation of the county.[24]

After a year as Columbia correspondent, N. G. was promoted. Enthusiastically, he went to Washington on October
5, 1881, to describe the special and regular sessions of Con-

---

[23] *Ibid.,* November 2, 1880.
[24] *Ibid.,* October 6, 1880. If a Democratic rally proved to be a fizzle,
Gonzales' enthusiasm waned and his space shrank—although not without
blaming whatever lukewarm Democrats were responsible. His boss, Editor
F. W. Dawson, was a member of the state executive committee and was
South Carolina's representative on the Democratic National Committee.

gress for the *News and Courier*. When he left Columbia, he confidently expected never to return because his orders called for his moving to the Charleston office the following summer.[25] For the moment, however, he would enjoy such marvels as the asphalt streets "as smooth as the summit of Charley Bell's pate," his first electric lights, or the many huge thirty-cent meals to be eaten on his improved salary of eighty-seven dollars a month.[26]

"Our Special Correspondent" altered his style and approach very little for the larger capital. In a single column he revealed himself as a congressional reporter, court reporter, news gatherer, gossip columnist, news analyst, editor, and forecaster of things to come—all rolled into one. His opinions still flowed freely with his heaviest guns now trained on dissident Democrats. For example, he rebuked William Mahone's "swallowing the Republican party": "He is a Dictator. He rules the State [of Virginia]. . . . He also rules the President. . . . He is a very able traitor."[27]

Naturally most of the Washington column was devoted to Congress and congressmen. At first, the sometime resident of Varnville was impressed by the statesmen, but proximity soon bred contempt and indifference. In general he praised Southerners in his column, although his private letters revealed less awe and reverence for the Confederate Brigadiers. N. G. perhaps shocked his Aunt Emily when he privately classified Senator Wade Hampton as a nonentity living on his old reputation—one who even himself realized his failure.[28] With this outlook, Gonzales developed a reporter's arrogance:

25 N. G. Gonzales to W. E. Gonzales, September 25, 1881, and to Gertrude Gonzales, October 7, 1881, in E.G.P.

26 N. G. Gonzales to Ralph E. Elliott, October 7, 1881, in E.G.P. This letter is a lively, nine-page description of Washington.

27 *News and Courier*, November 14, 1881.

28 N. G. Gonzales to Emily Elliott, March 1 and May 18, 1882, in E.G.P.

If he [Hampton] gets too lofty I will put in a little criticism. That is one delight of my position. . . . Hampton . . . is careful to come to me when he wants anything put in that will show him off. . . . If you consider this sacrilege, remember that this is the age of brass. . . .[29]

N. G. frequently stripped away all the glamour and respect with which the Senate was cloaked and revealed to his readers the picture of ordinary men at their worst. One whole dispatch was devoted to "A Politician's Two Faces"—the one he had for his constituents while "on the stump" and the one he had for Washington.[30] Soon wearied by the empty words of pompous orators, Gonzales noted a good speech by a man who had spoken only ten minutes in five years, thereby proving

that if a statesman wants to make a hit with his utterance he must bottle himself up for some time and ferment thoroughly, then loose the cork and the missile flies briskly. The men who keep their mouths open all the time are like bottles with the same fault—they yield an insipid, tasteless stream that would otherwise be a foamy, spirited outburst.[31]

An unvarnished view of the cloakrooms appeared. There, "it is very peaceful and quiet, but wholly lacking in the characteristics of intelligent legislation. . . . There are too many sleeping beauties on the leathern couches, and there is no knight to waken them."[32] But the disillusioned readers of the *News and Courier* probably no longer believed in knights anyhow.

As a court reporter, N. G. merely enlarged on his earlier

[29] N. G. Gonzales to Emily Elliott, March 1, 1882, in E.G.P.
[30] *News and Courier,* February 10, 1882.
[31] *Ibid.,* April 26, 1882.
[32] *Ibid.,* June 28, 1882.

experiences. In Washington he described in detail the trial, conviction, and execution of Charles J. Guiteau, assassin of President James A. Garfield. Frequently departing from the full testimony, Gonzales interspersed his reports with observations on judges and juries, prophecies of Guiteau's conduct, and one penetrating analysis and description of the spectators at the trial.[33] When it ended, N. G. wearily wrote his aunt, "Well! Guiteau is doomed. I still believe . . . that he is cracked, but in spite of that I will have to try my powers of description on his hanging."[34] For such sensations, his powers never failed the morbid *News and Courier* readers in Charleston, Branchville, Yorkville, or Abbeville.

Although a reporter of news, N. G. had gone to Washington with a clear understanding that he could express his own views even in disagreement with the policy of the *News and Courier*.[35] Besides this *carte blanche,* his opinions were also stimulated by his expressed conception of himself as an extra member of the South Carolina delegation, responsible for unhampered and frank reports to his constituency—the state population and the subscription list being synonymous in his eyes. His readers therefore learned:

There is an excess of verbal husk to the small kernel of legislative action.

When every other grab is made they all unite on a big effort for Mississippi River "improvements." A bold scheme which was hatched up a few days ago to open the Treasury for the "Father of Waters" was consigned yesterday to a watery grave, which it filled very appropriately.[36]

[33] See *ibid.,* November 22, 1881. The trial ran from November 1881 into January 1882.

[34] N. G. Gonzales to Emily Elliott, January 25, 1882, in E.G.P. To facilitate such work, Gonzales studied shorthand in 1881. N. G. Gonzales to A. E. Gonzales, March 15, 1881, in E.G.P.

[35] N. G. Gonzales to Emily Elliott, February 19, 1882, in E.G.P.

[36] *News and Courier,* January 23, 1882.

Likewise frank were the following observations: "Jeffersonian Democracy is not popular where the river and harbors bill is under consideration"; "The whiskey bill very properly . . . collapsed . . . today"; or, after a passage of a pension bill, "Only a foretaste of the squeezing we are to have for all the bummers of the Union armies."[37]

As earlier in Varnville, Savannah, and Valdosta, N. G. became increasingly restless and disgusted while in Washington.

With very little reverence for existing statesmen and an unfortunate deficiency in the powers of admiration, I became accustomed to Congress in a week . . . and tired of it in a fortnight. . . . Saturated with Congressional proceedings, sated with the cry of "Mr. Speaker," revolting against a study of the *Record,* I shudder at the thought that the session must last until July. . . . With this . . . truthful outline of the situation, I conclude my confession and revert to THE EVERLASTING CONGRESS.[38]

Part of his irreverence was personal gratification or ego, for N. G. claimed "there is but one power, The News and Courier, and Gonzales is its prophet." Another time he candidly explained: "Felt sour Sunday, so I abused the Congressmen. I do that on principle, lest they should think me an 'organ.' " Actually, he was on close terms with all the South Carolina delegation, and won some praise from Congressman George D. Tillman who once told him, "You have an *awful* gravity for a young man, Narcisse. You show very mature thought for a boy. And damne! you're independent as hell!"[39]

Very little good could N. G. find in any Republicans, but he was particularly unsparing of those from South Carolina, whom he unfavorably described as "bogus representatives

---

[37] *Ibid.,* June 16 and May 18, 1882.

[38] *Ibid.,* May 18, 1882.

[39] N. G. Gonzales to Emily Elliott, February 19 and March 1 and 27, 1882, in E.G.P.

of the [E. W. M.] Mackey stripe," who were devout believers "in the Sunday-school dogma that 'Satan has some mischief for idle hands to do.' "[40] Even so, he frequently attacked the many Democrats who acted and voted like Republicans and who he said needed "a little politico-economical training and an infusion of ordinary common sense."[41]

Attacks on the G.O.P. of South Carolina did not go unanswered, for Mackey accosted Gonzales in front of Willard's and demanded that the reporter not allude further to his "social misdeeds." N. G. told him he would use his own discretion in the matter, whereupon Mackey departed. Robert Smalls, however, used a stick to impress his complaints on the correspondent, but he soon had to retire, leaving Gonzales in possession of the field. The reporter was particularly pleased to observe that the rival *Columbia Register* headed its story, "Bully for Gonzales."[42]

The Gonzales columns were not always serious and political. Often his pen strung together a potpourri that resembled a modern gossip column. In this way, his readers learned of the "aboriginal features" of "that unterrified advocate of the advantages of pantaloons on the 'female form divine,' Dr. Mary Walker." That same day they learned personal bits about Judge T. J. Mackey of Charleston; were warned that Washington lobbyists were "the country's real legislators, . . . innumerable in number and multiform in character"; and heard rumors about the Charleston collectorship that was "causing agony" in the Treasury Department.[43] One column was devoted to a hilarious crusade against four "Capi-

[40] *News and Courier,* July 29 and April 18, 1882. Mackey was a white Republican who became prominent during Reconstruction, was speaker of the Republican House in 1876, and was elected to Congress in 1878 and 1880.

[41] *Ibid.,* June 21, 1882.

[42] N. G. Gonzales to Emily Elliott, December 25, 1881, and January 8, 1882, in E.G.P.

[43] *News and Courier,* January 12, 1882.

tal Nuisances, . . . before they sap my young existence": the bootblack, the cigarette youth, Washington weather, and essence of musk.[44] N. G. also observed for his country readers that Washington women were more in evidence on cold, windy days. "Why? Simply because they want to show off their sealskin sacques. But I thought today, at least, the game was not worth the candle."[45] And like other Washington correspondents, Gonzales always could tell his readers "on the best authority" what certain statesmen would decide or do in the future, but at least he confessed fallibility: "But it is pleasanter to guess for the amusement of the public than to neglect the future entirely, so I run the risk of errors."[46]

Besides such mosaic columns, N. G. also wrote lengthy feature stories that contained both information and entertainment, not unlike some of the features in the modern *New Yorker*. For example, once he devoted well over a column to the customs, traditions, and inner workings of the Supreme Court, including little-known details that would interest readers of any time.[47] On other occasions, he gave thumbnail sketches of congressmen, cut short only to give rest to "my overworked adjectives." For example, he characterized S. S. ("Sunset") Cox of New York thus: "The genius of perpetual motion. Small, nervous, compact, versatile, he flits from one task to another, the bee of the legislative garden." Other irreverent descriptions of Cox included "second best record of noise—not brains—on the Republican [sic] side"; "horse face, but credited with horse sense also"; and "prefers to do silent work in the interest of protection."[48]

Several columns were given over to the woman suffrage

[44] *Ibid.*, April 29, 1882.
[45] *Ibid.*, January 27, 1882.
[46] *Ibid.*, August 5, 1882 (his last column from Washington).
[47] *Ibid.*, March 19, 1882.
[48] *Ibid.*, February 4, 1882. Evidently Gonzales erred carelessly: Cox was a Democrat.

movement. Bachelor Gonzales attended one meeting and confided to the readers of the *News and Courier,* "I confess that my preconceived ideas of strong-minded women received a shock in one respect," for instead of "vinegar features" he found that "a majority of the Convention were decidedly stout and their raiment was as vivid in color as any ordinary slave of fashion." One was even "tolerably good looking. I should pronounce her to be a school teacher"; after her came "a wild Western woman," who from her own account kept her husband and children "pretty well under her control." N. G. predicted that "there will continue to be fanatics forever, and before many years the agitation will bear fruit. . . ."[49]

All of N. G.'s life in Washington did not rotate around Congress and political movements, however. The young writer was just beginning to "feel his oats" and for a time enjoyed the bright lights of Washington as well as the sensation that he now was "Somebody." Living at a boardinghouse, the journalist roomed next to George D. Tillman, South Carolina congressman. The latter roomed with James R. Randall, author of "My Maryland" and then a correspondent for the *Augusta Chronicle.* The three became fast friends and mutual admirers. Of Colonel Tillman (the only person ever to call N. G. "Narcisse") the newsman said, "I have the run of his books and papers, and better than all, his hard sense and legislative experience."[50] To his family, N. G. wrote numerous descriptions of Randall, of which the following is typical:

He writes beautifully and rapidly, and is as lazy as yours affectionately, and, as Col. Tillman says, "loves good eating better than any poet I ever saw, damne!" . . . He . . . joins me in my

49 *Ibid.,* January 23, 1882.
50 N. G. Gonzales to Emily Elliott, January 25, 1882, in E.G.P.

frugal style of eating and then, disgusted, rushes off to a big dinner and gets sick.

I assure you that he is infinitely more tragic when condemning a 35¢ dinner than while reciting "My Maryland"—and he has reached the stage of life where a good meal is sweeter by far than oceans of panegyric.[51]

As in earlier days, the Washington correspondent tried to economize in order to send money to the family, although he confessed that sometimes he did "hanker for a square meal of hominy and bacon."[52] His aunts saw no reason why he could not arrange immediate compensation in Washington for their confiscated lands, and N. G. had to warn: "Congress is a queer animal, a sort of humanized lottery. . . . Hence impatience is not only useless but injurious. . . . Brace up. . . . Encourage hilariousness as I do—*I*, with all the ills of life upon me."[53]

Although his newspaper work was attracting wide comment and was frequently copied by other papers, N. G. admitted, "I am a South Carolina alligator, and am not happy except in my own swamp."[54] The flowers and plants sent frequently from Oak Lawn to him did naught to alleviate his growing aversion to the nation's capital. His tune again sounded like that in his impatient letters from Varnville:

Gayety, and fashion and wealth—are not pleasant subjects to a dull and tired drudge who can't participate, . . . who hates to have luxury thrust before his impecunious eyes, and who in truth is very much of a Communist. . . . I want to be among some

[51] Same to same, *ibid.* and February 5, 1882, in E.G.P. As George Tillman expressively said, " 'If that man don't put his stomach on a pedestal and worship it, I'm a fool, by dam!' " Same to same, February 19, 1882, in E.G.P.
[52] Same to same, February 19, 1882, in E.G.P.
[53] Same to same, April 9, 1882, in E.G.P.
[54] Same to same, March 12, 1882. Also, see his letters to her, January 8 and February 19, 1882, in E.G.P.

poor people. . . . I abhor the sight of a lot of rascals who have made their money by government thefts or usury.[55]

Since Ambrose was now working as a telegrapher in New York, N. G. occasionally went there, hoping to bring himself out of "the slough of despond." Gloomily he reported, "No money, no companionship and an infinite quantity of tread-mill routine and hard and unavailing thought are not vivify-ing or cheering."[56]

This growing disgust was mirrored in his reports which increasingly discredited Congress. He finally suggested as-sessing the people directly by monthly bills which would read: "You are charged $—— for ministering to the vanity of the Hon. ————. as per *Congressional Record,* Forty-seventh Congress." He had some hope of adjournment since "Hot weather stimulates conscientiousness in a Congressman wonderfully." When the summer heat failed to work that change, N. G. lamented:

> The Senate . . . is my *bête noir.* . . . The sternest rebuke in-flicted upon that agglomeration of garrulous geniuses this year was dealt by the House adjourning over three days. . . .
> This bad body may, however, be expected to do some work during the coming week. . . . I base my opinion upon the fact that the supply of free Apolinaris water has been cut off.[57]

Chief cause for Gonzales' impatience with Washington, however, was that he now had more buoyant personal hopes than at any previous time. Riordan and Dawson had plans to convert their property in 1882 into a joint stock company in which they would keep 70 percent of the stock. Riordan visited N. G. in Washington and told him they planned to

[55] Same to same, March 1, 1882, in E.G.P.
[56] N. G. Gonzales to Gertrude Gonzales, March 19, 1882, in E.G.P.
[57] *News and Courier,* August 4, 1882.

bring him to Charleston to "go into training for the editorship." Riordan said he definitely favored N. G. for the post,
and that he and Dawson wanted to retire from active work
soon. As proof of his faith, Riordan sold Gonzales a $500
share of his stock on easy terms. Dawson also wrote to praise
and encourage his work, but he never committed himself to
making N. G. his heir apparent.[58] With this goal, however,
the prospective editor left Washington for Charleston in
August 1882.

Arriving in that "Holy City," Gonzales found the place
"excruciatingly dingy, dull and dismal." Riordan and Dawson received their star reporter with considerable frigidity
and seemed interested only in knowing when he could go to
work. N. G. noted it was "not an encouraging reception. . . ."[59] In the home office, his work was varied—exchange editor, rewriter of "country correspondence," editorial writer, headline writer, letter writer, and proof reviser.
After going to Columbia in the fall to report the activities of
the legislature, he returned to Charleston and soon could
announce, "The Tycoon [Dawson] has been very amiable
indeed."[60]

The Charleston residence was brief, however. In early
1883 Dawson went to Europe, and James C. Hemphill, the
Columbia correspondent, was brought to the home office and
was replaced at the state capital by Gonzales. The latter believed that the swap was temporary during the absence of
the editor; Riordan always attended primarily to the busi-

[58] Detailed account of the Riordan promise is contained in N. G. Gonzales to R. E. Elliott, October 21, 1881, and N. G. Gonzales to W. E. Gonzales, October 22, 1881, in E.G.P. Riordan implied that Dawson approved
the plan, however. I have not seen any evidence of this plan in other
manuscript collections.

[59] N. G. Gonzales to his aunts, August 22, 1882, in E.G.P.

[60] N. G. Gonzales to R. E. Elliott, August 17, 1882, and N. G. Gonzales to
Emily Elliott, January 3, 1883, in E.G.P.

ness affairs anyhow, and Hemphill "has *cacoethes scribendi* and can fill up the editorial page on short notice and to order, which I can't."[61]

Gonzales believed that Dawson favored Hemphill as his heir apparent (a feeling confirmed by subsequent events) and that Riordan was backing him.[62] At least, he bore no animosity toward his old friend Hemphill, who probably was favored by Dawson because he was more tactful and had a less mercurial temperament. An affable soul from a well-known South Carolina family, "the Major" as he was always known (a mysterious title, the reasons for which apparently nobody ever fathomed) began his newspapering in Abbeville and enjoyed a successful journalistic career that lasted into the 1920s.[63] Gonzales accepted his assignment back to Columbia as a pleasant one where "the escape from Dawson's continual ordering and hectoring is quite refreshing."[64] Meanwhile, he still continued to contribute occasional editorials to the paper.

N. G.'s improved fortunes enabled him now to provide for the education of his youngest brother, Willie—a responsibility which he had begun in 1881.[65] Such a task was almost beyond his ability and was made doubly difficult by Willie's reluctance to seek a formal education because of his severe stuttering. In early 1881 he set forth for the King's Mountain

[61] N. G. Gonzales to Emily Elliott, January 14, 1883, in E.G.P.

[62] Same to same, January 21, 1883, in E.G.P. Here he quotes at length from Riordan.

[63] For a too-brief sketch, see Lewis P. Jones, "James Calvin Hemphill," in Sass, *Outspoken,* pp. 75–80. Dawson had been subjected to some badgering and snubbing because of his English and Catholic background, and may have therefore bypassed Cuban Gonzales for the quite conventional Associate Reformed Presbyterian "Seceder" from the up-country. It is interesting that of the five editors of the *News and Courier* to date, only one—the present one—has been a Charlestonian.

[64] N. G. Gonzales to Gertrude Gonzales, December 1, 1882, in E.G.P.

[65] A. J. Gonzales to Ignacio Gonzales Gauffreau, August 5, 1884, in possession of Major R. K. McMaster.

Military School conducted by Colonel Asbury Coward in Yorkville, rough and rustic town of the up-country.[66] The timid boy was constantly homesick for the plantation but promptly received demerits for fighting that he reported "had to be dun." Like his oldest brother, he always had an eye for the fairer sex and expressed grave regrets that the Yorkville girls "will not set the world on fire with their beauty."[67] Despite this disparagement, his aunt gave him permission to fall in love with a new girl every Sunday. His reply shows similarity to his grandfather's personality—although not to his syntax.

I have not found a sweethart in york, yet, for I am very gready. I want one alto myself not those that drive by here and kiss there hands to all the boys weather they know them or not. There was a party here the other night. . . . but I did as I would be done by and did not go, for I knew . . . that if I had gone none of the other boys would have had a chance to have spoken to a girl for I would have flung them all in the shade and though none of them have thanked me openly I can see that they are greatly moved by my noble generosity.[68]

Ambrose felt constrained to warn the fifteen-year-old Lochinvar, "You must be careful & not let the girls run off with you. Having the traditional beauty of the Gonzales, it behooves you not to make public exhibition of your charms."[69]

N. G. took seriously his responsibility for his young brother and sent frequent admonitions and advice which resembled

[66] This small academy, founded in 1855 and closed in 1886, claimed to be the "Pioneer and Oldest Existing" private military school in the South. It is now the site of an Episcopal orphanage. For a history of it, see *The State*, October 29, 1913, which republished an article from the *Rural Carolinian* of February, 1874. On Colonel Coward, see *The State*, April 29, 1925.

[67] W. E. Gonzales to A. E. Gonzales, March 4, 1881, in E.G.P.

[68] W. E. Gonzales to Emily Elliott, March 10, 1881, in reply to her letter of February 21, 1881, in E.G.P.

[69] A. E. Gonzales to W. E. Gonzales, March 19, 1881, in E.G.P.

letters by his grandfather, William Elliott. Often he had difficulty in providing the necessary expenses for his less energetic brother, but never did he fail him. In 1883 Willie joined Ambrose in New York and there attended a school to improve his speech.[70] N. G. then sent the boy to The Citadel in October 1883, and although the young cadet liked military training, he constantly complained of being embarrassed by his stuttering and prevailed on his guardian to let him drop out of school in April 1884.[71]

N. G.'s responsibility was but one aspect of a scattered family that still remained very much knit together. All of their income was virtually pooled, and both Ambrose and N. G. kept trying to supply the needs of those on the plantation.[72] The aunts, Misses Emily and Anne Elliott, took summer boarders at their Flat Rock home, and Gertrude Gonzales began teaching both her younger sister and the neighbors. And in 1883 Hattie, the youngest, embarked for a Baltimore school where she was financed by her father and Ambrose. Always uninhibited, she had difficulty adjusting to the restraints, though pridefully she went to her first Sunday school "and got through it remarkably well considering."[73]

Numerous letters helped maintain these close family ties. Like N. G., Ambrose was generally pleasant in his letters

[70] W. E. Gonzales to Miss Anne Elliott, August 2, 1883, and A. E. Gonzales to Emily Elliott, August 29, 1883, in E.G.P.

[71] Major Lewis Simons, assistant registrar of The Citadel, to the author, February 9, 1951; N. G. Gonzales to Gertrude Gonzales, February 22 and April 8, 1884, in E.G.P. Despite the short stay, he was always a very loyal alumnus.

[72] N. G. Gonzales could be irritated when their requests became too frequent or nagging. In 1884 he tried to set aside money to buy stock in the *News and Courier*, despite just having spent $1,500 on Willie. See N. G. Gonzales to R. E. Elliott, July 22, 1884, and to an aunt, April 5, 1885, in E.G.P.

[73] Harriett R. E. Gonzales to Emily Elliott, February 18, 1883. Also, see W. E. Gonzales to Emily Elliott, October 13, 1882, and A. E. Gonzales to Emily Elliott, October 9, 1882, and December 30, 1883, all in E.G.P.

although occasionally he did weary of having to "contribute any more to the maintenance of joint grass and dog fennel (and dogs) which seem to be the outcome of agricultural ventures there under the present régime. . . . With any kind of management the place could make at least a winter support for the family . . . and I'd be ashamed to wear breeches if I couldn't do it."[74] Such unproductivity did not bother or shame Uncle Ralph, however, although he in turn frequently chided Bory's propensity for sleeping, swearing, and visiting barrooms. Ralph also dabbled in local politics, but, as on most things, he soured on that, reporting that the county convention was "remarkable for the absence of lawyers, decorum & grammer [*sic*]— the baptist preachers and stock thieves had it all their way."[75]

At no time could the family get planting out of the blood, and in 1883 Ambrose Gonzales was planning to return from New York to Social Hall Plantation where N. G. would go shares with him. The latter also proposed grandiose schemes for settling German immigrants on the land. The brothers' most tangible aid for the family, however, was the erection of a new cottage at Oak Lawn late in 1883.[76] They were also continuously sending cash contributions to those two gentlemen of leisure, Uncle Ralph and Bory.

Although the family letters were numerous, N. G. never ceased complaining about their inadequacy. Once he wrote his fond brother as follows:

Dear Brosie:
    Your note received. You suffer from a constitutional shortness of breath in regard to letter writing. . . . If the ancients had

[74] A. E. Gonzales to Emily Elliott, October 5, 1883, in E.G.P.

[75] R. E. Elliott to Emily Elliott, July 13, 1882, in E.G.P.

[76] N. G. Gonzales to Emily Elliott, March 13, 1883, and to W. E. Gonzales, March 29, 1881; A. E. Gonzales to R. E. Elliott, December 15, 1883, in E.G.P.

hated writing descriptive letters as much as you do, we wouldn't have any history. A description of Caesar's assassination would read thus: "Dear Blank. Caesar was killed today. Weather splendid. No news. Write soon. Yours, Blank."[77]

None of the wanderers could ever get enough reports on the planting, the hunts, the jessamines, or the cattle of Oak Lawn.

One reason for N. G.'s family attachment was the fact that he made few very close friends in Columbia. His sole recreation was chess, but he did insist that his arduous work was the only explanation of his being known "for abstemiousness in the matter of womankind."[78] Always he had a reputation for aloofness and introversion. Such a coldness was partially due to a personality marked by extreme timidity and shyness. His few friends always recognized this trait, while others saw only arrogance and superciliousness. Despite his distant ways, he was one of the thirty-two charter members of the Columbia Club in 1884, an exclusive social organization for gentlemen of the capital.[79]

When he returned to Columbia in 1883, N. G. resumed his old routine of energetically making daily rounds of hotels, government departments and offices, the South Carolina College, all courts, railroad shops and stations, the city hall, the penitentiary, lawyers' offices, and—above all—the legislature. One installment of his news gleanings went to Charleston on the afternoon train and more items followed by telegraph late at night. Variety still marked a column that might read in part as follows:

The Governor's Guards gave a grand hop tonight.
The Penitentiary Board will meet tomorrow at 10 o'clock.

[77] N. G. Gonzales to A. E. Gonzales, March 15, 1881, in E.G.P.
[78] N. G. Gonzales to Emily Elliott, May 7, 1883, in E.G.P.
[79] *News and Courier*, March 25 and April 30, 1884; *The State*, July 11, 1893. A history of the club is in *The State*, November 4, 1913.

Dr. Howe's condition is cheering.

The Congaree is slowly falling tonight.

It is warm enough today. Maximum, 84, minimum, 49, rainfall none.

Before Judge Hudson today an involved land case of no public interest was protractedly argued.[80]

Of course, significant events received more detailed coverage and often used all of the space allotted to "N. G. G." And, as always, the correspondent's opinion was aired; after stories of shootings or stabbings, he usually added a laconic prognosis: "He will die" or "He will recover."

Several types of events received routine treatment that would seem unique to modern readers. Gonzales reported all major funerals in the capital and sometimes told much more about the pallbearers and parson than he did about the deceased. He devoted great attention to churches, and on Mondays synopsized the themes of all the services the day before. Revivals were covered in detail, especially those of the famous Moody and Sankey who jammed the Opera House in 1886. However, such wrestlers with Satan as the Salvation Army and the Holiness evangelists drew unrestrained condemnation from this Episcopalian who said, "Alleged conversions of the ignorant or inebriate may be made by vociferations of impending doom, but they do not last."[81] Of the "vulgar," "insulting," "offensive" Evangelist Sam Jones, Gonzales asserted, "People must have pretty strong stomachs to digest the sort of spiritual food which this alleged preacher has offered to Columbia."[82] But they went in droves and

---

[80] For another example, see *News and Courier,* January 31, 1884, where six inches of type described ten events. The events in the text above were picked at random and did not appear together in one column.

[81] *News and Courier,* February 21, 1887. For more attacks, see *ibid.,* February 22–24, 1887.

[82] *Ibid.,* April 20, 1888.

later took special excursion trains to hear him preach in Charleston.

Every fall Gonzales played with all stops out when the state fair was held in Columbia. In addition to listing all the prizes and premiums, he gave full coverage to the balloons, "Japanese day fireworks," "grand torchlight parade and illumination," the "Invisibles of Columbia," the fire department parades, and the grand "ascent of Pain's prize asteroids." On top of this extra work, he always had the additional duty of entertaining Bory, who never missed a fair.

In the 1880s reporters rarely shied away from indelicate subjects. For example, in a story of a "disgraceful affair," N. G. gave the full details and names in an incident which involved a white man's horsewhipping a Negro out of jealousy of a Negro woman "who seems to be at the bottom of the affair."[83]

A more onerous reportorial task for Gonzales was the duty of reporting society events. A major event of the social calendar was the State Ball, given annually in the State Capitol by the exclusive South Carolina Club during the state fair. Dawson finally sent a female reporter up to help Gonzales describe the women's costumes, but her omission of some items brought feminine wrath on the luckless head of the Columbia correspondent.[84] In 1887, however, N. G. devoted his energy to the "unpleasant duty" of reporting most frankly a ball most unsatisfactory because of "a very picayunish economy or exceedingly bad judgment." The chief legislative reporter was unsparing in his criticisms of tables that "looked as if they had been raided by an army of white ants, Sherman's bummers, or some other devastating

---

[83] *Ibid.,* July 30 and 31, 1885.

[84] N. G. Gonzales to Gertrude Gonzales, November 25, 1883, in E.G.P.; *News and Courier,* November 19, 1883. For a history of the South Carolina Club, see *The State,* October 25, 1903.

horde."[85] College festivities also came under the reporter's scrutiny; once he cautiously and tactfully observed that he would have described the women present "but as there might also be some partiality displayed, it is probably wisest to desist."[86]

Although Gonzales quickly became known as Dawson's bright young reporter, he was, as usual, soon unhappy as Columbia correspondent for "this unthankful, bloated and insincere journal."[87] B. R. Riordan, who had been Gonzales' sponsor, left the paper in 1884, and even before he departed had come to agree with Dawson that Hemphill should be pushed to the top.[88] In 1884 "Major" or "Deacon" Hemphill was appointed virtual vice-editor and manager by Dawson, who clearly now had no big plans for Gonzales.[89] Nevertheless, the Charleston publishers appreciated their capital reporter, gave him a free rein, and noted that their paper, published 130 miles away, outsold the rival *Columbia Register* in its own town. Such recognition was inadequate for Gonzales, who sensed his own importance and who never enjoyed taking orders.

In early 1884 N. G. and his old friend A. B. Williams started plans for launching a Charleston evening paper to compete with the *News and Courier*. Their leading financial backer was F. W. Wagener, a Charleston banker who had become most disaffected with Dawson because of the paper's support of a Republican fusionist candidate who de-

---

[85] *News and Courier,* November 15, 1887.

[86] *Ibid.,* June 17, 1885.

[87] N. G. Gonzales to W. E. Gonzales, December 23, 1883, in E.G.P.

[88] B. R. Riordan to J. C. Hemphill, February 15, 1886, in Hemphill Papers. Riordan's place in the business management was generally filled by General Rudolph Seigling, Charleston banker. See biographical sketch in *Columbia Register,* March 14, 1894.

[89] F. W. Dawson to J. C. Hemphill, December 29, 1884, in Dawson Papers. For Hemphill's reminiscences of his duties, see his "Report to the Directors," February 8, 1910, in Hemphill Papers.

feated his brother, Gen. John A. Wagener, for Charleston mayor in 1875. At that time he had set up the *Journal of Commerce* to oppose the *News and Courier,* bringing R. B. Rhett, Jr., up from New Orleans to edit it.[90] Now in 1884 Wagener and others agreed to make Gonzales and Williams a loan of the equipment of the defunct *Journal of Commerce.* N. G. was holding out for cash to finance the new paper, when Wagener suddenly changed his mind and demanded cash for the printing plant and thereby caused the whole enterprise to collapse. Gonzales had in the meantime been warned by Dawson that he did not consider an evening paper as a serious competitor but that he was determined to thwart Williams, "their pet abomination."[91]

During this maneuver, the *News and Courier* made several offers to keep N. G. in its fold, and at the end the directors accepted his terms: twenty-eight dollars a week and the chance to write three or four editorials weekly. N. G. was candid to his brother about the coup: "So now, 'out of the nettle, danger, I have plucked the flower, safety.' . . . I feel pretty jovial. There's nothing like audacity, and my grand 'bluff' game was highly successful."[92]

The paper soon thereafter further enhanced N. G.'s responsibility. For one thing, on September 20, 1884, he ac-

[90] Joseph W. Barnwell, "Life and Recollections of Joseph W. Barnwell," unpublished manuscript (1929), p. 408, in South Carolina Historical Society. As Dawson put it once, "The Rhetts . . . are mortal foes of mine. . . ." F. W. Dawson to Sarah Morgan, July 3, 1873, in Dawson Papers. In 1876 Dawson was embittered by a "scandalous attack" on him and sued the *Journal of Commerce* for libel and damages of $25,000. Dawson to his wife, "Monday" [1877?], in Dawson Papers.

[91] N. G. Gonzales to Gertrude Gonzales, February 22, 1884; N. G. Gonzales to Emily Elliott, March 26, 1884; and N. G. Gonzales to A. E. Gonzales, April 6, 1884, in E.G.P.

[92] N. G. Gonzales to A. E. Gonzales, April 6, 1884, in E.G.P. N. G. was now buying *News and Courier* and Building & Loan stock, saving $30 a month, providing $30 a month for Gertrude and Willie, and buying all of Willie's clothes.

quired an assistant, William E. Gonzales, who received five dollars a week for his labors.[93] In April 1885 the *News and Courier* established its Columbia Bureau, of which N. G. was made manager. The new organization handled not only news gathering but also circulation and advertising business for the paper in the capital city of ten thousand. From the beginning the Bureau was a financial success—a fact often paraded in Gonzales' Columbia column. Somehow N. G. schemed with Dawson to handle circulation on a commission basis and thus brought into the Bureau the sage services of Uncle Ralph, Captain R. E. Elliott, as supervisor of three newsboys and as bookkeeper at ten dollars a week. As the nephew admitted, "The Captain's work will be more sedentary than anything else."[94]

As a team, the Gonzales brothers functioned smoothly. Although the Captain was horrified that they earned their pay by working from nine A.M. until midnight, seven days a week, N. G. was soon pleased with Willie's work, though he acknowledged that his younger brother was "beginning to be touched with acute enlargement of the bump of self-appreciation . . . like all dudes. But entirely too big to spank."[95] When Narciso left Columbia to report big murder trials, political campaigns, and other events, the "City on the Congaree" was signed "W. E. G." Willie also accumulated extra cash by serving as Columbia representative for

[93] W. E. Gonzales in *The State*, September 20, 1934. N. G. contributed $10 a week and his lodgings to this reporter "green as grass when summer rains have been 'copious.' " N. G. brought him there in the hope of "teaching him business habits and ameliorating his stammering, which is worse than ever." N. G. Gonzales to A. E. Gonzales, July 22, 1884, in E.G.P.

[94] N. G. Gonzales to an aunt, April 5, 1885, in E.G.P. All three of the family roomed together. On the Bureau, see *News and Courier*, April 20, 21, 28, 1885; April 21, 1886; April 21, 1887; and Helen K. Hennig, *August Kohn: Versatile South Carolinian* (Columbia: Vogue Press, 1950), pp. 75–76.

[95] R. E. Elliott to Emily Elliott, May 21, 1885; fragment, N. G. Gonzales to ———, n.d., in E.G.P.

the *New York Sun,* which preferred stories of hangings above everything else.[96] With this increasing prosperity and with Willie now more independent, N. G. soon was able to buy more stock in the paper.[97]

One reason why Dawson had never accepted Gonzales as his editorial heir undoubtedly was the temper which had been evident since N. G. was a child at Oak Lawn. The testy correspondent was constantly involved in controversies and "scrapes," and although his indignation was righteous and his cause perhaps right, his language was rarely restrained.

Gonzales' first "difficulty" after the Robert Smalls fight in Washington occurred in 1883. In his column he painted an unfavorable picture of the action of Secretary of State James N. Lipscomb in removing from office his chief clerk, M. C. Robertson. J. P. Thomas, Jr., private secretary to Governor Hugh S. Thompson and close friend of Gonzales, remonstrated with Lipscomb, and the two eventually resorted to fisticuffs. N. G. published a thoroughly pro-Thomas account of their fracas. Lipscomb questioned the validity of this account, whereupon Gonzales proclaimed to the world that he would call on the secretary of state to "denounce him in unmistakable language." Hearing of the threats, Governor Thompson swore out a peace warrant against Gonzales when the latter refused to promise to restrain himself. Appearing before a trial justice, the reporter had to put up a $500 bond to keep the peace for a year and a day. Despite the restrictions, his printed words fairly bristled as he recounted the duplicity and "misstatements" of Lipscomb.[98] As a matter of fact, N. G. was privately pleased with

---

[96] *The State,* August 3, 1933.
[97] F. W. Dawson to N. G. Gonzales, December 3, 1886, in Dawson Papers.
[98] *News and Courier,* May 30, 31, 1883, and September 15–19, 1883; also, *Columbia Register,* same dates.

himself: "Instead of simply telling Lipscomb to his face that he was a liar I have been able to advertise the fact in the papers all over the country."[99]

This matter of "giving the lie" to a man was a serious problem in the violence-ridden South. Honor was as delicate a thing in the New South as the old *code duello* had been before the war, and a veritable arsenal traveled in Southern hip pockets. Personal dignity was kept alive in an atmosphere of vengeance, and Southerners were unreasonably touchy about their veracity and good names. Recognized perpetrators of embezzlement, usury, adultery, too-sly trading, or even killings could wander in the community with impunity and often with swagger. Reference to their past deeds might evoke either a sneer or a smile, but such reference was not necessarily dangerous. But an implication that a man was a liar and a blackguard necessitated "satisfaction." Often shrewd maneuvering might follow and end with both parties "satisfied"—the accuser that he had proved to the world that the other was a liar, the accused as agreeably pleased that his survival had convicted the other of cowardice. Endowed with the Gonzales temper and the Elliott pride and sense of honor, N. G. Gonzales frequently ventured dangerously close to the violence and lawlessness which he so vigorously condemned in his writing. In his own mind and in print, he also boldly proved some men liars and then, by circuitous arguing and bluff, also proved them cowards—or so he always claimed until one shot him to death.

A year after his clash with Lipscomb, N. G. Gonzales received a visit from one John Agnew, his two sons, and his cane. Survival in this case hinged on the fact that Gonzales had not written that article which had offended Agnew, who

[99] N. G. Gonzales to Gertrude Gonzales, September 20, 1883, in E.G.P.

was still angry from an incident which he had instigated a few weeks before by publishing "cards" in the *Columbia Yeoman* to accuse Gonzales of cowardly conduct during the arrest of W. B. Cash, son of Colonel E. B. C. Cash. In that exchange, N. G. had been defended and his honor saved by a retort signed by one of the constabulary who assured readers that Gonzales actually was in the posse "where he could easily have been shot." Thus his good name was preserved at the same time that he had been "scooping" his rivals by cutting the telegraph wires and tapping out his own story of Cash's arrest.[100]

More serious clashes often centered around the *Columbia Register,* whose editor had been baiting the *News and Courier* before Gonzales appeared in his bailiwick.[101] His advent merely superheated the temper and words of the ill-humored publisher of the *Register,* Charles A. Calvo, Jr. Beating the *Register* to many news items, the Columbia Bureau never failed to gloat over its victories "even at the risk of introducing the people of Columbia" to the "cantankerous doings of their local journal." The Calvo family could absorb many shafts, but not the salt which the Gonzaleses gloatingly poured in the wounds.

The weakness of the *Register* was its martyr complex when scooped and its plaintive appeals to Columbians to bear with it, despite the intrepid competitors from Charleston who, it said, suffered from "continuous self-magnification." Such pleas only evoked jibes and chiding sermons from "N. G. G." In 1885 he told the public that the reason he gave better coverage to the South Carolina College than Calvo did was that the *Register* was not interested in the

---

[100] *News and Courier,* October 6, 1884; March 12 and 21, 1884; April 7, 1884; May 16, 1884; *Columbia Register,* April 6, 1884; N. G. Gonzales to Emily Elliott, May 12, 1883, and to A. E. Gonzales, April 6, 1884, in E.G.P.
[101] See *Columbia Register,* April 26, 1880, on the *News and Courier.*

college nor in boosting the state. From what N. G. called "the mudbanks of his imagination," the *Register* editor then unloosed "a shower of abuse" on Gonzales, who in turn admitted it was "unpleasant to be assailed, even by the vicious and vulgar" but stated that "friends who believe that the 'tar-baby' of the *Register* cannot be touched without defilement have induced me to let it alone."[102]

Six months later the Bureau and the *Register* were at it again. N. G. had suppressed a story of a prospective bankruptcy, but the *Register* "characteristically perverted" the facts. For several days, scurrilous charges appeared in both papers, and finally, according to the *News and Courier,* "Mr. Gonzales . . . found Mr. LaMotte [*Register* writer] . . . and forcibly impressed his answer . . . upon the left eye of Mr. LaMotte. Being restrained . . . from further emphasizing . . . his resentment, Mr. Gonzales took his usual rounds about the State House." Two hours later, Charles Calvo, Jr., accosted N. G., who struck the *Register* owner who thereupon retaliated with a cowhide. Gonzales then pulled a pistol, belabored Calvo over the head, and, according to his own news story, "could have killed Mr. Calvo with ease but preferred not to do so." Calvo retired, "bloody and disheartened." Within three hours, William Calvo called on Gonzales and cursed him, and both drew pistols, only to be disarmed by bystanders. Net result of the stormy day was a small fine and peace bonds for all participants. All of it was thoroughly (and relatively calmly) written for the *News and Courier* by N. G., who noted that "The Register, as usual, is malevolently incorrect in its report" and thanked his "many friends who volunteered hearty muscular and financial aid." He admitted he had intended to shoot Charles Calvo but changed his mind because he "rather admired

---

[102] *News and Courier,* June 5 and 6, 1885.

Mr. Calvo's pluck in standing up for his delinquent reporter." When the well-publicized shouting died down, all participants were assuring their readers of the complete cowardice of their opponents.[103] If Calvo's readers were loyal to him, then N. G.'s harsh words were ineffective because "his [N. G.'s] vanity and conceit are so colossal that he does not conceive it possible . . . that the public shall accept any statement as true unless it first passed through the crucible which he 'manages' at the Bureau."[104]

Four months later the war was renewed because the Bureau was swaggering over beating the *Register* to a story of a train wreck. Again, the local paper cowered and complained of the "malignant representative" whose success was really the fault of Columbians who refused to give the *Register* adequate support. Gonzales replied that the natives would continue to buy the Charleston paper until it "ceases to be a *newspaper,* or—the *Register becomes* one." No blood was shed this time, but such ill-tempered competition became more and more frequent.

Before N. G.'s peace bond had expired, he tested his employer's equanimity again by breaking the peace. In this case his antagonist was a former friend, W. C. Robertson, whom he privately relegated to "the pillory of public shame, where he rightly belongs." When this "covert, habitual, and cowardly slanderer of women . . . a creature unfit to be recognized by gentlemen," heard of the Gonzales invective, he awoke N. G. at two A.M. to challenge him. The aroused sleeper refused to break his peace bond, and the offer by his bedfellow, Willie, to substitute for him failed since Uncle Ralph refused to permit such hostile activities in his room at that time of day. A long series of technical challenges ensued, and in the effort to avoid the violation of

[103] *Ibid.,* February 1–10, 1886; *Columbia Register,* February 2–9, 1886.
[104] *Columbia Register,* February 2, 1886.

the peace bond N. G. offered Robertson a chance to start shooting on sight, in which case N. G. could legally defend himself. The challenger held out for the *code duello,* outside the state if necessary. When Robertson published a handbill denouncing Gonzales as a coward, the latter published in full their correspondence to show that he had offered satisfaction, respected the law, and felt Robertson a coward. Much printer's ink but little blood had flowed.[105]

Such frequent turbulence must have made Dawson look askance at his valuable correspondent. Their relations were harmonious and their respect mutual, but on several occasions the editor's patience was sorely tried. Even N. G. admitted his impetuosity, having said truthfully during *l'affaire* Lipscomb, "I don't think I am especially vicious, but I don't mince words in defending the right as I see it, and this always enrages some crank or scoundrel."[106] Dawson warned him that his style was "bad-tempered or querulous" and made enemies unnecessarily; the editor admitted that Gonzales was usually right and that his own criticism involved the manner of his statements and not the statements themselves. Furthermore, the Englishman warned:

I object most strenuously to controversies with any of the petty newspapers . . . , the Register included. . . . It is practical to be fearless & independent & outspoken without dropping into controversies. . . . You can pitch in just as much as you please on the facts, or on your beliefs, . . . but the war must be conducted so as to save the News and Courier from . . . controver-

[105] *News and Courier,* October 28, 1886, contains a summary and all the correspondence. Dawson, whose religion restrained him from dueling, had followed the same tactic: Rather condescendingly decline the challenge but tell his antagonist on which sidewalk and which street he habitually walked at a certain hour and dare him to "draw first." In this way, Dawson could claim to be "defending himself" if he lived to get the chance to "draw second"—or to "beat him to the draw."

[106] N. G. Gonzales to Gertrude Gonzales, September 20, 1883, in E.G.P.

sial writing which is the delight of half-baked Western journalism and . . . utterly abhorrent to me.[107]

Many such warnings were sent the boisterous reporter, and they reveal the painstaking patience of an impresario both blessed and cursed by the control of a valuable but temperamental prima donna. Always they reasserted friendship and respect; always they pleaded for moderation. Dawson's fury never showed in these admonitions.[108] And despite his anxiety for the Gonzales manner, Dawson always trusted his lieutenant's integrity, veracity, and ability and defended his right to express his opinions freely.[109] Gonzales keenly resented the editor's criticism, writing his superior, "You must be aware that I am not pachydermatoris, and do not require any goad save my own sense of duty and responsibility."[110]

With the freedom allowed him, Gonzales continuously used his talents to wage vigorous crusades in the *News and Courier*. In doing so, he set patterns which he was to follow for years. In most of his opinions, his ideas ran parallel to those of Captain Dawson. For example, over and over again he attacked the convict lease system as he reported the arrival and departure of the unfortunate prisoners at the penitentiary. To add strength to his case he wrote features revealing the revolting conditions under which they worked and lived. His constant theme was that it was "impossible

[107] F. W. Dawson to N. G. Gonzales, July 23, [1885], in Dawson Papers.
[108] Once he became furious with Gonzales when the latter charged him with unfairness in business relations. See F. W. Dawson to N. G. Gonzales, May 27, 1886, in Dawson Papers.
[109] F. W. Dawson to J. C. Hemphill, July 25, 1885, and to D. M. O'Driscoll, November 30, 1886, in Dawson Papers.
[110] N. G. Gonzales to F. W. Dawson, January 9, 1889, in Dawson Papers. In this lengthy communication, Gonzales virtually seemed to be saying that he would quit unless he were left alone: "I will do my fullest duty to the paper, without other incentive than my own sense of right."

to secure proper treatment for convicts out of sight of those who are officially responsible for their well-being."[111]

Despite his own altercations, Gonzales was "Dawson's first lieutenant in his war against violence" and lawlessness.[112] But however much he deprecated the South's shame, he at the same time satiated his curious readers' appetite for sensational details of murders, hangings, and lynchings which he so frequently reported. As such a reporter, N. G. went throughout the state where crimes had been committed and, careless of real danger, investigated and wrote the facts temperately but without mitigation. For this candor, he made enemies. Once, after the bodies of Negroes were found in a Laurens County stream, he spent several days there interviewing suspects. Warned not to return except at the peril of his life, he went back on the next train and spent a day in what he headlined as "Lawless Laurens."[113]

Gonzales also condemned lynchings as evasions of legal processes, although his most outspoken diatribes on this crime did not appear until maturity tempered his own precipitate reactions. Like his chief, the reporter opposed dueling, despite his provoking others to challenge him.[114] He also stigmatized in his column "sports" founded on violence, particularly the "so-called entertainment" of prize fighting and cockfighting.

[111] *News and Courier,* June 11, 1883. Also see *ibid.,* August 15, 1883, and June 27, 1885, for strong expressions. For this cruel penal practice, see Fletcher M. Green, "Some Aspects of the Convict Lease System in the Southern States," in Fletcher M. Green, ed., *Essays in Southern History* (Chapel Hill: University of North Carolina Press, 1949), pp. 112–23; and George B. Tindall, *South Carolina Negroes,* chap. 13.

[112] W. W. Ball, *The State That Forgot* (Indianapolis: Bobbs-Merrill Company, 1932), p. 173.

[113] W. W. Ball, "An Episode in South Carolina Politics," in Tillman Pamphlets, no. 13, in South Caroliniana Library.

[114] As early as 1883, he received "cards" from readers but refused to take notice of " 'you're another' replies" which came from subscribers whom he called "curs and cowards." See N. G. Gonzales to Gertrude Gonzales, August 26, 1883, in E.G.P.

All of his crusades were not denunciations, however. On the positive side, his unflagging interest in education headed the list. Certainly it was not an area in which South Carolina excelled. Before the Civil War, no real public education system existed. The Bourbon emphasis on economy and reduced spending hardly advanced the cause. The fact that the public school system had been an innovation of the Radical government was almost a kiss of death. A two-mill statewide property tax provided income but not enough. The amount spent on the state's school system in 1895 was not much more than was spent in 1876. Negroes suffered the most. The amount spent on Negroes per pupil went down while it went up for whites; Negro enrollment increased 55,952 to 119,292 (1876 to 1894) while expenditures on Negro schools actually went down.[115]

Gonzales did not revolt against the Conservatives' parsimony, nor did he seem unduly concerned about the poor Negro education. His "campaign for education" was not so much by direct editorializing as by innumerable news and feature stories about happenings in education. If ever South Carolina College had friend and able defender, it was Gonzales. He fed his readers a detailed recounting of all official and student activities; often he devoted whole columns to an investigation of the current status of the institution.[116]

But the subject nearest to N. G.'s editorial heart was the incessant boosting and extolling of his adopted town. His vision foresaw a future that less optimistic or less vivacious natives could not see, but if they read his column, they were

[115] George B. Tindall, *South Carolina Negroes,* pp. 211–17. At least, Negro illiteracy decreased from 78.5 percent in 1880 to 52.8 percent in 1900. *Ibid.,* p. 223.

[116] For such interesting and factual surveys, see *News and Courier,* May 14, 1883, and October 2, 1883. He usually wrote such a report every fall when the college opened.

soon surfeited with the prophecies of this one-man chamber of commerce. Joyfully, he recorded every new advance of "progress"—the new street car system in 1886 ("Mules are to be used, which is a fact distressing to aesthetic minds"), the first electric light system in 1889, a new hotel (The Jerome), or his favorite railroad (the C. N. & L.) projected in 1885. Nevertheless, the Gonzales brethren devoted less attention to applauding progress than they did to stressing opportunities and making constructive criticism. Incessantly they complained of the sea of mud that was Main Street, suggesting that a ferry would be a "profitable enterprise" across that "veritable canal." Their persistence finally produced brick crossings at corners and, eventually, pavements and sidewalks.[117] When Willie's crusade for an electric fire alarm system lagged, he produced a whole column of "facts and figures which the majority of the City Council do not seem inclined to consider." Such documented demands often led to success, not only for the fire alarm system but also for a pure water system and other civic improvements. In such campaigns, the Gonzales brothers restrained their tempers and maintained their good humor, which, coupled with cogent arguments, brought more success than they attained in the controversies where their words were brilliant and passionate but so ill-humored and inflammatory as to alienate many potential supporters.

Two of their pet projects were revealed in one sentence: "What Columbia needs more than any other institution except a factory is a first class hotel."[118] Over and over in his column N. G. called for industries and tourist hotels, and when the former at last began to come to Columbia, his cup of joy ran over. As part of his campaign, the Columbia Bureau in 1888 published a special edition, "A Complete

[117] *News and Courier,* February 25, 1887; *The State,* September 21, 1904.
[118] *News and Courier,* April 23, 1883.

Presentation of Life and Industry at the Capital of the State,"
then a town of 6,866 whites and 5,899 Negroes. This complete survey of all phases of Columbia life concluded:
"Unity, and liberality and a progressive public spirit can
make Columbia in a very short time what her position en-
titles her to be. . . ."[119] The following year, in the "graphic
and picturesque style" of N. G., the *News and Courier*
again published an "annual review of the trade, resources,
and prospects of Columbia," a thorough study that included
eight pages of statistics compiled by William Gonzales.[120]

The "City on the Congaree" column also revealed many
other views of its authors. Although an eternal advocate of
railroad expansion, N. G. Gonzales also recommended railroad regulation. In 1883 and 1884 he was shocked at the
bribery and corruption used by railroad presidents to
thwart the railroad commission; although "muzzled" on
the subject, he took an active part in making the rounds of
saloons to locate senators "unable to walk by reason of the
liberality of their railroad friends" and to get them to a roll
call that preserved some state regulation of the roads.[121]

Besides his news coverage and crusades, N. G. also wrote
many features which perhaps show his writing at its best, as
well as furnishing today a thorough reflection of the 1880s.
True, modern readers would tire of four verbose columns on
the dedication of yet another in the endless parade of Confederate monuments, but they would enjoy an account of the
initial trip of a narrow-gauge railroad (Carolina & North
Western) or N. G.'s efforts to expose hoaxes.[122] An onerous
trip to "the Chester volcany" enabled N. G. to be "happy to
report that South Carolina is in no immediate danger of

[119] *Ibid.*, September 4, 1888.
[120] *Ibid.*, October 2, 1889.
[121] N. G. Gonzales to R. E. Elliott, December 23, 1883, in E.G.P.; *The State*, February 21, 1901.
[122] *News and Courier*, June 21, 1883, and May 24, 1884.

consumption by the fires thereof," although it was "no doubt still being kept in eruption for the benefit of Northern newspapers."[123] Likewise, humbuggery took him to the small town of Ninety Six that had

a private earthquake of her own, a seismic tremor antedating the Charleston affair, a growling, shaking fiend . . . [which] refuses to receive its initiative from any low-country point and does business by itself, and a pretty lively business too . . . which can be depended on for regular duty.

N. G. added that if he worked for the *Atlanta Constitution,* he could go further and tell of "crevices in those fair fields, cotton blasted by sulphur fumes, the terror of women and vast religious revivals, and any number of incidents which didn't occur," but as it was, he could only reveal the stories told and embellished in the "Earthquake Court in Mr. H. J. Kinard's store."[124]

Frequently he wrote factual and descriptive essays on Carolina towns. At other times, he reported on his own lengthy investigations of conditions in some of them. For example, in the series, "Laurens Lawlessness," he tried to find out if that town were as dangerous as his paper had been portraying it. The exposé followed the defiance of the law by John L. M. Irby, a rowdy planter who compelled an enemy at the point of a pistol to submit to a horsewhipping by a Negro. Although Irby threatened to kill Gonzales on sight, the reporter published a full account of Irby's vagaries (under such captions as "Irby Drunk Again") and a careful investigation of the machinations of the law in Laurens County (under "Dastardly Assassination" or "Civil War at Waterloo") . Perhaps as penance, a few months later he wrote

---

[123] *Ibid.,* March 28, 1884.
[124] *Ibid.,* October 11, 1886.

a feature on that town as "the future Atlanta of South Carolina" and "the crossroads of the upcountry."[125]

N. G.'s duties in Columbia also included reporting athletic events, which by 1886 accounted for an increasing proportion of the Columbia column because the baseball craze helped sell papers.[126] In the first league game played, "the Columbias" were defeated largely because "an epidemic of heavy batting . . . disheartened the locals."[127] Amateur games received quaint but lengthy descriptions. A contest between the "Fats" and "Leans" occurred on a very hot afternoon when "the condition of the Fats can better be imagined than described." Since the catchers "preferred giving the board fence the honor of stopping the balls, [they] were invariably carefully passed." Darkness ended the game after seven innings with the score 26-25. "Errors only the most unpardonable being noticed, Fats, 27, Leans 16. The Fats want to go on the road, but the YMCA preferred that they remain domesticated."[128] Such a whimsical report was but one among many that were written by N. G. and W. E. Gonzales.

Despite N. G.'s occasional truculence, Dawson evidently valued the family, for in October 1885 he added Ambrose Gonzales to the payroll. His health had failed; so, leaving his several New York jobs, Ambrose accepted a job as traveling agent for the business department of the *News and Courier*.[129] Rambling all over the state in the interest of circulation and advertising, the likeable Ambrose was soon a popular figure in the small towns where his story-telling

[125] *Ibid.,* July 20, 27, and August 1, 1885; October 10, 1885; and August 14, 1897. F. W. Dawson to N. G. Gonzales, July 25, 1885, in Dawson Papers.

[126] N. G. Gonzales to an aunt, April 12, 1886, in E.G.P.

[127] *News and Courier,* May 22, 1886.

[128] *Ibid.,* July 21, 1886. For two of the more hilarious games, see *ibid.,* September 19, 1886; June 15, 22, 1887.

[129] *Ibid.,* October 4, 6, 1885; N. G. Gonzales to an aunt, April 12, 1886, in E.G.P.

capacity, his baritone voice, and his generosity became
legendary. It was no easy job for even the energetic Ambrose.
He worked in a town all day, often riding rough passenger
and rougher freight trains at night with his satchel as a
pillow or sharing rooms with snoring drummers in country
hotels. For such services, the zealous agent received ten
dollars a week, gradually raised by the appreciative Dawson
to fifteen.[130]

Although a member of the business department, Ambrose
contributed many items to page one of the *News and Courier*.
Some of them were straight news reporting: a farmers' meeting in Spartanburg, a firemen's tournament in Anderson, a
Democratic meeting at Barnwell, a stock show at Ninety
Six, and others. Of interest to the local historian would be
his long, descriptive articles—complete with pictures—that
appeared in 1889 and treated the towns that he visited:
Darlington, Abbeville, Laurens, Greenville, Rock Hill, and
others. Although his enthusiasm portrayed each as an embryo
metropolis, he gave statistics and numerous facts that undoubtedly aided the circulation of the paper in the flattered
communities. He also wrote some essays to encourage new
agricultural developments and to record industrial development.[131]

In 1886 and 1887 Ambrose Gonzales also published in
the *News and Courier* a series of sketches in the Gullah
Negro dialect, "the worst English in the world." Many of

[130] F. W. Dawson to A. E. Gonzales, September 24, 1887, and February 10,
1888, in Letterbook, 1887–1894, of Hemphill Papers. Some of A. E. Gonzales'
best writing was composed of humorous reminiscences of his early days; see
"Chips from an Old Log," in *The State*, January 4, 11, 18, 25, 1925. Ambrose
Gonzales later said he hardly met Dawson over twenty times. A. E. Gonzales
to W. W. Ball, March 23, 1925, in Ball Papers, in Duke University Library.

[131] Issues too numerous to list here. See also W. E. Gonzales to F. C.
Withers, June (?) , 1923, in the Snowden Papers.

these were later reprinted along with other compositions of this unique type, but even at this time he gained some fame for the "Kinlaw' tales"—especially "A Dante from Dahomey."[132]

Ambrose's two brothers in Columbia were also leading a busy life in the late 1880s. As well as being manager of the Bureau, N. G. was agent for Walker, Evans & Cogswell Company, commercial printers of Charleston.[133] He also served as agent for the Columbia Board of Trade, forerunner of the Chamber of Commerce,[134] and was active in the Richland County Democratic organization, where his participation can best be classed as stormy.[135] The youngest brother, Willie, was a director in the Broad River Bridge Company; correspondent for several Northern newspapers; an active member of the militia (Richland Volunteer Rifle Company) after 1885; and champion rifle marksman of the state.[136]

N. G. briefly became more sociable and became engaged to a young lady, only to have the affair broken off mysteriously after a year.[137] The more genial Willie had more success, however, and in 1886 became engaged to Miss Sara Shiver, one of the most striking belles of Columbia. Daughter of a Columbia merchant who was more successful in business than in society, she was endowed with unusual beauty and charm. Coming from a social stratum considered beneath the

[132] First appeared in the Charleston *Sunday News*, September 2, 1886; reprinted in *The State*, December 25, 1925.

[133] J. P. Richardson to N. G. Gonzales, May 24, 1888, in Governor Richardson's Letterbooks, in the South Carolina Department of Archives.

[134] *The State*, July 1, 1923.

[135] *News and Courier*, May 13, 1888; N. G. Gonzales to A. E. Gonzales, April 6, 1884, in E.G.P.

[136] *News and Courier*, January 18, 1888, and July 2, 1885.

[137] N. G. Gonzales to Gertrude Gonzales, December 15, 1887, and to an aunt, November 10, 1888, in E.G.P.

Oak Lawn altitude, she was not too well accepted by the Elliotts, despite N. G.'s reassurances to the aunts.[138] Nevertheless, the romance culminated in a brilliant wedding, complete with twenty-eight members in the bridal party. The "densest crowd ever seen in its walls" packed the First Presbyterian Church. The governor appeared, the Richland Volunteers attended in full uniform, Mrs. Shiver gave a reception at her "palatial residence . . . on Arsenal Hill," and the Columbia German Club honored the couple with a ball.[139]

N. G. Gonzales generally had much of his attention riveted on the less charming subject of politics. A very large proportion of his printed words dealt with this topic, which had interested him since his boyhood. His most vibrant stories dealt with Democratic rallies and the tours of the "campaign party"—wet carriages, arrivals on freight trains at two in the morning, cornet bands, torchlight parades, barbecues, Red Shirt parades, mounted men, barrels of flaming tar, swarming country hotels, gallant gentlemen, demagogic speeches, eloquent speeches, long speeches, eloquent prayers, applause, jeers, and rebel yells. Such rallies until 1885 were relatively cut-and-dried despite the Democratic leaders' effort to keep up enthusiasm. Whenever he sensed lethargy, Gonzales appealed to the Democrats' conscience, with such reprimands as, "The failure of the authorities to close the barrooms ensured the absence of a lamentably large portion of the bibulous Democrats during the speaking."[140] He was always obviously happy to end his reports with "The Democracy are united and vigilant."

[138] N. G. Gonzales to an aunt, April 12, 1886, in E.G.P. The beauty of the bride was vividly recalled by some of the elderly people whom the author interviewed.
[139] Account from the *Columbia Record*, n.d., reprinted in *News and Courier*, February 6, 1887.
[140] *News and Courier*, October 12, 1882.

But even the most vigilant Democrats, like N. G. Gonzales, failed to see a cloud coming from an unwatched sector of the political horizon. The leaders in control since 1876 were satisfied with their regime and saw no need for basic changes in South Carolina government and politics. To them, existing grievances were few and inconsequential, and correction of them would necessitate no major alteration of the *status quo*. But in the Bennettsville courthouse on a hot day of 1885, Gonzales witnessed the ascension of a new comet destined to strike through recently calm political skies. At the time, he failed to recognize the importance of the event, although its consequences were to constitute the dominant course of his career.

The man who appeared was to alter the course of N. G. G.'s career and that of South Carolina history. Since the newcomer threatened the Conservatives and the ancient planters' values to which they claimed to cling, Gonzales could only view him with alarm. The journalist became a man obsessed by this new arrival in the political arena—Ben Tillman.

CHAPTER IV

Agrarian Revolt against Bourbonism

IN BENNETTSVILLE THE STATE GRANGE AND THE SOUTH Carolina Agricultural Society met in 1885 in a joint session that was supposed to be an innocuous, pleasant gathering of gentleman farmers. There Gonzales' reportorial path crossed that of Benjamin Ryan Tillman, unsuccessful and disillusioned Edgefield farmer who had an invitation to address the planters. Thus N. G. Gonzales wrote of a man launching a revolution, a man he was later to detest with unrelenting passion:

Mr. Tillman of Edgefield, (brother of Congressman [George D.] Tillman), contended that farmers . . . were poorer than they were fifteen years ago. . . . Mr. Tillman then made a long and rambling speech containing many hard truths, mingled with a great deal of dry humor.

Mr. Tillman defended his resolutions in a speech full of hard sense, keen satire, and good-humored badinage.[1]

---

[1] *News and Courier,* August 7, 1885.

Around this "agricultural Moses" rallied the disaffected and discouraged farmers who saw in him a leader against the evils that he denounced so vigorously and colorfully: demagogues and lawyers in the pay of "the money trust"; the agricultural department of South Carolina College; and "the ring" that ran state politics for the benefit of the Bourbons and planters. Charging that their numbers were carrying no weight in state affairs and making demands for a separate agricultural college, experiment stations, and farmers' institutes, Ben Tillman slowly but surely rallied the rude farmers in agrarian revolt. Cautious at first, they became bolder as Tillman told them that they constituted three-quarters of the white population but did not govern the state because they had been "bamboozled." Here was the South Carolina version of the nationwide agrarian crusade of the 1880s and 1890s.

As the *News and Courier* said, there was much hard sense in Tillman's charges, but—somewhat just as N. G. Gonzales himself did—the farmer by his vituperative methods alienated many fair-minded men who might otherwise have subscribed to his demands for changes. His strategy of appealing to the mass of poor farmers against a broad, enlightened class horrified many who saw in this the danger of class war and an ominous subdivision of the white rulers. Others saw heresy in his daring to attack the hitherto inviolate Carolina gentlemen. Among the most shocked Conservatives were the unorthodox Gonzales brothers who normally had also fought oppression, urged agricultural reforms, advocated extension of education, and detested dictatorial government. But, on the other hand, this rude farmer and his "red necks" were challenging the integrity of a benevolent government run by gentlemen and aristocrats, the Confederate Brigadiers, and spiritual descendants of their grandfather; if the Tillmanites felt aggrieved, why then should they not come with wool hats in hand and respect-fully seek amelioration from the ruling class—the Elliott class? His experience and wisdom tended to make N. G. Gonzales a liberal, but his training, intuition, and outraged class pride dictated that he defy this threat to an old order that to him was innately sound. He therefore followed William Elliott, not Ben Tillman. And with a Gonzales in a controversy, there were no halfway measures or compromises with an archenemy.

Briefly the *News and Courier* hesitated. Tillman had said that the state was ruled by a "ring," which the Columbia *Register* identified as the Democratic executive committee, " 'and that Ring is on Dawson's little finger.' "[2] Nevertheless, the editor in 1885 and 1886 opened his columns to letters of the "agricultural Moses" who said that he himself was only an unintentional leader for the elevation, encouragement, and protection of farmers. Although eschewing political action, he wrote, "This is a farmer's State and farmers should govern it."[3]

Political overtones were given to the agrarian movement by the call for a farmers' convention for April 29, 1886. As the summons said, "We may justly claim, then, that we constitute the State, yet we do not govern it, nor are the laws administered in our interests, and few are passed for our benefit."[4] To remedy these grievances, agricultural clubs sent delegates to the April convention which was to organize the movement; they were described by N. G. as "a sturdy and substantial looking set of men." "It is a convention of intelligent South Carolina farmers, with a few black sheep

[2] S. Frank Logan, "Francis W. Dawson, 1840–89: South Carolina Editor" (M.A. thesis, Duke University, 1947), p. 267.

[3] *News and Courier*, January 28, 1886. Despite their differences, there was a good deal of correspondence between Dawson and Tillman.

[4] *Ibid.*, March 9, 1886.

among them."[5] As for Ben Tillman, Gonzales said his face "gives no indication of the brain power which it undoubtedly conceals." Although this organizational convention made plans for a Farmers' Association which would meet each November and demanded a number of projects for farmers, N. G. still was not too alarmed and believed that the "conservatism of the State will be made manifest at the nominating convention. . . . There will be no clean sweep."[6]

Tillman was to prove one of the major figures in South Carolina politics, perhaps the most powerful political personality yet since the Civil War. A native of Edgefield County, he belonged to a family long associated with farming, violence, and tragedy. His formal schooling was limited to a rural academy, but he read widely and thereby gave himself a rather impressive education. Although he did not become affluent on his 400-acre farm adjacent to his mother's land, he was hardly the small operator of a garden-sized collection of weeds (the typical "wool hat" farmer that often springs to mind when the "Tillman movement" is mentioned).

His entry into politics had come in 1876 when he participated in the Ellenton and Hamburg riots. His patron saint at the time was Martin Witherspoon Gary, "the Bald Eagle of Edgefield," who introduced the "Mississippi Plan" into the 1876 campaign and led the Red-Shirt campaign of terror and intimidation to prevent or limit Negro voting that year. The potentially explosive tactics were disavowed by Hamp-

[5] *Ibid.*, April 29–30, 1886.

[6] *Ibid.*, June 7, 1886. On the convention, see Francis B. Simkins, *Pitchfork Ben Tillman* (Baton Rouge: Louisiana State University Press, 1944), pp. 100–105 (hereinafter cited as *Tillman*); *News and Courier* and the *Columbia Register*, April 29–30 and May 1, 1886.

ton who sought the Negro vote and who made moderate promises to the Negroes. Before 1880 Gary and his young henchman Tillman had broken with Hampton (partially because the latter had thwarted Gary's ambitions for high office), and they dared to criticize the Bourbon oligarchy. Gary died in 1881, but Tillman remained disaffected and in effect was reviving "Garyism" in the 1880s and 1890s. Neither Gary nor Tillman was awed by the Confederate Brigadiers (Gary himself was a general), not sharing B. H. Mitchell's view of how South Carolinians were

wild about getting commissions from *Governor Hampton*. I believe they think if they can get a piece of paper with the Great Seal on it, and *his* name signed, with theirs in the belly of it, that their salvation is assured on this & the other side of the Grave. Peter they think (who is in General Command up there) will recognize the signature and pass in the bearer free of challenge or expense.[7]

But neither Gary nor Tillman looked to Hampton for their tickets through the pearly gates nor bowed passively before him.

Until 1885 Tillman had not attracted statewide attention. A one-eyed rustic, unprepossessing in demeanor, he did not seem "the type" accepted by South Carolinians of that era as being of leadership timber. According to his excellent biographer, Francis B. Simkins, "Careless in manner, unattractive in personal appearance, and possessed of a rasping voice and irascible disposition, he was not even liked by his neighbors."[8] But after his Bennettsville appearance, he became a figure to conjure with.

[7] B. H. Mitchell to James Conner, April 23, 1877, in James Conner Papers, South Carolina Historical Society.
[8] *Dictionary of American Biography* (1936), XVIII, 547.

During the 1886 campaign, Editor Dawson trusted the "absolute political and personal honesty of Capt. Tillman" and provided him a major outlet for his opinions.[9] The editor wrote Tillman that he had originally supported the farmers' movement and still did but that they had gone too far, and for his own part he refused to join them in arraigning the Democratic party.[10] Nevertheless, Dawson continued to counsel the "agricultural Moses" to adopt moderation.[11] At a June conference, the two agreed to support John C. Sheppard for governor against the more conservative John P. Richardson, friend of Gonzales. With the farmers not fully organized and with Sheppard hedging on issues, Richardson won with little difficulty. The brains and energy for his candidacy were supplied by N. G. Gonzales, who thus overcame his own chief.[12] But after the election, Dawson continued to give Tillman good advice on the best methods for obtaining desirable, moderate goals.[13]

In November 1886 the Farmers' Association held its first annual meeting. The enthusiasm of the previous session of the farmers was lacking, and N. G. Gonzales, still unruffled, wrote: "The personnel of the Convention is very fair. There are cranks and nuisances and political aspirants in it, but the mass of the members seem to be really striving after agricultural betterment."[14] Although not confessing failure,

[9] *News and Courier*, October 21, 1886. Dawson strongly defended the need to keep a newspaper's columns open to any responsible citizen, saying that the press is the only channel through which grievances can be presented and reach the public. This he considered especially essential when the issue involved a public official or public issue. See Dawson to Wm. A. Courtenay, in Courtenay Letterbooks, I, 105–6, in South Caroliniana Library.

[10] F. W. Dawson to B. R. Tillman, May 13, 1886, in Dawson Papers.

[11] For example, see F. W. Dawson to B. R. Tillman, June 28, 1886, in Dawson Papers.

[12] Ball, *The State That Forgot*, p. 214.

[13] F. W. Dawson to B. R. Tillman, December 1, 1886, in Dawson Papers.

[14] *News and Courier*, November 10, 1886.

the Tillmanites saw that their revolution could not come
overnight, and farmer leaders in the legislature, such as
John L. M. Irby (of "Lawless Laurens"), won few "reforms."

With Tillmanism temporarily routed in 1886 and 1887,
the Conservatives had little fear of the public censure frequently broadcast so vociferously from Captain Tillman's
farm near Trenton, in Edgefield County. Even Ben himself
temporarily gave up his campaign—"I am simply too poor to
attempt it . . . so I sing my last song"—admitting at least
to Dawson at the time that he had come to "have a much
better opinion of you personally than I ever expected. . . ."[15]
The movement was not dead so long as the farmers had to
contend with a lien law, credit merchants, fertilizer trusts,
defeats because of ignorance, and a "selfish and proud
'ruling ring' of the Columbia Club." They did not charge
"the ring" with dishonesty or scandal, only stupidity and
negligence. As his legislative program failed miserably, it
became obvious that Tillman himself would either have to
fade away or embrace politics. Since the leader continued to
arouse intense popular enthusiasm on the debating stump,
it was soon apparent which road would be taken. Ben did not
fade away.

At the Democratic convention of 1888, Tillman called for
a state primary system for the nomination of state officials
as an alternative to the nominating convention which he
said was undemocratically controlled by conservative cliques.
Although his resolution failed, a concession was made by
providing that potential candidates might tour the state for
joint speeches and debates on the stump and thereby let
county delegates to the state convention judge popular sentiment. The "one-ring circus" that had been a pep rally now

[15] B. R. Tillman to F. W. Dawson, January 20, 1888, in Dawson Papers.

would be replaced by a real circus in which differing views would be heard, but it unfortunately promoted as much demagoguery as democracy.[16]

In July the 1888 campaign opened in Hodges with Tillman, although not a candidate for office, speaking for his cause. His coarseness and rough-and-tumble harangues were in marked contrast with the polished oratory of Governor Richardson, a gentleman of the old school, who was seeking reelection. Many of the tense sessions were reported by N. G. Gonzales, who (according to Tillman's biographer) "combined stenographic accuracy with interpretations almost tactless because they were startlingly unfair or startlingly truthful."[17] But N. G. did not believe that tact was a desirable attribute for an honest reporter who now thought he saw a monstrous threat to all that he believed good in his state.

Because of his reports, N. G. became one of "Pitchfork Ben's" targets, as at Chester where Tillman "once more distinguished the representative of the News and Courier" by referring to his "sneering pen."[18] When Tillman criticized the captions over his reports, Gonzales took the stand himself to explain heatedly that they were inserted by the home office. At this meeting, "Great confusion prevailed."[19]

As his candidate, Richardson, seemed unequal to his task, the reporter supplemented his fiercely partisan reports by interruption at the rural festivals. In Blackville, Captain Tillman said Gonzales' reports so misrepresented the meetings as to be unreliable, whereupon the enraged correspond-

---

[16] Simkins, *Tillman,* pp. 124–25; *News and Courier,* May 18–19, 1888. Gonzales opposed statewide primaries because he thought they gave too much power to the populous up-country counties which were the stronghold of Tillmanism. See *News and Courier,* September 5, 1888.

[17] Simkins, *Tillman,* p. 558.

[18] *News and Courier,* July 31, 1888.

[19] *Ibid.,* August 2, 1888.

ent arose and shouted, "If you say that I misrepresent you, you are an infernal liar." Amid great commotion and threat-ened bloodshed, he repeated the ultimate in Carolina anath-emas. The sardonic speaker from Edgefield promised to see the reporter later. That night, amid a tense crowd of rabid partisans, the two met in the lobby of a little Blackville hotel and verbally skirmished for position. Finally, Tillman said his remarks were directed at the reporter and the paper and not at Gonzales personally; when he withdrew the charge that N. G. intentionally misrepresented him, the "Reporter withdrew his impeachment of Captain Tillman's veracity."[20]

The farmers' friend respected Gonzales enough to say that "if Gonzales had the reporting to do he (Tillman) would always get beaten" and that "This reporter, Mr. Gonzales, would elect the next Governor."[21] Actually Till-man's attack was on the newspaper monopoly enjoyed by Dawson, who had now broken completely with Tillman, and whom Ben characterized as "some buzzard who has escaped from the market house in Charleston and gone into the *News and Courier* office, where it was spewing its slime all over me." Even in Charleston itself, Ben told an audience of hostile natives that they were "the most arrant set of cowards" and the "most self-idolatrous people in the world."[22] Dawson, he said, was "clinging around the neck of South Carolina, oppressing its people and stifling reform."[23] Al-though the paper denounced him as "the leader of the Adullamites, a people who carry pistols in their hip pockets, who expectorate on the floor, who have no tooth brushes and comb their hair with their fingers," Dawson finally ordered Editor J. C. Hemphill to conduct a campaign of silence and

[20] *Ibid.*, August 7–8, 1888.
[21] *Ibid.*, July 12 and 31, 1888.
[22] *Ibid.*, July 21, 1888.
[23] *Ibid.*, August 29, 1888.

mention Tillman only when it was not possible to avoid doing so.[24]

The 1888 campaign did little to weaken the Conservatives' control of the convention, but it did enhance the general popularity of Tillman. Although he supported Conservative Joseph H. Earle, the more conservative Richardson was renominated in September 1888. And with this defeat, the prophet from Edgefield left the stage for about a year.

Despite the victory over the "Reformers," Dawson and Gonzales began to drift apart. Never did they have wide differences on politics,[25] but the irrepressible correspondent would have been a trial to any employer. Gonzales was not amenable to suggestion and resented criticism; on the other side, Dawson was willing to read the riot act and let his subordinate know who was editor.[26] Even so, the Gonzales brothers continued staunchly to defend Dawson against " 'fellows of the baser sort.' "[27]

Gradually the Gonzales ties to the *News and Courier* were being parted. In September 1888, as a retrenchment move, the directors of the paper dispensed with the services of William Gonzales—who only a few months before had vainly sought a raise.[28] Almost immediately he replaced Louis Chazal as private secretary to Governor John P.

---

[24] Wallace, *History of S. C.*, III, 340; F. W. Dawson to J. C. Hemphill, September 11, 1888; December 14, 1887, in Hemphill Papers. Dawson promised not to discriminate against Tillman if he limited himself to "courteous criticism." *News and Courier*, August 31, 1888.

[25] Yates Snowden to P. S. Barry, July 5, 1931, in Dawson Papers.

[26] F. W. Dawson to N. G. Gonzales, January 10, 1889. Also, see Dawson to N. G. Gonzales, December 14, 1887, and Dawson to B. R. Tillman, in Letterbook, 1887–1894, of the Hemphill Papers. The result: Gonzales threatened to quit. Gonzales' complaints to Dawson: letter of January 9, 1889, in Dawson Papers.

[27] N. G. Gonzales to J. C. Hemphill, March 23, 1889, in Gonzales Manuscripts, South Caroliniana Library.

[28] F. W. Dawson to N. G. Gonzales, September 8, 1888; and Dawson to W. E. Gonzales, May 2, 1888, in Letterbook, 1887–1894, of Hemphill Papers.

Richardson.[29] Late the following year, Ambrose Gonzales left the paper to become secretary to the State Board of Agriculture.

The Gonzales-Dawson friction abruptly ended March 12, 1889, when the brilliant editor was murdered by a Charleston doctor in a difficulty centering around a French governess in Dawson's home. N. G. Gonzales, an active pallbearer at the funeral, was profoundly affected by the sensational tragedy, as was much of South Carolina.[30]

At first, Gonzales cheerfully accepted the colorful Major Hemphill as his new superior while assuring him of his own indispensability and importance in Columbia.[31] Undoubtedly he would have welcomed for himself what Christie Benet, lawyer and circuit judge, called the "chair of the perpetual governor of South Carolina."[32] N. G. accepted Hemphill's request to define what a newspaper should be, and, in effect, he stated his journalistic creed in a ten-page letter to "the Major." Included was this advice:

I hope that the editorial management will not be hampered . . . by the owners. . . . Care should be taken that the paper is not so lamblike as to be inane. Fair, hard blows . . . will quicken public respect. . . . It must hold opinions and express them boldly or it will lose moral force. . . . If I had a paper, I would, under reasonable limitations, let my worst enemies have access

---

When Willie Gonzales sought an increase, he was married and had been making $12.50 a week for the previous eighteen months—an amount which he said made it difficult to live "in a respectable manner" in Columbia. W. E. Gonzales to F. W. Dawson, April 28, 1888, in Dawson Papers.

[29] News and Courier, September 27, 1888, and N. G. Gonzales to an aunt, November 2, 1888, in E.G.P.

[30] For an account of the murder, see News and Courier, March 13, 1889. The doctor was acquitted. See Logan, "Dawson," chap. XIII; also, S. Frank Logan, "Francis W. Dawson," South Carolina Historical Association Proceedings, pp. 13–28.

[31] N. G. Gonzales to J. C. Hemphill, March 23, 1889, in Gonzales MSS.

[32] W. C. Benet to J. C. Hemphill, April 11, 1889, in Hemphill Papers.

to its columns. . . . The paper should be . . . a State institution, and every county . . . should feel that it is its active friend. . . . Every new enterprise . . . should be "written up." . . . Manufacturing activity . . . should be encouraged to the fullest.[33]

Gonzales was writing a prospectus of *The State*. Soon after Dawson's death in 1889, Gonzales was assisted by an enterprising young man who idolized him: August Kohn. This admiration for the shining light of Columbia's journalistic world had developed while Kohn was a student at South Carolina College. In 1889 the cub reporter substituted for N. G. when the latter suffered an attack of typhoid fever, and thereafter the two cooperated harmoniously in the coverage of South Carolina news.[34]

Exciting news began to break as Tillman's movement became a real revolution. In 1889 John L. M. Irby and Tillman met and decided to call a convention early in 1890 to present the latter to the state as Democratic candidate for governor. From this decision came the Shell Manifesto, published January 23, 1890, and bearing the name of the president of the Farmers' Association but drawn up by the Edgefield leader. A "farmers' convention," called for March 27, was to designate candidates for the Democratic nominations to be made that summer. Such a preconvention within the party was declared necessary so that "the common people who redeemed the State from Radical rule" could now redeem it from those who "are running it in the interest of a few families and for the benefit of a selfish ring of politicians." This clique of "an aristocratic oligarchy" was vituperatively attacked, as were the "pets of the aristocracy," such as the South Carolina College, The Citadel (called "the

---

[33] N. G. Gonzales to J. C. Hemphill, March 23, 1889, in Gonzales MSS.
[34] Hennig, *August Kohn*, pp. 32, 44.

dude factory" by Tillman), the state Department of Agriculture, and the Columbia Club—all of which were closely associated with the Gonzales brothers. The Manifesto also indicted the Conservatives' legislature for being "bamboozled and debauched."[35]

"Shell's Bombshell" split both "the Reformers" and others who feared such a convention would wreck the Democratic party, but the famed March Convention of 1890 carried out the dictates of its proponents. The *News and Courier* account was written by Gonzales:

> The Convention was in many respects one of the queerest deliberative bodies ever assembled in the State House. There was plenty of new material, men whose faces have not often been seen in such assemblages. There was but a slight sprinkling of the old war horses of the Democracy. The speeches, as a rule, were good, and many an earnest appeal was made in protest against nominating candidates.[36]

N. G. bluntly asserted that the convention was bamboozled by its leaders, John Gary Evans and John L. M. Irby, who carried the day for making nominations amid great consternation and unparliamentary disorder by sheer lung power and misstatement of votes. Seven years later Irby admitted that the reporters had been right in their charge that he had cheated the will of the delegates. The convention "suggested" Tillman as the best candidate for governor.[37] The aroused farmers thus became a political machine within the

---

[35] *News and Courier*, January 23, 1890; Simkins, *Tillman*, pp. 140–42.

[36] *News and Courier*, March 28, 1890.

[37] *Ibid*. Reporters agreed that the vote was 117-116 against nominating a slate of Reform candidates; officially, the vote was announced as 121-114 in favor of nominating. On Irby's confession, see *News and Courier*, August 28, 1897, as cited by Simkins, *Tillman*, p. 146; also, Thomas J. Kirkland, "Tillman and I," in *The State*, July 7, 1929.

Democratic party and were known thereafter as the Reform Movement.

Aiding the new organization was the Charleston *World,* the first "Tillman organ" to be bitterly attacked by N. G. Gonzales. Another ally was the Farmers' Alliance, doubly suspect in the eyes of Gonzales since it—like Tillmanism— seemed to threaten white supremacy by risking a Democratic schism.

The canvass which followed the March Convention of 1890 was no timid affair. The Conservatives held no organizational preconvention but they generally united on Joseph H. Earle. A second Conservative candidate was General John Bratton. These and other aspirants undertook the first county-to-county campaign in their efforts to harangue and allure support for the state nominating convention.[38]

During this lung contest, politicians sought the support of the masses not only on their merits but also because they were opposed by certain newspapers; as a whipping post, the *News and Courier* served Tillman well. The 1890 candidates resorted to blasphemy and vituperation, and the aroused partisans made each meeting a near-riot. N. G. Gonzales' coverage of the hustings did little to cool a populace more aroused than any since the 1876 election. Although his reports were slanted, they were lively and thorough and included verbatim the banter, retorts, and reactions. From his very first report he beat the drums for the Conservatives by assuring his readers that Tillmanism was a lost cause: "The Tillmanite who can extract comfort from today's meeting of the Democracy of Fairfield is hopelessly abandoned to delusions . . . , and indeed [is] an irreclaimable optionist [*sic*]."[39] At least his

[38] See Simkins, *Tillman,* pp. 152–68. During the 1888 campaign, one meeting was held in each Congressional district. For activities and thinking of the Conservatives, see Joseph W. Barnwell, "Life and Recollections of Joseph W. Barnwell," pp. 466 ff.

[39] *News and Courier,* July 2, 1890.

opinionated accounts were readable, as witnessed by a typical opening of a Gonzales story:

> Although Andrew Jackson today had the honor of being compared to B. R. Tillman, a compliment which will surely send the bones of the Sage of the Hermitage stalking abroad tonight, and though the descendants of Andrew Jackson's fellow-citizens didn't rise en masse and resent comparison, there is yet hope for the Lancaster Tillmaniacs, for they have not yet learned to stop their ears to the voice of truth. . . .

A fourth of July tone, strongly tinctured with Tillmanic gush, was, however, apparent.[40]

Some of N. G.'s Columbia reports were virtual editorials. One of his three-column taunts he urged all anti-Tillmanites to clip and carry constantly in their pockets. In it, he quoted Tillman's own words over the previous five years and "proved" that he had "an unalterable contempt for the intelligence of the average farmer" and was no reformer but only "for Tillman, first, last, and all the time."[41]

Columbia was a hotbed of anti-Tillmanism. When the "one-ring circus" performed there, Gonzales wrote ten columns about the joint debate in the capital, although he asserted that there were only seventy-four Tillmanites in Columbia, composed of "malcontents, ex-Greenbackers, time-servers, soreheads and disappointed officeseekers."[42] In Columbia, the Conservative scribe was active in the "Straight-out wing" of the Richland Democratic convention, a group of enraged "Antis" who wanted to make it hotter yet for "the Great Bamboozler."[43]

A state Democratic convention was called for August 13

40 *Ibid.,* July 5, 1890.
41 *Ibid.,* May 28, 1890.
42 *Ibid.,* July 18, 1890. Also, see *ibid.,* June 25, 1890.
43 *Ibid.,* July 24, 1890.

to determine the method of electing the nominating convention in September. Although the Tillmanites controlled a majority of the delegates to the August meeting, the old Conservatives still dominated the party's executive committee under Colonel James A. Hoyt. Gonzales reported another riotous session with ladies fleeing the galleries, "a hundred hands in a hundred hip pockets," and the uproar of malediction; the Tillmanites won control. Since it was to their advantage to do so, they now spurned the primary system which two years before they had endorsed. Going beyond the authorized agenda of this convention, they chose a new executive committee under John L. M. Irby and wrote a new constitution for the party. The Straightout delegates, including wily N. G. Gonzales, withdrew, charging the Tillmanites with usurping the convention and acting arbitrarily, foolishly, and undemocratically. At the same time, they asserted that the Tillman organization was not the Democratic party of South Carolina.[44] On August 26, a secret Straightout conference was held to map strategy; among those seceders (or "bolters") , who claimed to be the only true Democrats, were W. E. and N. G. Gonzales.[45]

As was expected, the Democratic nominating convention (with both Hoyt and Irby on the platform as rival chairmen) met September 10 and chose a Tillmanite slate of Democratic nominees for the general election.[46] Many who had opposed Tillman, including the *Columbia Register* and the

---

[44] *Ibid.*, August 14, 15, and 16, 1890.
[45] *Ibid.*, August 27, 1890.
[46] *Ibid.*, September 11, 1890. Hoyt stepped aside. He was criticized for "surrendering" to the Tillman faction, but considered that the rule changes of the earlier meeting were illegal and that Tillmanites had a majority anyhow. He and a boyhood friend, G. Wash Shell of the Tillmanites, had worked out his graceful abdication in a deal made earlier in the Ben Della Hotel in Laurens. Memo of James A. Hoyt, Jr., October 3, 1947, in James A. Hoyt Papers, South Caroliniana Library.

News and Courier, now unhappily fell into line rather than split the party over an obstreperous standard-bearer.[47]

But the "Advisory Committee of Straightout Democracy" did not surrender so easily. These independent bolters of 1890 were led by Alex C. Haskell, a sincere and conscientious Conservative who realized the danger of such a step in one-party South Carolina but sensed the deep resentment and fear of Tillman's Reformers, reflected by one outraged partisan who reported: "My family and many of my friends . . . would not vote for a saint from Heaven if suspected of a leaning toward Tillman and his rabble. . . ."[48] Secretary of the committee of Straightouts was Ambrose Gonzales, and active in its work were W. E. and N. G. Gonzales, the latter thereby again running counter to the policy of his editor. Posing as the only bona fide Democrat, and denying that he was a "bolter," Haskell announced to the state through the *News and Courier* bureau in Columbia that he would oppose Tillman in the general election in November. Having already committed heresy by leaving the organization, he now appealed for the Negro vote and promised the blacks justice but not offices.[49]

It is not certain that the Haskellites realized their sin would forever hang around their necks like the proverbial albatross, but for the moment they loudly compared themselves to the Hamptonites of 1876 and their opponents to the followers of Daniel H. Chamberlain. "Not for publication per either man, maid or matron," Ambrose Gonzales

[47] *Columbia Register,* October 1 and 15, 1890; *News and Courier,* October 1 and 8, 1890.

[48] George M. Ransome to John Gary Evans, July 2, 1890, in J. Gary Evans Papers, South Caroliniana Library.

[49] A. E. Gonzales to Gertrude Gonzales, August 23, 1890, in E.G.P.; *News and Courier,* September 30, October 7 and 10, 1890; *Register,* October 1, 1890.

wrote a long analysis of their predicament. By shrewd tactics, he said the opposition had "absolute control of three-fourths of the white vote," the "communistic 'po' buckra' element" of "the most ignorant men of the very lowest stripe." He admitted that able men interested in their own ambitions had allied themselves to Tillman and that lukewarm Conservatives felt that, given enough rope, Ben would "hang himself" by the errors of one administration. The Gonzales brothers, however, agreed with Haskell and Joseph W. Barnwell that in two years Tillman would "have all the election machinery . . . in his hands and will be in a position to make a trade with the National Republican party." They also feared that "once in, he can if unscrupulous enough, combine with the negro and control the decency of the State for a decade." The Straightout appeal to the Negro, said Ambrose, was simple: "Just let the ticket composed of gentlemen, and that composed of toughs, be put up and let him take his choice. . . . The question is, shall we allow them to come to us now or allow Tillman to take them two years hence?"[50] The Haskellites thus had "practical" and sincere reasons for their action, but they unnecessarily complicated their dilemma as they refused to recognize the simple fact that they had already been defeated. Master politician though he was, Tillman had no such nefarious and circuitous schemes as those of which the Straightouts suspected him. His victory had simply become possible because he had publicized deplorable conditions which gnawed at the very existence of a majority of South Carolinians. In this explosive atmosphere, he had convinced the oppressed citizens and others that he could and would give the state a new deal. Although the Straightouts were sure that his promise was folly and that

[50] A. E. Gonzales to Gertrude Gonzales, August 23, 1890, in E.G.P.

Conservative rule had been basically "good," they failed to realize that the most important facts of history are states of mind.[51]

During the hopeless campaign of the Haskellites, N. G. Gonzales' Columbia column became practically an organ of the Straightout conference. Much of his space was allotted to the last-ditchers' fight and his reports of them stressed the word "gentlemen," but the Haskellites received the kiss of death with the endorsement of the Republican party.[52] Tillman was confident that "Haskell and his dark legions will be met and beaten. I feel sure that as our people realize more clearly the deep-laid scheme to deliver the state over to the republicans . . . the more determined they will be to . . . punish the conspirators."[53] Wade Hampton, political saint of the Conservatives, refused to endorse the bolt, and many Conservatives judged Tillman less obnoxious than a threat to party solidarity. Even John C. Haskell, brother of the Straightout nominee, supported Tillman, though admitting, "to use a vulgar expression, I will not, while eating my crow, smack my lips and say I like it."[54]

Such a tide did not dampen the ardor of N. G. Gonzales, one of the leading campaign managers for Haskell. Never openly disheartened, he observed that the *Columbia Record,* one of the four or five papers in the state to support Haskell, enjoyed a marked increase in circulation, thereby proving that "Good deeds are their own reward."[55]

[51] For a keen analysis of conditions in the state and a background of Tillmanism, see Wallace, *History of S. C.,* III, 352.

[52] *News and Courier,* October 26, 1890, and September 18, 1890. The latter is one of N. G. Gonzales' most hilarious pieces of reporting.

[53] B. R. Tillman to Wm. A. Courtenay, October 20, 1890, in Courtenay Papers.

[54] J. C. Haskell "to a Columbia journalist," October 24, 1890, printed in N. G. G.'s column, *News and Courier,* October 30, 1890.

[55] N. G. Gonzales to Yates Snowden, October 23, 1890, in the Snowden Papers.

At the end of the strenuous struggle by the three Gonzales brothers—journalists all now turned politicians—N. G. had to write of an overwhelming victory in the general election for Tillman "and his woolhats," although he received some comfort from reiterating his view that most "prominent men" had supported Haskell and that allegedly only a minority of the white voters favored Tillman.[56]

Obviously, N. G. Gonzales' political dogma was influenced by class consciousness, but this only helped to crystallize his thinking, which arrived at its inflexible conclusions sincerely and honestly. He knew of the farmers' ills as well as Ben Tillman did, but these evils he could not and would not attribute to the ruling regime. In his view, progressive innovations for which he had crusaded, not simply the total overthrow of the Old Order, would wipe out the inequities and difficulties. His background convinced him that only in the Old Order could qualified leadership, ability, honesty, knowledge, statesmanship, and moral principles be found, not in Ben Tillman or such men as Irby, Talbert, or Evans.

Naturally this leading Straightout was unhappy writing for a Conservative paper that seemed to him tame and timid. In October, before the election was held, he had unbosomed himself in an eleven-page letter to Editor J. C. Hemphill, charging that the paper had abandoned principle as well as its best friends, who he said were naturally of Haskell's literate class. More serious, he accused the news department of suppressing Haskell news and of intentionally minimizing the importance of the Haskell movement and thereby discouraging many who might have supported it. Gonzales pointed out that victorious Tillmanites would never thank the Charleston paper for its help; at the same time many Conservatives—including advertisers and subscribers—were

[56] *News and Courier*, November 5, 6, 1890.

deserting such a spineless paper, "and there is serious talk of establishing a big paper here which shall represent the ideas of the Haskell movement and injure the News and Courier in the up-country." Concluding his lesson on how to run a "broad, high and independent" newspaper, N. G. had forecast: "I do not expect to remain here if Tillman is elected and it matters little whether what I may write during the next three or four weeks gets into print or the waste basket."[57] The conscientious correspondent carried out his threat, abandoning a post he had held for ten years "rather than be thrown, as . . . Columbia correspondent, into contact with B. R. Tillman, Governor, a man he despised and had charged with falsehood to his face."[58]

N. G.'s last column appeared November 23, 1890; a few days later he turned the Bureau over to M. F. Tighe, who was soon replaced by August Kohn. He also arranged for Captain Ralph E. Elliott to continue his work in the circulation department.[59] The editorial columns said that his own interests had induced him to leave a post where he had "made an enviable reputation as a journalist, the artistic work of his pen losing nothing from the fact that it was not artistic only, but expressed the real sentiments of a man and gentleman."[60] Having saved $1,000 after fifteen years of work, the truculent writer now planned to go to the South Seas.

The new state administration, which was inaugurated December 4, 1890, cast all the Gonzales brothers off into

[57] N. G. Gonzales to J. C. Hemphill, October 22, 1890, in Hemphill Papers.
[58] *The State,* July 15, 1892. This editorial summarizes the history of the Gonzales-Tillman relations to date and shows the grounds on which N. G. Gonzales based his charges of insincerity against the Reform Movement.
[59] N. G. Gonzales to J. C. Hemphill, November 17, 1890, in Hemphill Papers.
[60] *News and Courier,* December 15, 1890. A. B. Williams tried in vain to succeed Gonzales at Columbia; see Williams to Hemphill, November 18, 1890, in Hemphill Papers.

space. Naturally, W. E. Gonzales, private secretary to the out-going governor, found himself unemployed. Also at the end of the year, the Department of Agriculture that had been so often attacked by Tillman lost the services of its chief clerk, Ambrose E. Gonzales, who now turned his thoughts back to New York.[61] Truly, the election of 1890 and the success of Tillman constituted a revolution not only for South Carolina but also in the lives of the Gonzales brothers.

[61] A. E. Gonzales to ———, December 28, 1890, in E.G.P.; *News and Courier*, January 1, 1891. B. R. Tillman to J. Wilson Gibbes, February 21, 1916, in Letterbook, 1916, of Tillman Papers, as copied in F. B. Simkins' notes for *Tillman*, deposited in Southern Historical Collection, University of North Carolina Library; hereinafter cited as Simkins Notes, with citations referring only to the notes made on the Tillman Papers, subdivisions and locations of which (letterbooks etc.) are not being indicated. Many of these excellent notes by Professor Simkins are verbatim copies of letters in the voluminous Tillman Papers, which were closed to use at the time research for this study was done; hence, Professor Simkins' notes were particularly helpful in clear-ing a disconcerting obstacle. In effect Simkins Notes can be read as the Till-man Papers, which are now available for use at the Clemson University Library.

CHAPTER V

Gonzales Gazette

ANYONE ACQUAINTED WITH N. G. GONZALES, "AS INTENSELY South Carolinian in his prejudices and ideals as Till-man,"[1] must have known that he was unlikely to abandon his beleaguered state in favor of the South Seas. Almost as soon as he left the *News and Courier,* a group of Conservatives and Haskellites persuaded him to stay in South Carolina and launch an untrammeled Columbia newspaper that would show more boldness, brilliance, and spice in attacking the Reform Movement than the Charleston paper would do or than the *Columbia Register* could do. N. G. and Ambrose Gonzales were not willing to be tied to "an organ," but, with the idea of making a real newspaper that would be a big operation from the start, they both fell in wholeheartedly with the plan. Undoubtedly the scheme was as much theirs as it was that of their friends, but they knew that they could not initiate such an ambitious project without the backing

[1] Simkins, *Tillman,* p. 201.

of Conservatives and Haskellites who, although not a numerical majority of the population, nevertheless dominated much of the financial and intellectual wealth of the state. With the promise of such support, they were busy making plans before the end of 1890. In this work, they were without the services of Willie Gonzales, who now was a real estate promoter of Buena Vista, a resort spot near Asheville, North Carolina.

By early January 1891 a new company, The State Publishing Company, had been formed with a capital of $30,000, two-thirds of which was speedily subscribed. No halfway measures were contemplated; from the beginning, the publishers planned an eight-page, seven-days-a-week newspaper. (The *Register* consisted of four pages, six days a week.) [2] Efforts to buy the plant of the money-losing *Register* collapsed when Charles Calvo asked $25,000, and so the Gonzales bought a large, new Cottrell press.[3] Altogether, The State Publishing Company had 107 original stockholders, including such leading Conservatives as A. C. and J. C. Haskell, D. R. Coker, A. P. Butler, W. H. Gibbes, J. K. Alston, W. H. Lyles, J. P. Thomas, Jr., and J. P. Richardson. Various Columbia business firms also underwrote the new venture.[4]

Such a paper was an enterprising undertaking for a city like Columbia with a population of only 16,947. Mule-drawn street cars still traversed its muddy thoroughfares. Business was not booming, although some saw hope for the town as a future railroad center. Despite the fact that there had been a telephone system for ten years, only sixty-two subscribers felt that the pace of their lives demanded the new invention.[5] It was obvious to the Gonzales brothers that their big new

---

[2] *News and Courier,* January 10, 1891.
[3] *The State,* June 13, 1891; *News and Courier,* January 15, 1891.
[4] List of stockholders published in *The State,* June 25, 1941.
[5] For a sketch of Columbia in 1891, see John K. Aull's article in *The State,* February 18, 1931.

paper would have to lean heavily on a patronage outside of Columbia, while stimulating its home town to keep pace with its metropolitan daily. This important task fell to Ambrose Gonzales, who again had the title of "general agent" for a newspaper as he traveled all over the state seeking stock subscriptions, advertising, and circulation for their unborn brainchild; he admitted at the time that it was the hardest work of his life.[6]

With nearly all the stock subscribed, the stockholders (of whom N. G. Gonzales was the largest) met and chose nine directors,[7] who promptly elected N. G. Gonzales as editor and A. C. Haskell as president of the company. While Ambrose toured the provinces, N. G. stayed in the capital assembling both equipment and staff for his paper. The whole plant was in one storeroom of an annex of the old city hall at the northwest corner of Main and Washington Streets, with the new press in the basement. The press and all of the hand-set type was new, and by late January a number of printers had drifted in to apply at the new shop.[8]

Many of the men who joined the Gonzales brothers were as zealous partisans as they were, and equally as good newspapermen. Although N. G. Gonzales was to supervise the business department for two years, he hired John S. Reynolds, formerly on the editorial staff of the *Register* and editor of the *Evening Record*, as treasurer;[9] his "department" consisted of Asher P. Brown. The local staff was composed of Ebbie J. Watson, an indefatigable and intriguing personality. In all, the force consisted of one editor, one business manager, one telegraph editor, one reporter–city editor, one

[6] A. E. Gonzales to Gertrude Gonzales, February 8, 1891, in E.G.P.

[7] *News and Courier*, January 23, 1891; *The State*, March 30, 1892.

[8] See reminiscences of E. H. DeCamp and John J. Cormack in *The State*, February 18, 1916.

[9] *News and Courier*, September 28, 1888, and February 6, 1889; *The State*, February 18, 1916.

pressman, twelve printers, one foreman, and three apprentices.[10]

Endowed with pride and *esprit de corps,* this little group energetically and hopefully made preparations for the latest advent in South Carolina journalism. Already there were six daily papers in the state, but Ambrose Gonzales found N. G.'s reputation a decided asset as he met with surprising success in getting "subscriptions in advance for the unborn infant, which I expect to have almost as rapid growth as the precocious babe in the 'Bab Ballads,' although I trust 'twill not become 'a decrepid old dotard at 5.' "[11] He felt that four-fifths of the daily newspaper readers outside of Charleston were on their political side, "and I will make it warm for the opposition when I get started."

For a name, N. G. had borrowed from their Grahamville journalistic experiences and tried a "dummy" of the front page as "The Palmetto State." Finding this title too long for his large Old English type, he eliminated "Palmetto" and replaced it with the state seal containing that tree, and thus established the familiar colophon still appearing at the head of *The State.*[12]

All was finally in readiness for the first issue. Early on the morning of February 18, 1891, the brothers and the few other employees gathered in the basement of the city hall to witness the important event. They were proud of their little Cottrell two-revolution press, powered by the first gasoline engine in Columbia. The first issue began to run and soon 3,000 copies of *The State* were pouring throughout South Carolina.

This edition, eight pages of six columns each, was the largest paper ever published at the state capital. In addition

[10] Reminiscences of John J. Cormack, foreman, in *The State,* June 2, 1911, and February 18, 1916, and of E. H. DeCamp, compositor, in *ibid.,* February 18, 1916.

[11] A. E. Gonzales to Gertrude Gonzales, February 8, 1891, in E.G.P.

[12] C. M. Galloway to the author, April 25, 1951.

to the many "specials" from staff correspondents already contracted to give complete state coverage, the first edition contained the full Southern service of the United Press which
told of an Ohio River flood, congressional activities, "Jack
the Ripper," and the gory details of "A Duel with Axes." Ambrose had done his work well: the paper averaged seventeen
columns of advertising daily during the first week and began
with more bona fide subscribers than any other Columbia
paper. Besides a daily selling for $8.50 per year, the pub-
lishers also printed a semiweekly on Tuesdays and Fridays
for $2.00.

In volume one, number one, of a paper which the editor
said was "freighted with good intent and high resolve," the
objectives and policies of *The State* were set forth: "There is
room and work at the capital of the State for a newspaper
which will be fearless and consistent, true to its party faith
but resolute in its opposition to 'bosses' and 'cabals,' fair to
opponents as well as friends, pledged to principle rather than
policy. . . ." The editor promised that the paper would be
"Democratic, independent, fair, statewide, and progressive."[13]

Well publicized, the Gonzales gazette was received with
great curiosity and interest. The first editorial page took
notice of this excitement:

It has been abused and praised while its type was in the foundry
and its paper in the stock. It has been, by adventurous correspondents, endowed with a multiplicity of editors and a paucity
of common sense; and, before the breath of existence had passed
its metal lips, it has effected startling metamorphoses in the
policies and manners of some of its journalistic elders.

Interest in the controversial paper continued to run high and
to elicit many comments. Even Governor Tillman subtly ob-

[13] *The State*, February 18, 1891. The often-quoted editorials of the first
issue can be conveniently read in N. G. Gonzales, *In Darkest Cuba*, pp. 26–29.

41

served: "I really have no desire to appear in print concerning the new paper, but I will say this: I hope the State will have all the success it deserves."[14] Even after a year of *The State*'s diatribes, Tillman admitted that it was a "bold, dashing, spicy and aggressive sheet, edited with spirit and ability."[15] The editor of the *Columbia Register* welcomed his competitor but mentioned that its opening editorial compared itself to a ship starting on a long sail; hence he wondered if it were to be propelled by hot air. Confident, he said, that the stockholders had "a *dear* privilege, and it is not for us to deny them that delectable privilege."[16]

Even the first felicitations caused N. G. to joust with his "eminent contemporaries." Since the *News and Courier*, like Tillman, wished for *The State* " 'all the success in life that it deserves,' " he thanked it for "a wish, of course, concerning a prosperity almost unqualified." After all, said he, that paper should be kind since it was really a foreign missionary that always preferred "good stubborn heathen at long range, like the Indianapolis *Journal*."[17]

Many readers and editors ridiculed the name of the new paper, but Gonzales said his enterprise would live up to its name, in contrast with others that led a misnomer existence:

The "Worlds" wobble, and the "Suns" are frozen out, and "Registers" fail to register the news, and the "Advances" stop still, and the "Heralds" hide out and don't proclaim, and the "Sentinels" sleep in the sun. . . . and the "Peoples" represent only one class of people, and the "Timeses" are untimely, and the "Spartans" are literary epicures, and the "Couriers" ride backward. . . . and the "Newses" are newsless.[18]

14 *The State*, February 20, 1891.
15 B. R. Tillman to C. A. Calvo, Jr., January 30, 1892, in Simkins Notes.
16 *Columbia Register*, February 19, 1891; hereinafter cited as *Register*.
17 *The State*, February 23, 1891.
18 *Ibid.*, February 27, 1891.

Actually, most exchanges admitted that the new paper was spicy and well produced, and nearly all praised its full news coverage. The *Greenville News* said "it promises to excel all other dailies in South Carolina" because it had "abundant brains and energy behind it."[19]

In general, what were the normal characteristics of this journal that made such a splash? Editorially, it reflected the keen ability and opinionated wisdom of its alert, bright editor. Writing swiftly and rarely rewriting or correcting, he composed nearly all the editorials for years, finally turning the Sunday edition over to others. Obviously, the chief characteristic of his policy was "Tillmania" since the Gonzales brothers "felt with their murdered colleague [Dawson] that the integrity of the commonwealth was threatened by the hegemony of the back country proletariat."[20] N. G. Gonzales' animosity toward Tillman was political and not personal, their one personal clash (at Blackville) having been "settled on the spot in such a way as to leave no grievances behind and no legacy of retaliation."[21] To the dishonest, the hypocrite, the sycophant, and those threatening the state, he gave verbal lashings as brilliant as they were indiscreet.

In its coverage of the news, *The State* was similar to other papers of the time but perhaps had more zest and barbed humor in the stories written by its own staff. Although for years no headline was wider than a single column and many consisted of only one line of type, they often were tantalizing enough to stimulate the reader to peruse the story below, for example: "PRETTY PRIZE FOR A POLITICIAN," "DEVILISH!" "THE EARTH YAWNED," "A CORPSE HELD UP," "WASHED OUT OF BED," "A ROYAL

[19] Comments of sixty-five papers in *The State,* March 1, 1891.

[20] Virginius Dabney, *Liberalism in the South* (Chapel Hill: University of North Carolina Press, 1932), p. 232.

[21] *The State,* March 19, 1892.

HOWDY-DO OVER IN AUSTRIA," or "BISCUITS
KILLING INDIANS." Violence was the keynote of many
news stories, as was indicated by such captions as "CRE-
MATED IN THEIR BEDS," "WADED IN BLOOD,"
"TERRIBLE HAND OF FATE," "PISTOLS PULLED
AT PELZER," "FOULLY MURDERED," "HIS ARM
GROUND OFF," "DISASTER IN THE DEEP," "DIS-
ASTER AT A DEDICATION," "SICKENING SLAUGH-
TER," or "BLOWN UP AND BURNED." A classic
headline was "BULLET IN THE BOWELS." This same
overworked headline writer took his recreation in long and
short alliteration: for example, " 'Jaggers Not Jugged' | Al-
though the Justice Knew He Had a Jug of Jolly Juice";
"Sinful Smith's Society Sequel | Swell Supper in Silvery
Swim Required 'Stuff,' So He States | Some 'Society' Slang";
"Board Buys Many Barrels of Booze"; "Holocaust in a Hotel"; or "Ben 'Busts' a Bomb."

Despite a relatively thorough coverage of the news that
from the first was rivaled in South Carolina only by the *News
and Courier,* the paper could hardly be called objective. This
was particularly true of anything associated with Tillmanism,
as can be seen by such headlines as

WELL!! WELL!! WELL!!
Governor Tillman Rewards Another
of His Richland Followers

INDIGNATION IN CHARLESTON
Over the Elevation of a Fifth-Rate
Lawyer to the Supreme Bench

When a prohibition bill passed the House, *The State* headed
its story, "Ears Shut to Reason and the Bill Pushed
Through." Another example of objectivity:

TAKING TILLMAN TO TASK
Colonel Keitt Reviews the
Great Blower.[22]

Needless to say, the stories themselves overworked the adjectives necessary to instruct the readers as to who were the heroes and who the villains. Nevertheless, as N. G. Gonzales had said he would, he opened the columns to the correspondence of friend and foe alike, and authors of "letters to the editor" had a field day taking full advantage of his invitation and their own invective.

Financially, the most difficult years for *The State* were 1891–1897. On many occasions in this period, employees were sure each week was their last. On the surface, however, innovations and improvements seemed to substantiate the optimistic boasting in which the paper often engaged. Certainly the size of the initial circulation list and its steady increases were heartening, especially since for years the ambitious *State* had to get five-sixths of its readers outside of Columbia.[23] In 1892 *Ayer's Newspaper Annual* showed that the circulation was already double that of the *Register* and larger than any Southern daily published in a city of equal white population.[24] But even the Columbians were *State*-conscious, as John A. Rice explained:

The only newspaper read widely by the living was published there—the rest read the Charleston *News and Courier* then as now. . . . Meanwhile, to be mentioned favorably in *The State* was a desideratum, even in the days that did not know the word "publicity."[25]

[22] *Ibid.*, April 20, 1892; December 4 and 9, 1891; January 7, 1892.
[23] *Ibid.*, February 17, 1901.
[24] *Ibid.*, December 9, 1892.
[25] John A. Rice, *I Came Out of the Eighteenth Century* (New York: Harper and Brothers, 1942) , p. 48.

Within three months after *The State* was founded, Calvo cut his own *Register* advertising rates in half and reduced his subscription rates, but Gonzales shrugged it off as a compliment and went merrily on. Nor did the *Columbia Annual Trade Review*, first published ten months after *The State* was launched, indicate any shaky footing; prepared by Ambrose Gonzales, it claimed to be the largest paper ever published in South Carolina.[26]

Purchase of another paper also beguiled those who regularly foresaw and forecast the end of *The State*. In early 1893 H. P. Clarke and a group of Columbians, primarily bankers, bought the *Evening Record* at auction and tried to continue it as the *Columbia Journal* with John P. Capers as editor. After seven months of losing up to $250 a week, the owners sold out to The State Publishing Company in September 1893. No money changed hands, only stock, but Clarke and his cohorts were persuaded that it would be impossible to lose as much as theretofore. *The State* owners felt that with only the editorial departments of the two papers separate, the new operations would necessitate only one or two extra men.[27]

Much astonishment was expressed by others at this expansion. The Charleston *Sun* unkindly said it was a case of Jonah swallowing the whale, and Calvo was frankly pleased, since "if one of them fails it will carry the other along to the grave."[28] Gonzales replied to his mockers by saying that his partisanship was not a sign of weakness: "The fact that it [*The State*] was outspoken and uncompromising in behalf of its faith gave it strength instead of weakness."[29]

[26] *The State*, April 18, May 14, and November 9, 1891.
[27] August Kohn to General Rudolph Seigling, n.d., in Kohn Papers, in South Caroliniana Library; *The State*, January 15, 17, February 1, September 24, 1893.
[28] Same to same, [date blurred], 1893, in Kohn Papers. Part of these papers have apparently suffered considerable damage from water.
[29] *The State*, September 27, 1893.

Ambrose Gonzales brought William Watts Ball, editor of
the *Laurens Advertiser,* to Columbia to edit and manage his
new paper in February 1894. After a few months, Ball and
his cousin, Larry W. Boyd, purchased the little nonpartisan
paper for $1,500—money which the Gonzaleses badly needed
at the time, according to August Kohn.[30] The mechanical
work of the *Journal* was still done by *The State.* Ball drew
no money from his venture since he was then earning a good
living as correspondent for other papers. Although he was
praised by *The State* as "the most promising of the young
journalists of South Carolina," he and Boyd closed down the
local *Journal* in December 1894, and soon thereafter Ball
went to Charleston as managing editor of the *Evening Post.*[31]

In 1893 Gonzales also mocked *The State*'s Cassandras by
becoming the first newspaper owner in the two Carolinas to
install linotype machines to replace the old hand-set type.
Costing $12,000 on the installment plan, the four machines
helped make *The State* office a public institution; for some
time after their purchase the plant held open house for interested spectators. Kohn told his superiors that the machines
gave a great deal of trouble, and Calvo again rejoiced at his
own prophecy that such newfangled contraptions would not
pay at all in small offices.[32]

It is understandable that the critics of *The State* were
shocked at such expansion. During the national economic
panic of 1893 the *State*'s editor and managers were drawing
no salary, and often the staff was paid late; some of them once
went unpaid for eleven weeks.[33] All of the traveling men

[30] August Kohn to J. C. Hemphill, n.d., in Hemphill Papers.
[31] W. W. Ball to the author, January 30, 1951; *The State,* February 8, June
19, 20, and December 24, 1894; April 5, 1895.
[32] August Kohn to General Rudolph Siegling, date blurred, and August
Kohn to ———, [date blurred], in Kohn Papers. Also, see A. E. Gonzales to
Gertrude Gonzales, May 10, 1893, in E.G.P., and *The State,* September 25,
October 2, 4, 1893, and February 18, 1916.
[33] Reminiscences of John B. Rodgers in *The State,* June 25, 1941.

were called off the road, and Ambrose Gonzales undertook all that work as well as superintending the home office. Neither Kohn nor Calvo could understand how the paper kept running.[34]

But it did keep running, and there was one explanation: Ambrose Gonzales. If ever a man was trusted by his employees, it was this Gonzales. Smiling and joking despite overdue notes, drafts, and bills, he inspired them to be as determined as he that their paper should survive. When linotypes displaced compositors, he established a job printing office to give them work. When one printer was killed by his machinery, "Mr. Ambrose" voluntarily undertook to support his family thereafter. When he had any money, his men always knew they could get it—although one said his gifts and loans were more generous than his pay scale. But the employees stuck by him when they saw N. G. not drawing his thirty dollars a week and going ragged while his men got what little came in. Not having enough money to unload their C.O.D. shipments of newsprint, they helped "Mr. Ambrose" persuade a railroad agent to dole out a day's supply at a time. Even the post office held up the papers for postage, and once in 1893 a judge's order placing the paper in the hands of a receiver was averted only by two hours of frantic stock raising. Persuasive Ambrose, insolvent and in debt, could always prevail on friends like W. H. Lyles and Chris Fitzsimmons to help prevent emergencies, even after the original stockholders had long since abandoned hope of their capital or any dividends.[35] Despite its weaknesses, *The State* was

[34] August Kohn to J. C. Hemphill, [June 1893?], in Kohn Papers. Hard times hit *The State* early; see John S. Reynolds to R. R. Hemphill, October 13, 1892, in Hemphill Papers.

[35] Reminiscences of John J. Cormack, E. J. Watson, Asher P. Brown, and W. W. Watson (original employees) in *The State*, February 18, 1916; and of E. H. DeCamp in *ibid.*, July 11, 1903; also, see editorial, *ibid.*, February 17, 1901.

within a year considered by many Columbians as a civic institution in which many took a pride and interest that was almost personal.

During these difficult days of the not-so-gay nineties, Ambrose himself worked like a Trojan, glumly writing his sister:

I can't make three dollars a week for myself and yet . . . I am forced . . . to trampoose around the State in quest of more stock and more money to keep it from going to the devil, and of course I'll get neither thanks nor profits for my pains.[36]

But "trampoosing" around, he made hosts of friends for himself and his paper. Always he showed a real interest in the little towns where he became well known. On these travels he demonstrated the generosity which brought streams of widows and orphans to his office (some regularly on the first of the month). Once in Spartanburg, he accidentally went to a meeting where funds were being raised for Converse College, enthusiastically subscribed $500, and somehow managed later to raise the money—and always thereafter loved and boosted Converse! Although as partisan as N. G., he affected his political antagonists differently from the testy editor. As W. W. Ball put it,

He laughed at the politicians . . . to their faces and made their friends laugh with him. He made them absurd, told them of their buffooneries and hypocrisies, and never one of them could take offense. How he did it Heaven knows, but many a fool or knave actually seemed to relish his exposures of them; while the bystanders roared.[37]

By 1895 such a leader and his loyal employees began to find a path out of the financial woods. Even N. G. himself

---

[36] A. E. Gonzales to Gertrude Gonzales, August 23, 1892, in E.G.P.
[37] Ball in *The State*, July 25, 1926. Similar observations in Mrs. W. P. Greene (Abbeville newswoman) to the author, January 20, 1951.

had almost given up in 1893, having futilely sought from the new Democratic administration a consular post first in Shanghai and then in Brazil; he never publicly explained whether the move was a temporary expedient to relieve the paper or whether he had less faith in "Mr. Ambrose" than the others had.[38]

Besides raising subscription rates rather than cutting the size of the paper (as the *Register* had to do), the publishers undertook much reorganization. In 1892 Judge Haskell resigned as president and was replaced by Colonel C. Quitman Marshall; at the same time, Tazewell T. Tally replaced John S. Reynolds as secretary-treasurer, and $10,000 worth of preferred stock was issued.[39]

With these new leaders, the paper rocked along. A few months after the paper had started, Willie Gonzales (then signing himself "W. Elliott Gonzales") had come to the firm. In 1890 he had gone into partnership with John R. Crapo of Vermont to develop real estate and a hotel at Buena Vista. Willie was to furnish the money (his wife's), and his partner the experience; by summer of 1892 Willie had the experience and the partner the money. In the fall of 1891 his full-page advertisements were devoted not to the hotel but to explanations of its failure and strong denunciations of the duplicity of Crapo.[40] By the summer of 1892 he was with *The State* and soon was simultaneously the telegraph editor, proofreader, and headline writer for that paper, and telegraph and news editor of the *Columbia Journal*. For this grind, seven days a week, he earned a gross emolument of $19.20.[41] He was

---

[38] *The State*, March 19, 24, 25, 30, April 2, 9, 11–16, and May 8, 1893.

[39] The new rate was $10 annually for seven issues a week; the *News and Courier* charged this rate for only six a week. *The State*, January 21, 1894. On the reorganization, see *ibid.*, November 30, 1892.

[40] See especially *The State*, August 30, 1891, or December 3, 1891.

[41] A. E. Gonzales to Gertrude Gonzales, April 7, 1892, in E.G.P.; Helen K. Hennig, *Great South Carolinians of a Later Date* (Chapel Hill: University of North Carolina Press, 1949), pp. 296–97.

therefore present in the 1893 reorganization when Ambrose Gonzales became president and also business manager.

More drastic financial finagling was needed if *The State* was to survive, however. Needled by the Charleston *Sun,* "that microbe of common sense," the editor admitted in 1895 that their friends had a mortgage on the property, but the paper was not, as the *Sun* said, "notoriously plastered over with mortgages, debts and judgements"; and furthermore it had "lived over four years . . . without a dollar of commercial capital, through panic, four cents cotton and all that." By then, however, it was finally on a self-sustaining basis.[42] Two months later, when the original stock of $30,000 had been exhausted, The State Company was organized with a capital of $10,000 and leased the paper from The State Publishing Company, which had "inherited from the panic year [1893] a floating debt which embarrassed and threatened it." Without buying the assets of the old corporation, the new organization profited and by 1901 was able to increase its stock from $10,000 to $100,000, buy out the old company, and pay off its debts. The new firm was dominated by the Gonzales family with three of the brothers, William H. Lyles, and A. R. Stewart making up the board of directors.[43] Not until then was stability achieved.

Such an uphill struggle had been made in the face of fierce competition. In 1892 there were eight daily papers in South Carolina.[44] Chief competitor was the *News and Courier,* the policy of which Gonzales ridiculed in good humor while

[42] *The State,* April 22, 1895. August Kohn to J. C. Hemphill, January 25, 1895, in Hemphill Papers, confirmed some of the suspicions of the *Sun.* Kohn, however, had been very optimistic about *The State* only a few months before; see Kohn to Hemphill, August 30, 1894, in Hemphill Papers.

[43] *The State,* June 11, 25, 1895; A. E. Gonzales in *ibid.,* July 12, 1926; F. C. Withers (business manager) in *ibid.,* February 18, 1931. The new company agreed to pay a sum equal to 20 percent of the common stock of The State Publishing Company and 25 percent of the preferred stock.

[44] *Rowell's American Newspaper Directory,* 1892, p. 47.

staying on friendly terms with August Kohn, who had become Columbia correspondent in February 1892.[45] Up in Greenville, *The State* contended with A. B. Williams' *News* and Colonel James A. Hoyt's *Enterprise and Mountaineer*. In Charleston, Octavus C. Cohen published a Tillman organ for four years until Gonzales ran his eye-catching headline, "THE END OF THE WORLD HAS COME."[46] N. G. left finances up to Ambrose, but at the time the *World* folded he explained his sole theory of newspaper survival: "A newspaper devoted to principle *may* fail; but one without principle *must*." In Spartanburg, there were the *Herald* controlled by J. C. Garlington, the *Journal* by Charles M. Henry, and the *Spartan* by Captain Charles Petty. In Columbia there were the *Register* and the *Record* (and then briefly the *Journal*), and in Charleston, beginning in 1894, the *Evening Post*.

N. G.'s editorial attitude toward these rivals varied. He sneered at those "more familiar with the bludgeons than the rapiers of discussion" and who thus did not always understand the subtle sallies of *The State*. "If contemporaries can't understand *The State*, they ought not to criticize it. It is published for the delectation of the intelligent, and doesn't undertake to present a bottle of brain tonic with each copy."[47] Although he obviously enjoyed witty controversies, N. G. could also wield the bludgeon; when the *Florence Times* predicted the financial collapse of *The State*, he blasted: "The writer of the above falsehood is a despicable slanderer."[48]

Relations with Calvo's *Register* can be better termed enmity than rivalry. Always contemptuous of it, the Gonzaleses

[45] *The State*, February 15, 1892.
[46] *News and Courier*, April 21, 1888; *The State*, October 7, 1891. For a condensed history of the *Greenville News*, see that paper, September 25, 1949.
[47] *The State*, October 19, 1892.
[48] *Ibid.*, September 17, 1892.

began to hate the *Register* when it embraced Tillmanism
and was rewarded with state printing contracts which offset
its continuous operating losses. Annually, *The State* exposed
"the printing steal" and minced no words in showing how
Calvo continued his paper.[49]

Of course, the Calvo-Gonzales feud was one of long standing. In the first year of *The State,* a row developed over circulation claims of the two papers. The law provided that
certain public advertising be placed in the largest Columbia
paper, and the Tillmanites—accepting the exaggerated
claims of the *Register*—gave the contract to that organ. Ambrose Gonzales then approached J. Walter Gray, clerk of the
House, in the Grand Central Hotel and accused him of fraud
in placing such advertisements. Gray pulled his pistol, whereupon Ambrose called him "a damned coward" and dared
him to throw away his pistol; according to *The State,* "This,
of course, Gen. Gray would not do." At that moment, Dr.
Sampson Pope, recent editor of the *Register* and then clerk
of the Senate and also responsible for aiding the *Register,*
entered the lobby and threatened anyone who accused him
of fraud, whereupon N. G. belabored him "while Dr. Pope
attempted in plug-ugly fashion to gouge out his eyes." Ambrose, "unable to get any fight out of Gen. Gray," eliminated
Dr. Pope and offered to take on any three of the gathering
hostile crowd. Word of the near-riot reaching *The State,* all
of the printers seized available weapons—side sticks, foot
sticks, mallets, column rules, and other printing shop imple-
ments—and invaded the hotel in full battle array. The "case
of the *Register*'s honor" did not end in the mayor's court,
where the Gonzales brothers were exonerated. A day later
a bloody battle took place between Ambrose Gonzales and

[49] *Ibid.,* December 28, 1891; July 9–13, August 4, 20, September 3 ("The
Organ Is Rewarded") , 1892; October 26, November 23, 1894; February 10,
1897. The last is a history of public printing in the state.

M. F. Tighe, *News and Courier* correspondent who in his news dispatch had said Ambrose did not fight fairly in the battle of the Grand Central. Although Tighe "scratched and gouged," Ambrose gave him a thorough drubbing.[50] Later, the two legislative clerks hired as an "expert investigator" one W. M. Rodgers, late of the *Register* staff, to determine the circulation of Columbia papers. He, according to Gonzales, "lied, deliberately and maliciously" to aid the *Register*, "a moribund newspaper, which seeks to live by grace of the alms of the [Tillman] administration." The editor warned: "We shall make these unfaithful public servants as sick of their slanderous work as we have made the Columbia *Register*, their tool."[51] And this *The State* did, forcing the legislature to investigate Rodgers' figures and methods; they found the *Register*'s circulation padded by 2,000 for the single day of the survey made by Rodgers, "a knave" and "a scapegoat," according to N. G. G. Actually, the circulation of *The State* at the time was almost triple that of the *Register*.[52] Thereafter, Gonzales gleefully wrote of the "Tillrodgerster."

After this controversy, there was no bloodshed until 1893 when C. A. Calvo with the aid of his son attacked N. G. Gonzales from behind on the street at night. As usual, both sides claimed victory and made charges of cowardice. *The State* noted that "the *Register* yesterday failed to extend thanks to Engineer Smith [a peace-making bystander], whose kind offices saved its proprietor from another humiliating position." On the other side, the *Register*, in its news story, "Bully Gonzales Beaten | He Received a Much Deserved Castigation," said that Calvo had reached the stage where he could no longer abide "the lowest and vilest abuse" of *The*

<hr/>

50 *Ibid.*, November 25–28, 1891; *Register*, November 26, 1891; John J. Cormack's reminiscences in *The State*, February 18, 1916.

51 *The State*, November 24, 1891.

52 *Ibid.*, November 26, 27, December 9–17, 1891.

State and that "all who know Mr. Calvo know that he is an honorable and courageous gentleman who would not take advantage of anyone."[53]

In 1896 N. G. again tangled with the *Register,* this time in the person of its editor, George R. Koester. On this occasion Gonzales' charges were based on misinformation which he eventually admitted, but the dispute continued to gather adjectives. Finally, Koester sent a challenge to a duel, and as in earlier years, N. G. declined to break the law although conceding to Koester the opportunity to take action since the editor of *The State* was "personally responsible for what he has said, and is within easy, everyday reach. Koester should put up or shut up." Koester did not shut up, but the next day printed a long editorial on Gonzales, "a dirty, low, cowardly ruffian," "a cowardly scoundrel" who hurled epithets at gentlemen and then tried to save "his dirty carcase [*sic*]," a "contemptible bully and confessed coward." In turn, Gonzales washed his hands of "a persistent liar and a blackguard by nature and preference" who conducted "long-range abuse" in "a scurrilous sheet." Both retired from the field disdaining to further contaminate themselves by contact with each other.[54]

Fortunately for delicate readers of *The State,* many of its clashes with its rivals were more gentle. Once it even offered to arbitrate a row between the *Baptist Courier* and the *Southern Christian Advocate* and thus "to prevent inkshed."[55] Gonzales always enjoyed baiting his old friend Alfred Williams of the *Greenville News.* Once when the latter misquoted *The State,* he chided it:

Wherefore, O! dweller in the mountains, it [*The State*] beseeches you to follow its own example, not only in the matter of temper,

[53] *Ibid.,* May 6, 1893, and *Register,* May 5, 6, 1893.
[54] *The State,* April 25–27, 1896; *Register,* April 26, 1896.
[55] *The State,* March 12, 1891.

but of credits, and when you comment on the saying of a contemporary, set down exact language of that contemporary. So wilt thou be reverenced as a just man throughout all Israel.[56]

Never did Gonzales let anyone have the last word:

Our contemporary [again the *News*] is too acute not to recognize a logical argument against it, too sensible to meet it with flimsy reasonings, and too . . . polite to . . . use abuse as a substitute for proof. It smiles, waves the white flag, and declares itself the victor.[57]

Frequently, Gonzales ridiculed the poetry in the *News* but conceded, "Possibly, by some providential metamorphosis, it may yet become a true political seer. If that should ever happen, *The State* will welcome it to the ranks of prophets and sages. Meantime it will delight itself with the brimming poetry of the editorial page."[58]

Some members of the country press were not amused by Gonzales' needling so he suggested "an editorial night school in which several otherwise intellectual journalists may be taught the difference between polite irony and impolite rage and to distinguish generally between fun and fury."[59] One in particular was chided: "Editor Holmes of the Barnwell *People* is too frisky. He should be inoculated with lymph from . . . the Charleston *World*. That would bring him down several points in the scale of liveliness and make him a better balanced citizen."[60]

But the favorite target was the *News and Courier,* dubbed "The Ostrich" for its evasion of warm issues. When "The Old Lady of Broad Street" sneered at the jibes of *The State,*

[56] *Ibid.,* March 7, 1891.
[57] *Ibid.,* October 23, 1891.
[58] *Ibid.,* September 22, 1891.
[59] *Ibid.,* March 14, 1891.
[60] *Ibid.,* March 20, 1891.

the latter said it was not alarmed by " 'the awful ban of ex-communication' " by "our modern St. Simeon Stylites on its pillar, bowing to Boston, Indianapolis and Rumtofoo, while oblivious to what is being said in Greenville, Spartanburg and Charleston." The staid old paper seemed irritated that any of the press should poke fun at it, but "Even in its most grand and gloomy moments our esteemed contemporary . . . manages to amuse the irreverent."[61]

No amusement was involved in a prolonged quarrel with the *News and Courier* about train schedules which would be advantageous to circulation. In this competition, the Charleston paper for a long time had the upper hand with trains putting it in the up-country at the same time as *The State* and with few trains going from Columbia into the low-country until the *News and Courier* had already pervaded the area with the day's news. Some trains even seemed to be mysteriously removed for the benefit of the Charleston paper. For thus eliminating schedules for the traveling public, the *News and Courier* editorially praised the railroad, but, as *The State* said, "For cold and naked cheek we don't think that anything but a porcine jowl in an ice-house could surpass the *News and Courier's* editorial. . . ."[62] When Hemphill (editor on the *News and Courier*) got the Southern to institute a 3:20 A.M. departure from "the Holy City," Gonzales gleefully observed it was presumably run for the mass of Charlestonians who wrote and mailed letters at two A.M. and for the convenience of an energetic traveling public who liked to arise at three A.M.[63] Hemphill even used his influence

[61] *Ibid.*, November 2, 1893. The rivalry was not too bitter, since the *News and Courier* helped *The State* in its financial troubles, even lending it rolls of newsprint. *News and Courier* ("per J. H. L.") to August Kohn, July 21, 1898, in Kohn Papers.

[62] *The State*, January 28, 1892.

[63] *Ibid.*, November 7, 13, 1902; J. C. Hemphill to P. I. Wells, November 5, 1902, in Hemphill Papers.

to get trains out of Columbia delayed. Actually, schedules from Columbia improved with the growth of the city (*The State* vigorously denied ever actively intervening in behalf of advantageous schedules), and in a few years the paper was in much of South Carolina by breakfast time. Hemphill gave this as the primary reason that the *News and Courier* had ceased to dominate the state by 1910.[64]

The State also engaged in another life-and-death struggle with other papers, this one for wire service. When the paper began in 1891, other Southern dailies subscribed to the New York Associated Press but *The State* proudly joined the new United Press which supplied news until three in the morning. In June 1891 the U.P. installed a special leased wire and an operator in *The State* office, the first such service south of Richmond. All other papers got their dispatches via Western Union wires and through the regular offices of the telegraph company. The first operator there was George V. Hobart, later known as a writer but at the time noted for his unique feat of recording the news reports directly on a typewriter.[65]

Trouble came in 1893. By a contract of October 1893 the United Press abandoned the Southern field, turning its few papers over to the newly formed Southern Associated Press, consisting of Southern papers which had seceded from the New York Associated Press and dominated by such old papers as the *News and Courier,* the *Augusta Chronicle,* and the *Savannah Morning Press.* Thus *The State* was thrown to the wolves it had been baiting.[66]

Pushed into the S.A.P., *The State* was at the mercy of Calvo, who already had the exclusive franchise of that service for the city. Provision was made that no existing paper be

[64] Hemphill's report to the *News and Courier* directors, February 8, 1910, in Hemphill Papers.
[65] *The State,* June 1, 2, 1891; February 18, 1916.
[66] *Ibid.,* January 4, 1893; December 3, 1892.

squeezed out by such franchises; hence Calvo had to let Gonzales have the service too, but he objected strenuously to the
division of the cost. *The State* for its part later claimed ex-
tortion and said it had paid the cost for both papers.[67] In
1895 the cost of the S.A.P. service was divided equally between the rivals, although Major Hemphill constantly sought
to have the press service increase its rates to *The State* which
was paying only about half what it cost his paper.[68]

The new compromise brought no peace. With the early
collapse of both the S.A.P. and the U.P., the Columbia *Register* successfully exercised its earlier contract with the New
York Associated Press and obtained exclusive rights to the
new A.P. for the city, thereby leaving *The State* without any
wire service.[69]

For six weeks in the spring of 1897, *The State* nearly suf-
focated for lack of news; the staff finally thought "Mr. Ambrose" was beaten. This time, however, Hemphill intervened
with the Associated Press in New York in behalf of fair play
and Gonzales' rights.[70] Meanwhile the intrepid staff printed
the news. The prolific E. J. Watson ground out column after
column of local news, and by devious means the paper obtained outside news. Calvo suspected the *Augusta Chronicle*
of "leaking" its A.P. wire service to Gonzales, and by paying
regular Western Union rates *The State* received so many

[67] August Kohn to J. C. Hemphill, date blurred [summer of 1892?], in
Letterbook, 1893–1896, of Kohn Papers; *The State*, February 22, 1897.
[68] The figures he gave in his complaints varied considerably. For his
anguish, see J. C. Hemphill to J. H. Estill, July 29, 1895, and to Patrick
Walsh, July 5 and October 5, 1896, in Letterbook, 1894–1896, of Hemphill
Papers.
[69] *Register*, April 8, 1897; *The State*, May 10, 1897; J. C. Hemphill to
Chas. S. Diehl, April 30, 1897, in Letterbook, 1896–97, of Hemphill Papers.
[70] The A.P.'s usual exclusive franchise contract was not to be applicable
to papers that had been receiving U.P. service on October 15, 1892, as *The
State* had. See J. C. Hemphill to A. E. Gonzales, April 29, 30, May 6, 11, 1897,
and to Chas. S. Diehl, April 30, 1897, in Letterbook, 1896–1897, of Hemphill
Papers.

"specials" that the public probably never knew of the feud.[71] The A.P., controlled in New York, was aware that its reports were "being stolen at some point on the circuit for the benefit of The Columbia State" and issued dire warnings to operators, but the Gonzales gazette continued to get the news.[72] In early May, *The State* obtained a ninety-year contract with the new A.P. combine and the latest battle of Columbia was over.

Survival in such crises obviously depended on an alert staff. Small in number, this loyal group made up in energy, verbosity, and ability for whatever else they lacked. As has been noted, N. G. Gonzales handled all of the editorials except for help from John S. Reynolds on the Sunday paper.[73] The rest of the staff made up one big rowdy family whose ambition in life was to "scoop" the *Register* and the *News and Courier*—a feat they performed with regularity. Kohn, Columbia correspondent of the latter, said there was no hope of beating *The State* staff and "a small army of volunteer workers" because "these people up here are wild on 'The State.' It makes no difference what happens they run post haste to tell The State people."[74]

From 1891 to 1904, E. J. Watson was chiefly responsible for the paper's thorough news coverage. "Ebbie" became a legend in Columbia journalism. It was said that everybody in town was eager to tell him a story; within ten minutes after a dog fight half of Columbia would pour into his office to give him the details. He had the title of "city editor," but he was actually a one-man staff who frequently enjoyed the services

[71] August Kohn to J. C. Hemphill, April 17, 1897, in Letterbook, 1897–1898, of Kohn Papers.
[72] A.P. memo cited by J. C. Hemphill to A. E. Gonzales, April 29, 1897, in Letterbook, 1896–1897, of Hemphill Papers.
[73] *The State*, October 26, 1909; August Kohn to J. C. Hemphill, August 6, 1895, in Hemphill Papers.
[74] August Kohn to J. C. Hemphill, April 1, 1901; see also September 19, 1898, in Kohn Papers.

of two or three volunteer "apprentices." Daily, Watson set out in his rounds atop an old bicycle with a huge and a small wheel, and within hours had four to eight columns of local stories; the only trouble he ever had as a reporter was that the composing room reported the paper filled up long before Watson submitted all his gleanings. Nothing stopped him. He stole rides on cowcatchers of freights to secure distant stories; he perched on a limb outside of the Grand Central Hotel to cover secret meetings of Tillmanites; and he obtained copies of significant letters to Tillman and printed them before the governor himself received them through the mail. Only once did he fail. When the morning train to Sumter (forty miles away) was eliminated, Ebbie grandly volunteered to deliver the paper there on his bicycle; on his maiden (and last) voyage, he eventually reached his destination on the night train.[75]

Others were almost as determined. James A. Hoyt, Jr., *State* reporter, was arrested in Greenville for breaking into a Western Union office to get his story to the paper.[76] Staff members like Sam McGowan and J. Wilson Gibbes were as eager, and *The State* never hid its lights under a bushel. For example, when Watson intercepted a letter from Governor W. J. Northern of Georgia to Governor Tillman, the front page gloatingly explained why "Passers-by may have heard hilarious sounds issuing from *The State* office last night, and may have wondered what . . . made the office cat stand on its hind feet in the window and grin at them, and why the local man had to hold his sides. . . ." The reason, of course,

[75] Reminiscences of A. P. Brown in *The State*, February 18, 1931; of E. H. DeCamp, in *ibid.;* of E. J. Watson in *ibid.*, February 18, 1916. Also, see August Kohn, "How To Get the News," in S. C. State Press Association *Proceedings* (1899), p. 12.

[76] *The State*, August 9, 1899. The exploit was performed in vain; the *Atlanta Constitution* intercepted the story en route and failed to relay it to Columbia. To put it mildly, *The State* was irritated.

was that *The State* had gotten out its "old reliable 'scoop' that it keeps on hand for emergencies."[77]

A less energetic member of the staff was Captain R. E. Elliott, who moved to the paper when it was founded by his nephews. As at the Bureau, his duties consisted of supervising the carrier boys, propagating ante-bellum philosophy for everybody who came to the office, and holding forth in the raconteur's chair perched on the street in front of *The State* office. Well known for his long beard and his evil-smelling pipe, this inveterate spinner of yarns was a landmark of Columbia.[78]

Watson's news collecting was amply supplemented by the three Gonzales brothers themselves. N. G. limited his signed news reports primarily to political affairs and national conventions. Even here he vented his spleen always on Pitchfork Ben. Under the headline, "AND 'BUST' HE DID," his "news report" told of the farmer's performance at the 1896 Democratic convention:

Ben Tillman is a fizzled firecracker. His egotism and snarling bitterness disgusted the convention. . . . He has been snubbed and sat upon by the silver men and hissed and flouted by the gold men—the local frog could not expand himself into the national ox. . . . I should say that the idolatry of our mock Moses has begun to wane.[79]

Ambrose Gonzales occasionally contributed florid outpourings about events he witnessed in his business travels. Although too verbose to be accepted as news stories in modern journalism, they had a certain literary charm and imagination which seemed to justify their length. For example, he

[77] *The State*, February 26, 1892.
[78] A. E. Gonzales to Gertrude Gonzales, February 18, 1891, in E.G.P. For a picture, see the frontispiece of A. E. Gonzales, *The Captain: Stories of the Black Border* (Columbia: The State Company, 1924).
[79] *The State*, July 10, 1896.

accompanied the first "cannon ball" train that was to get *The State* to the up-country in the morning. Even his description of the weather was real literature. The weather produced a flood that stopped the train at "the copper colored Hellespont" of the Saluda River. "Hero may beckon, but Leander swims not. . . . When the waters shall have subsided, *The State* will bear its message on to the hills beyond."[80]

On other occasions, "Mr. Ambrose" wrote a review of a traveling opera company at Greenville, described new cotton mills at Gaffney, gave "Something about the Summer Life" at Glenn Springs, reported a new building at Converse College, and described the magnificent new Merchants Hotel of Spartanburg, which was "heated by steam distributed through handsome radiators" and "equipped with bath rooms . . . on every floor."[81] Perhaps the luxuriant flow of his prose justifies a lengthy quotation to show what he could do with the story of the opening of an unpretentious railroad to the small town of Bennettsville:

The union of the Palmetto and the Pine! A commercial union, and, withal, a love match, was celebrated yesterday. Bennettsville was the altar and John H. Averill [railroad manager] the high priest; the bride was wreathed with cotton blossoms, and spiked rails of Bessemer steel were worn in lieu of "spiked tails."

Up from the ocean, where the blue waves danced in the sunshine and tossed their white caps in the air as they romped over the deep bar where the sea gull poised a scimitar wing and anon drifted on the billow's breast. Up from the beautiful bay, wrinkled by the breeze. . . . Up and away . . . from the sparrows twittering among the dwarfed live oaks of the battery, from the music of St. Michael's bells, from the dagger-voiced vendor of "wah shrimp" on to the borders of the Old North State where the pine cones swung emerald green, . . . on to the town of

80 *Ibid.*, March 10, 1891.
81 *Ibid.*, September 19, 1892.

Bennettsville, instinct with industrial life, and soon to be a city.
. . . Bennettsville on the Pee Dee was yesterday linked to Charleston on the Ashley.[82]

Willie Gonzales, news and telegraph editor, also contributed his share. His best work was done on feature stories that were highly literary but also chock-full of facts. Every summer he did lively, lilting pieces on Carolina resorts which he visited. In 1896 he wrote a series of eleven articles on "The New Columbia," an enthusiastic encomium which stressed the recent growth of various institutions and industries.[83] He also followed in N. G.'s steps with his detailed coverage of famous murder trials.

Nobody could say that *The State* during its first twelve years lacked color or life. Even a cursory comparison of it with its "eminent contemporaries" will reveal a sparkle. Its headlines showed an original twist unmatched by the *Register* or the *News and Courier*. Some "scare heads" told a story in themselves, with sentences spread over several changes of type. The following sample was one column wide:

SAD SCENE IN COACH
OF RAILROAD TRAIN

A Bright Little Child Dies
in Convulsions

THE PASSENGERS SHED TEARS

A Scene That Will Long be
Remembered by Those Who
Witnessed It
How It Occurred[84]

[82] *Ibid.*, July 12, 1891. The story consumed four-and-a-half columns and included a full account of the trip by the first train on the road.
[83] *Ibid.*, June 3–July 13, 1896.
[84] *Ibid.*, March 23, 1900.

Criticized for such heads, *The State* defended its flamboyance against the *News and Courier,* "a journal founded in 1803 and possessed of nonagenarian prejudices and more than nonagenarian conservatism."[85]

The reports from correspondents in South Carolina towns were labeled by whichever of the multitudinous items therein struck the fancy of the headline writer. For example, the first item in a Camden report was a flowery account of a wedding in the town, but the headline over the Camden column was:

WEAKENED THE BRIDGE

Passing of Trains Over Temporary
S.A.L. Bridge at Camden Stopped

A Spartanburg correspondent's story was headed:

SPARTANBURG WILL SPEND
FIFTY THOUSAND DOLLARS

For the Improvement of Her Streets
White Forger Escapes From the Chaingang

but the report told of three news events and gave the details of a family reunion.[86]

News stories also demonstrated the long-winded qualities of the staff of *The State.* When the cornerstone of Winthrop College was laid, E. J. Watson wrote one story seventeen columns long on the event.[87] Observance of Columbus day, the death of Tennyson, the first execution by electrocution—all could monopolize the paper for days. Local news stories often were "folksy" in phraseology: "Mr. D. A. Tompkins, the

85 *Ibid.,* February 26, 1900.
86 *Ibid.,* January 27, 24, 1900.
87 *Ibid.,* May 13, 1894.

Governor's private secretary, went up the road yesterday";[88] readers were presumed to know where he went—just as they were supposed to know men's first names or the background of the day's news, which was rarely filled in for the new reader. On the other hand, these same readers got more unvarnished facts than they would today: many obituaries listed the insurance policies of the deceased; a person's improprieties were aired before the reading public; and a plainspoken writer of the "personals" column might print, "J. Gregg Maxcy, appointed trial justice Tuesday, was drunk on the streets of Columbia last night."[89]

From 1891 to 1897, various regular features appeared in *The State*. A column, "People You Know and People You Don't Know," dutifully listed all arrivals at the three hotels. In vacation season, the "personals" or "Coming and Going" column was transformed into "Summer Swallows." Bill Nye's syndicated hilarity appeared weekly, and in serial form syrupy fiction was published on Mondays. Antidote to it could be found in the brimstone sermons of Dr. Thomas De Witt Talmadge who was a weekly feature for years. The first Columbia paper to publish on Mondays, *The State* piously gave much space to synopses of Sunday services and sermons, but gradually over the years it beat a timid retreat from the custom.

Several types of stories must have pleased many Carolinians. Any time two Confederate veterans got together copious columns described the event (all veterans being "our gallant heroes"), and if Wade Hampton made public utterance, the whole front page seemed to renew its frequent efforts to beatify the General. Every year on the anniversary of General W. T. Sherman's pyrotechnics at Columbia, *The State* all but reenacted the conflagration, again made a schol-

[88] *Ibid.*, July 30, 1892.
[89] *Ibid.*, April 21, 1892.

arly search for the originator of the deed (always getting the same answer), and regularly said the matter should be forgotten and harmony restored between the sections. Another annual feature was the copious Confederate eulogy poured out on the birthdays of Lee and Davis.

The many circuses that came to Columbia received their share—and more—of *State* space, but nothing warranted the ink allotted to activities of the legislature, which nevertheless could draw an irreverent headline, "ASSES IN SOLON'S GARB."[90] News of the South Carolina railroad world appeared with greater frequency than any other single topic. Although progressive improvements were discussed in detail and with pride, readers must have decided that the trains ran off the tracks about as much as on them; and the theme that "the fireman jumped before the crash" recurred so often that these men must have received training in that neck-saving activity. Still, none of these favorite topics was given a head wider than a single column, even though the reporter's prose on one topic might fill all of page one.

By 1900 the paper began to adopt several modern features and to become even less like the *News and Courier* of the 1880s. For one thing, the Sunday issue now became larger than the others, the added space being filled with more "feature stories," "boiler plate" material or patent pages, and the photographs which were introduced that year. Sometimes on Sunday a "Sports of the Week" page was inserted. Also by the turn of the century, numerous little "chit-chat" columns of minor events in Columbia were published: "Quips and Cranks for the Sunday State," "Town Talk," and others.

National and international affairs were reasonably well treated by *The State* although most of its attention was devoted to sectional events. Sensational news—the Boxer Rebellion, the Boer War, any activities of European royalty—rated major attention, but in general both news and editorial columns lingered longer over Benjamin Tillman than Benjamin Harrison, a Dutch Fork murder than the Venezuelan Crisis.

Some readers must have been surprised to read an 1899 editorial in which *The State* said "out of consideration for innocent relatives and solicitous friends" it suppressed many stories of violence.[91] Actually, the more discriminating readers must have gotten a superfluity of the violence and disaster for which the news editor appeared to have a predilection. The sensitive reader perhaps swooned often over the detailed sensational reports of train accidents, complete with sickening details of the victims under such aesthetic headlines as "Ground Up by the Locomotive," "Beheaded by an Engine," or "Death on the Rail." A single front page, picked at random, contained the following headlines of news stories for its bloodthirsty readers: "HORRIBLE BEYOND DESCRIPTION" (but described nevertheless in gory detail), "CASE OF MURDERER KING," "DALY THE DYNAMITIST," "FIST FIGHT TO FINISH," "WORK OF THE GUILLOTINE," "HIS BODY BLOWN TO ATOMS," "DROWNED IN THE LEHIGH CANAL," "A CONDUCTOR SHOT AND KILLED," "DEATH AT A RAILROAD CROSSING," "NOT A STORE LEFT STANDING," "FUNERALS WERE FREQUENT," "CRUSHED TO DEATH," and "CONVICTED OF MANSLAUGHTER." Only one of these items happened in South Carolina.

In contrast to this sensationalism was the constant attention given to education. All through the year special features gave information about the atmosphere, student and faculty

[91] *Ibid.*, July 15, 1899.

activities, plants, purpose, and personnel of the numerous colleges in the state. In June *The State* forgot such stories as "Butts His Brains Out," "Bullets and Buckshot" or "Baptized in Blood" and ecstatically turned to commencement activities when the little towns adopted a holiday atmosphere for the week that was the highlight of the year. In *The State,* readers could get the excursion rates for the occasion, sense the crammed little hotels, see the bright bonnets in the crowded opera houses, get the complete texts of the oratorical contests, and read in full the "most eloquent sermon" as the long-winded speakers and preachers relieved Atlas of his task for a few days. When it was all over, the Gonzales gazette could drop its benign manners and go back to "Murdered His Mother," "Died at the Dinner Table," "Eaten to Death by Rats," or the favorite—"Blown to Atoms."

In the news coverage *The State* owners insisted on accuracy. As Willie Gonzales once told a new reporter in the early days, "Oliphant, a reporter must write the truth as he sees it or hears it. Make all the friends you can; but truth comes before friendship."[92] The trouble was that the Gonzales brothers so colored and described "truth" as they saw it that their unquestioned accuracy was half concealed by the overtones of opinion. About his paper, N. G. Gonzales said that "no one could tell its views by reference to its news columns . . . ,"[93] and yet even a society event could be narrated as follows: "Deprived of the use of the Hall of Representatives because of the jealousy of a band of political parvenus [Tillmanites] who were beyond the pale of social recognition, the South Carolina Club has managed to give . . . two beautiful balls."[94] Certainly the political news of the early *State* could hardly be classed as unbiased any more than

92 Reminiscences of A. D. Oliphant in *ibid.,* February 18, 1931.
93 *Ibid.,* February 22, 1893.
94 *Ibid.,* November 18, 1892.

it could be called colorless, and no one "by reference to the news columns" would have thought the author of the following story (apparently N. G. G. himself) to be a Republican:

There was a terrible rattling of the marrowless bones of the Republican party in the State House yesterday. . . . Rattle! Rattle! Rattle! went the skeleton, but unlike the Royal Marionettes the bones were unable to get together. . . . Not over a dozen Caucasian countenances shone through the rows of sable beings.

The old familiar voices were there—the blasé Purvis, with his velvet voice and Republican platitudes; Dickerson, . . . chock full of oratory and common sense; Dr. Crum, the courtly . . . canary from Charleston; Fordham, the "Black Demosthenes" from Orangeburg; Tolbert, the lone white star from Abbeville; Deas, with his jagged English, elevated beaver, and striped pants; Prioleau, the fearful and wonderful professor of Africanese. . . .[95]

Accurate, undoubtedly yes; but neutral, no!

The writers of N. G.'s early *State* paid little attention to society events. Late in 1896 the editor began using some of page two on Sundays for "Woman's World," but generally space was given mainly only to outstanding events like the State Ball, the germans (dancing parties) at Glenn Springs and other resorts, and notable weddings. Descriptions of the weddings were about as lush and stereotyped as such accounts today, with a favorite headline being "At Hymen's Altar." The writer would sometimes become so fascinated by the sound of his (or her) own words that the names of the bridal couple would not be revealed until after three paragraphs of extravagant description.[96]

In general, then, it can be concluded that the news service of *The State* was thorough and, for its day, dependable. In

[95] *Ibid.*, September 30, 1892.
[96] See, for example, *ibid.*, November 3, 1901.

general it was accurate, sometimes almost too much so, since it could conclude a story: "Thompson has always been a vagabond worthless boy. . . ."[97] It was also written by a sprightly staff, who enjoyed composing such headlines as: "Mecca of the Drunkards | Columbia Will Soon be Overrun by Them | A Keeley Institute to be Established Here | Oh, All Ye that Have a Jug Come and Get Cured Forever."[98] The news reporters also gave a complete picture and strove for accuracy with all the facts, although on partisan issues their readers had to strip away innuendo and prejudiced adjectives to follow the thread of events in a story that might be captioned "Governor, as Usual, Tries to Muddy the Water." And for years readers seeking only pleasure reading had to avoid such stories as "Blood! Blood! Blood!" "Bullets in His Breeches," "Given Both Barrels," or "Booze and Blood"; they had to select instead "Jackass Justice," "Whiskey's Wondrous Ways," or "The Setting Senate."[99]

Outside of its straight news coverage, the Gonzales gazette presented many significant feature stories—factual or entertaining articles of no special timeliness, essays which would generally have been about as suitable one day as another. In this department the paper rendered probably better service than modern newspapers do; some of these articles could be reprinted without change today and still be enlightening and entertaining. Among the contributors to such features was Ambrose Gonzales, who published a series of fourteen "Sunday Silhouettes" in 1892. These were a continuation of the Gullah dialect vignettes which he had earlier written for the *News and Courier*.[100]

Other features with the emphasis on long factual surveys

[97] *Ibid.*, January 15, 1892.
[98] *Ibid.*, February 9, 1892.
[99] All of these samples come from 1894.
[100] *The State*, February 21–May 22, 1892; a fifteenth, "De Fuss Luck," was printed March 17, 1895.

of different towns and institutions of the state were written by Willie Gonzales and other staff members. Another favorite topic was a description of the mountain resorts and the numerous springs to which Carolinians flocked in the nineties. The daily life of these places was depicted fondly, and readers who never left home could become quite familiar with the flavor and life of Harris, Glenn, Chick, or Cherokee Springs: the violent games of pins and tennis or the more sedate whist and euchre; the excitement of everybody's flocking to meet the afternoon train; the evenings of the waltz or two-step with "a fine Italian band"; and the endless promenading or incessant piazza rocking. Staff reporters always felt moved by the muse after a trip to one of the places; E. J. Watson typically headlined his outpouring, "Harris' Health Harbor | Handsome Hospitable Hotel and Hamlets as Habitations | Healing Waters Help All | A Haven Heralded." According to Ebbie, the "aqua pura impregnated with the chemical products of the earth" would surely "bring about an instantaneous reformation and rejuvenation."[101] Perhaps not incidentally, Harris Springs was one of the biggest advertisers in *The State* and may have even provided Watson with his vacation.

Willie Gonzales wrote a story on the same resort when the state teachers' meeting "descended upon the peaceful inhabitants . . . as the waters of the Brazos engulfed the valley country of Texas." He was there at the time and thankful not to have been "swept away by the avalanche of 'living learning' " and happy to return to such activities as hayrides with the "chaperones at Harris [who] are . . . very beautiful and accomplished women." He compared the teachers to a swarm of buzzing bees, "But the storm has passed; the orchestra can once more be heard; there is room for the two-

101 *Ibid.*, August 25, 1895.

step, and Col. Bacon has descended from his retreat in the garret, murmuring frequently and fervently, 'Thank God.' "[102]

Even the youngest Gonzales, Harriett, wrote of the springs, taking Glenn's as her province and showing that even Mecca had detractions:

> The combination of a mellow moon, a sober man and a satisfied maid may be seen at almost every turn of the broad piazzas. . . .The ubiquitous child is here in flocks from the impish brunette to the angelic (?) little blond with ringlets. They play all sorts of things—notably, havoc with their neighbor's nerves. . . . So one . . . soon finds himself dreaming happily of a heaven where all the little angels have wings instead of feet. Would that there were more little angels![103]

Not surprisingly, a favorite topic always was the Lost Cause. Confederate veterans wanting to reminisce flooded *The State* with tales of heroic exploits. Although the editor decried sectionalism and advocated a forgive-and-forget attitude, his paper regularly reopened old wounds as pseudo-historians refought battles and issues in which they regularly justified Southern extremism. The stories of the siege of Charleston and the Battle of the Crater were favorites, perhaps because of General Stephen Elliott's prominence in both. Willie Gonzales even joined in this halo manufacture.[104]

In the 1890s the feature writers of *The State* as well as the editor unbosomed themselves in tongue-in-cheek ecstasy over J. Gordon Coogler, "author of purely original verse" and "the bard of the Congaree." All of this attention was gentle and good-humored and may have puzzled the Columbia

[102] *Ibid.*, July 20, 1899.
[103] *Ibid.*, July 30, 1899.
[104] See his story of the blockade of Charleston in *ibid.*, February 21, 1897.

printer-poet who must have wondered whether the effervescent words of the paper constituted approbation or derision. But on went his best publicists, who said they had "been accused by a poetess of no mean powers of persistence of having contributed largely to the making of Coogler. . . . None but he ever touched with the wand of illuminating fancy the dingy waters of the Congaree. None but he declared the poet's pleasure

> '—in the zephyr breeze
> On the electric cars to Shandon.' "[105]

In its treatment of the world of sports, Gonzales, Watson and company happily mingled news and entertainment. In no part of the paper were the prose and opinions as unrestrained as in the sports columns. The rule of prejudice was simple: the teams representing Columbia or South Carolina College were always right, although the *State* writers did render them much free advice. Even the editorial page would occasionally get involved: "One would think that the Columbia baseballists had never played beyond the shadow of their own grandstand. Their diffidence when visiting is something to make cranks and angels weep."[106]

In the 1890s, baseball was the most prominent sports topic. Even college games were fully reported, such as "a fine game between the gallant youths of Furman university and the chivalrous young collegians of South Carolina College."[107] Sometimes the reports rambled enthusiastically for several paragraphs before giving the final score—and some never

---

[105] *Ibid.*, March 25, 1901. For biographical data about Coogler, see *ibid.*, April 4, 1897, and September 10–12, 1901; also see Irene L. Neuffer, " J. Gordon Coogler: Bard of the Congaree," *S. C. History Illustrated,* I (August 1970), 29–32.

[106] *Ibid.*, May 11, 1892. The word *crank* is the modern *fan.*

[107] *Ibid.*, April 10, 1897.

did. Lead sentences avoided vital statistics; one story started, "Blessed are they who expect little, for they shall not be disappointed."[108] And headline writers on this page also avoided the sedate, preferring "ARMIES OF CRANKS," "A GOOSE EGG DIET" (a scoreless game), or "WOFFORD'S GALL."

Reporters were frank about dull games. The writer of "WATERLOO FOR SPARTANBURG" (score, 21-2) alleged that after the sixth inning, "The rest of the game was burdensome." However, an "unusual event occurred when . . . McGowan became rather insulting to Umpire Fetner, than whom no fairer umpire can be found." But the arbiters did not always remain docile in the face of contentious players and "cranks," and used *The State* for rejoinder. For example, "A Card from Umpire Moorman" stated:

It seems that some of those in attendance upon the ball game . . . yesterday were under the impression that I did not decide Mr. W. H. Dukes out at third base in the eighth inning, and . . . I beg leave to say that immediately upon his being touched I *did* declare him out, and adhered to my decision from first to last.

C. Wardlaw Moorman[109]

The comparatively new game of football presented difficulties to *The State* writers. N. G. Gonzales, a baseball fiend, shared their bewilderment:

How the soul of the "baseball crank" must sicken when he reads of an attendance of 37,000 at a football game. We do not know much about the game down here. . . . The roughness and danger of it suggest that it might be a good thing to introduce for the adoption of our opposing politicians.[110]

108 *Ibid.*, April 20, 1897.
109 *Ibid.*, August 15, 1891.
110 *Ibid.*, November 27, 1891.

Staff members of the paper soon wrote of football, however, with the same abandon which they used for baseball. After several paragraphs of purple prose on the crowds, colleges, and the weather, they might begin the fourth or fifth paragraph with "Well, as to the game. . . ."[111] For the edification of their readers, they printed the yells and cheers in full.

The sports writers' partiality was plainly and almost painfully evident. In an 1894 game a reporter concluded his story thus: "In Georgia's estimation, every tackle made by Carolina was a foul, but it is only due to our boys to say that Georgia did not know a foul tackle from a covey of partridges."[112] Nor were opinions concealed: One game was seriously marred by "Charleston's 'jawing' and unnecessary delays."[113] In 1896 the state's largest sports crowd in history, 2,000, witnessed a "most scientific game" between Carolina and Clemson in which "Both teams played clean ball, as gentlemen should." As for the crowd, "The large grand stand was filled to overflowing with the 'beauty and brains' of the State. . . . The din of their yells and horns sounded as if the inmates of an insane asylum had broken loose."[114] Occasionally reporters became righteously indignant at charges of college professionalism, as on the occasion when Wofford students "passed the hat" to raise funds to hire a coach.[115]

The editorial policy of the paper was to condemn frequently the brutality and bestiality of prize fights, but the news policy provided hundreds of inches of news on these bloody affairs. Minute details concerning the principals were printed on the front page for days both before and after the

---

[111] *Ibid.*, November 11, 1894.
[112] *Ibid.*
[113] *The State*, November 2, 1896.
[114] *Ibid.*, November 13, 1896. Spectators presumably got their money's worth—twenty-five cents.
[115] *Ibid.*, November 12, 1895. Space prevents reprinting the most amusing football reports; see especially *ibid.*, November 15 and 27, 1891.

fights. And in 1897 *The State* gave all of its front page and one of its rare two-column heads to the Fitzsimmons-Corbett contest.[116]

Ambrose Gonzales was in charge of the business department, which was little different from that of most Southern newspapers of the day. Much of the advertising was "boiler plate" or "ready print" material prepared by some syndicate which supplied such service to hundreds of papers.[117] From these services *The State* obtained numerous advertisements of nostrums for every known disease with which its readers might have been afflicted. Students of the paper might judge that the children of the subscribers cried continuously for Castoria and the subscribers themselves survived hundreds of maladies only because of the miracle powers of Dr. Niles' Nervine Cure, Brown's Iron Bitters, Magnetic Nervine, Parson's Great Nerve Restorer, Mrs. Joe Parson's Remedy, Shaker Digestive Cordial, Paine's Celery Compounds, or Simmons Liver Regulator. Local merchants also advertised widely and enjoyed the services of the bloodthirsty headline composers, special sales being labeled in huge type, "THE CARNAGE CONTINUES." Largest of all ads were those of the resorts—Cleveland, Harris, Chick, Griffin, and Glenn Springs—which used half- or full-page displays to make their claims, print pictures of their establishments, and list the guests who had arrived during the previous week.

This was the early *State*. And, of course, *The State* was the Gonzales brothers, especially in the days when the three composed a large proportion of its writing staff. Nevertheless, some parts of the family life were not major topics for the paper. As they had been for years, N. G. and Ambrose in the

---

[116] *Ibid.*, March 18, 1897. Earlier (September 7, 1892), the editor had written: "There seems to be no color line in pugilism, which is one of the best indications of its depraving tendency."

[117] See Thomas D. Clark, *Southern Country Editor* (Indianapolis: Bobbs-Merrill Company, 1948), pp. 51 *et seq.*

1890s were responsible for the stability and solvency of their scattered family; Columbia now was the focal point of the Elliott-Gonzales empire.

There in Columbia, rooming with N. G., was Uncle Ralph, whenever that impressive and accomplished raconteur was not off at a Confederate reunion contributing his share of reminiscences. Veterans were not his only auditors, for "the Captain" was always a young man's man. As his "nevvy" Ambrose said, Captain Elliott was a seer who always had a verbal disguise to save his face as a prophet, for "no crop ever yielded quite so little, no racehorse ever ran quite so far behind, and no political campaign ever brought so deep humiliation upon State and Nation as the Captain predicted!" In any group he "talked slowly, oracularly, convincingly, but always entertainingly" and frequently used his "always loaded magazine of expletives" for picturesque "cussing," which was inoffensive and "never cursing." Always holding in contempt the purse-proud and the *nouveaux riches,* the old gentleman never was too old to touch his hat or bend over a lady's hand, "and the swish of a silken petticoat was ever to his ears as the whisper of an angel's wing."[118] Technically attached to the circulation department of the paper, the "personals" column revealed that he made frequent trips, took long vacations, and once was gone to Florida for three years.

The Captain could also be depended upon to be in Columbia for the state fair, at which time he could see all of his nephews, for even Bory never failed to come up from Colleton for that autumn event. The remainder of the time Bory rusticated at Oak Lawn with the ladies of the place or took vacations. One midnight in 1893 while on a trip to Tybee Beach, he walked in his sleep and fell forty feet from a third floor window. Seriously injured, his back was put in a cast and for several weeks it looked as if Bory had taken his last

[118] Ambrose Gonzales, "The Captain," in *The State,* December 24, 1922; later incorporated in his book of the same name.

vacation. Ambrose brought him to Columbia and provided every possible care for him until he was able to return to Pon Pon—after all, the hunting season was near at hand.[119] The Oak Lawn aunts and sisters still partially depended on the Columbia brothers. For example, they arranged for John C. Haskell to rent Myrtle Bank plantation as a hunting preserve.[120] For years the Gonzales brothers aided in the aunts' litigation to get some damages from the federal government for the confiscation of lands during Reconstruction, and at last in 1893 the Court of Claims rendered judgment in their favor for their direct tax claims for Cedar Grove, Shell Point, and Ellis Place.[121] And as might be expected, the aunts willed the Flat Rock place to the Gonzales girls and the South Carolina lands to the boys, "their father to have no claim, part or parcel in the same."[122]

That gentleman, General A. J. Gonzales, had during the years at least been consistent: he had never settled down nor ceased agitating to promote the freeing of Cuba from Spanish domination. In 1884 he wrote some autobiographical articles on the López expedition for a New Orleans newspaper. He had held minor posts in Latin American embassies in Washington. He pulled wires to get into the United States consular service, and in 1889 was a translator at the First International Conference of American states held in Washington.[123]

[119] A. E. Gonzales to Gertrude Gonzales, August 13, 16, September 19, 1893, in E.G.P.; The State, July 17, 18, September 2, 1893.

[120] Lease of December 17, 1892, in E.G.P. Myrtle Bank, located on Hilton Head, was one of several of William Elliott's plantations.

[121] James Lowndes to A. E. Gonzales, July 14, 1892, and to Miss Anne Elliott, May 11, 1893; A. E. Gonzales to Gertrude Gonzales, May 10, 1893, in E.G.P. These three were located near Port Royal.

[122] Will of Miss Emily Elliott, November 10, 1885, in E.G.P. She died in 1889. Miss Anne Elliott died in 1916 at the age of ninety-four.

[123] For a more detailed record of the General's later years see Lewis P. Jones, "Carolinians and Cubans: The Elliotts and the Gonzales, Their Work and Their Writing" (Ph.D. diss., University of North Carolina, 1952), pp. 330–36.

In 1890 General Gonzales was still to be seen at balls in Washington—tall, erect, gray, martial, and handsome. His conversation still repeatedly flashed back to the topic of his native land.[124] In the summer of 1891, however, he was struck down by an attack of paralysis. His estranged sons showed proof of their gradual softening toward him, for they took him to Columbia where a few months before they had established *The State*. Their uncle, the Captain, maintained the old Elliott venom as he wrote his nieces:

Ambrose, after depositing his illustrious male progenitor at the Gd Central Hotel, registered as "General A. J. Gonzales, of South Carolina" left on convenient *duty*. The following day—an unkempt, unshaved, very maltreated looking, aged tramp came in . . . and said "Ralph." My reply was "Excuse me, Sir." The aged man left with the simple words—"I did not think it," he wept a little at the door, and that is the last I saw of him until this A.M. . . . He was shaved, & had on a clean shirt, so I suppose he is to be one more load on the willing asses back, unless he can be induced to share with Beaury the responsibilities . . . of taking care of the females of the family. For myself . . . as long as I have a memory of the sacrifices endured, and the deaths caused, by his selfish neglect of his offspring, I shall never treat him as an equal or a gentleman.[125]

Fortunately for the aged man, his sons were less spiteful, for he wrote a friend that he was cordially and comfortably cared for by them.[126] After a few months, he was taken to Key West where it was hoped that his health would improve. In that town there took place a meeting in 1892 often reported by effusive Cuban historians. In that hotbed of patriotic planning a group of revolutionary leaders headed by José Martí,

---

[124] Gonzalo de Quesada in *Patria*, December 31, 1892.
[125] R. E. Elliott to Harriett R. E. Gonzales, November 21, 1891, in E.G.P.
[126] Indicated in Arthur Graboroski to A. J. Gonzales, December 21, 1891, in possession of Miss Harriett R. E. Gonzales.

came to call on the old lieutenant of López. In the session were three generations of liberators, representatives of the revolutions of 1850, 1868, and 1895.[127]

Suffering a relapse in the fall of 1892, Gonzales was carried to Fordham Hospital on Long Island. Again the most humane of his sons, Ambrose, rose to the occasion and "went to see the poor old gentleman several times and had to make some arrangements for him. Poor old fellow, his condition is very pitiable. . . . I did all I could to cheer him up and arranged to give him all the attention possible."[128] Earlier, Ambrose had tried to arouse some compassion in the Gonzales girls: "I wish you girls would send some message of sympathy or something to the old gentleman. It looks cruel not to do so. He is failing rapidly and suffers intensely."[129] A total invalid, he was in bed for four months. Death came August 2, 1893, and he was buried in Woodlawn Cemetery, New York.[130]

Other members of the Gonzales family led relatively orthodox and unexciting lives during the 1890s. The "personals" column of *The State* shows a regular migration of the Oak Lawn ladies to Flat Rock and Glenn Springs for the summers; generally such journeys were broken by visits with family members in Columbia. Gertrude Gonzales became exceedingly intrigued by genealogy and constantly tried to gather all the facts about the Elliott family tree, in which she showed much pride.[131] In 1895 she married Frank Hampton of Columbia, nephew of General Wade Hampton. Five

[127] Portell Vilá, *Vidas*, p. 380; *Patria*, December 31, 1892.
[128] A. E. Gonzales to Gertrude Gonzales, May 10, 1893, in E.G.P.
[129] Same to same, April 7, 1892, in E.G.P.
[130] Bill from J. P. Garniss, the mortician, and title to the cemetery plot, in possession of Major R. K. McMaster.
[131] Family papers include her copious correspondence on the subject, but for a condensed expression of her attitude, see Gertrude Gonzales to J. S. Moore, March 10, 1894, in Wade Hampton Papers of Southern Historical Collection, University of North Carolina Library.

years later she died at Woodlands, the Hampton home, leaving three sons and twin daughters.[132]

The home presided over by W. E. Gonzales and his strikingly beautiful wife provided a headquarters and residence for some of the newspaper staff who lived there—James A. Hoyt, Jr., for example, and later Charles M. Galloway, as well as "Mr. Ambrose." Frequent trips and long vacations kept the mother and her three children in the mountains or at the beach for long periods in the summer. It was on one of these excursions to Pawley's Island that Consuela, a daughter of twenty-one months, died in 1896. Two other children, Robert and Alida, however, were destined to reach adulthood.[133]

During this same decade, "Mr. Ambrose" was becoming one of the best-loved (although not necessarily best-known) figures of Columbia. His greatest fault was excessive generosity, and many took regular advantage of his emotional susceptibility to tales of woe and to high-pressure schemes. This quality, coupled with his loyalty to his state and his devotion to Columbia, involved him financially and otherwise in many promotions for the improvement of the city; he boosted all of them and subscribed to all that he could afford—and to some that he could not. He was equally loyal to friends and employees, and no amount of knavishness or duplicity could convince him that his friends sometimes took advantage of him. He would lend the shirt off his back to such people, and never pester or pursue them for the repayment of the loan; to him it was simply an act of loyal friendship, not business. Unhappily, when he was in the opposite situation, he expected the same treatment—an outlook that was hardly con-

---

[132] Her husband died in 1926. See *The State*, June 13, 1900, and May 29, 1926; also, Emma ———— to Gertrude Gonzales, July 31, [1894,] and Thomas della Torre [?] to Gertrude Gonzales, January 6, 1895, in E.G.P. Her son, Ambrose Gonzales Hampton, is the present publisher of *The State*.

[133] *The State*, August 25 and 26, 1896.

genial with the business principles and methods of the bankers whom he had increasingly persuaded to help him underwrite many of the enterprises which he thought would be beneficial for Columbia.[134]

His energy as well as his money went into whatever he thought worthwhile. For example, he maintained always his inherited love for music and became a moving figure in the music association which organized an annual spring music festival for Columbia. "Mr. Ambrose" also took part himself in many recitals and amateur productions in the town. Old friends even yet recall how he knew the entire score of many operas—a fact sustained by files of *The State* which tell of his singing the baritone part in many of these local entertainments. One old employee who worked in his office recalled the way he managed to evade night work there: he would start whistling an aria from an opera, soon "Mr. Ambrose" would join in, and eventually the entire force in his office would aid and abet while Ambrose sang the entire work; by then it would be too late to work and all would adjourn to Main Street with their music.[135]

In his day, N. G. Gonzales was perhaps more famous than Ambrose, although few were really close to N. G. True, many did know the editor, but in some respects the editor and the man were two different people. Because of his "unreserved candor and the unrivalled vigor of his editorial expression," some South Carolinians considered him "an habitual fomenter of discord, a stirrer-up of strife, of deepest

---

[134] Opinions expressed here are a condensation of those gathered in the interviews listed with the bibliography. J. Rion McKissick said of his efforts in support of his long-range optimism: "He did more for South Carolina and South Carolinians than any man in the last half century" (cited in *The State*, July 14, 1926) . In *The State That Forgot* (p. 138) , W. W. Ball characterized him as "the most important and greatest South Carolinian since Governor Hampton, though South Carolinians do not yet know it." One can find this sentiment in many of Ball's private letters.

[135] *The State*, February 18, 1931.

prejudices, of implacable disposition, of tyrannous temper set to rule or ruin."[136] He regretted the fact that he was not personally popular but felt that it was the price one paid for accepting the high responsibilities of an editor, and with the courage of his convictions he "felt honor bound to stigmatize evil wherever he saw it."[137] While still working for the *News and Courier,* he expressed this credo: "When confident of my own rectitude of intention I have never yet cared, and never will care, what the public choose to think of me or of my acts."[138]

Many efforts—mostly eulogistic—have been made to define N. G., but Ambrose, despite his close relationship, perhaps came nearest to success when he said, " 'The child is father of the man.' " He observed that his brother had been "quick and passionate as a child, tenacious of his opinions and unyielding as to what he considered to be his rights," and therefore he had found it hard to "modify either rights or opinions, even in the face of facts." In his later years, the rough edges of life had softened his spirit and made him somewhat more tolerant of the views of others. By then, "He suffered fools patiently tho' not gladly."[139]

His restricted boyhood associations did much to influence N. G. as a man. Always the introvert, he was quiet, reserved, and dignified. He sought no companionship, invited no confidences, and imparted none. Quite nearsighted, his intent expression or the occasional intentness of look which accompanies that defect of vision gave him the appearance of aloofness, which was not a genuine characteristic. Often because of this malady and his frequent preoccupation, he

[136] The Reverend Samuel M. Smith in *The State,* January 19, 1904.
[137] *Ibid.*
[138] N. G. Gonzales to R. Means Davis, March 30, 1888, in R. Means Davis Papers, South Caroliniana Library.
[139] A. E. Gonzales, in foreword to N. G. Gonzales, *In Darkest Cuba,* pp. 31–34.

passed close associates on the street without seeming to see them. Actually, those who did get to know him well asserted that he was definitely timid and lonely. One close acquaintance said that his friends found in him the gentleness of a woman. Always he spoke in low and gentle tones, and only the commands of conscience evoked the strong written denunciations against what he considered evil. By nature, he was reserved and never a mixer, not even on the frivolous excursions of the state press association. Once he admitted to his assistant that he wanted to break out of his shell and avowed that in his long years of work and self-denial he had never learned how to relax and let himself go.[140]

N. G. hurdled the fence that bound his personality once, however, for in 1901 he was married to Lucy Barron of Manning. Prior to their marriage, Lucy had been state librarian in Columbia.[141] Civic-minded herself with a charming personality, she came to be a greatly admired and valued citizen of Columbia.

The strength of the Gonzales gazette during its early struggle lay in its three leaders. Its survival and growth can best be explained not by the brilliance or energy of any one of them but by the balance of the three. Because of that fact *The State* reached its peak of color, life, and influence while all three were alive.

Willie, an able and thorough news gatherer, had the most

140 This appraisal is based on interviews with Mr. and Mrs. J. A. Hoyt, Jr., Mr. W. W. Ball, Mr. Ed G. Seibels, Mr. Robert J. Gantt, Dr. William R. Barron, and Mrs. Clarendon Barron; also, see opinions of the Reverend Samuel M. Smith in *The State*, January 19, 1904; the Reverend W. E. Evans in *ibid.*, January 25, 1903, and February 18, 1916; and George A. Wauchope, *Writers of South Carolina* (Columbia: The State Company, 1910) , p. 52. The emphasis on a dual personality—that of the editor and also "the essential sweetness of his character, his real gentleness and kindness, which his public never knew" is stressed in a reminiscing letter of James A. Hoyt, Jr., to W. W. Ball, December 14, 1938, in Hoyt Papers.

141 *The State*, September 24, 1901; November 15, 1901.

pleasing personality of the brothers and was more of a demo-cratic mixer than the others. Of a gentle disposition, this youngest brother grew in maturity with the years as he in-herited more and more responsibilities.

The "great balance wheel" of the newspaper was "Mr. Ambrose," a man loved by most people who knew him, but loved rather than admired. Although no businessman in the usual sense of the word and constantly in fiscal complica-tions, he brought the paper through many exigencies and emergencies when it would have failed if not for his persist-ence, energy, optimism, and ability to inspire confidence. While N. G. was feeling the public pulse, "Mr. Ambrose" was supervising the details of a paper that at first seemed al-most too ambitious. His radiant personality, his gentleness, and his human qualities all made up the vital parts of his leadership which kept *The State* afloat.

As Yates Snowden said, if Ambrose was the balance wheel of the great paper, then N. G. was the steering wheel. En-during the spiritual loneliness of a sensitive idealist in a world of materialists, N. G. did not enjoy sending his vibrat-ing missiles into the hides of his enemies, but he did so be-cause he had the courage and sense of duty to perform what he believed to be a public service. The danger, of course, lay in the fact that selection of targets depended entirely upon his judgment, discretion, and information—all of which were conditioned and flavored by what can be called "a Wil-liam Elliott background." J. Rion McKissick said N. G. was "a master of militant journalism for the public good" who " 'never sold the truth to serve the hour,' " "an editor un-rivalled in all the two centuries of South Carolina news-papers for vigor, courage, and force."[142]

[142] J. Rion McKissick, "Newspapers," in Helen K. Hennig, ed., *Columbia, Capital City of South Carolina, 1786–1936* (Columbia: R. L. Bryan Company, 1936), p. 238.

CHAPTER VI

Tillmania

THE REPUTATION WHICH N. G. GONZALES EARNED FOR ACID-
ity came primarily from his incessant attacks on Tillmanism. He made no secret of the fact that *The State* had
been founded with the object of opposing Tillman and his
Reform Movement. The first issue appearing less than three
months after the inauguration of Tillman, *The State* thereafter for several years never moderated its flaming onslaughts
in both news stories and editorials. Wherever weaknesses
appeared in Ben's armor, N. G. G. pounced. If any folly or
blunder should be committed by Tillmanites, they could be
sure that it would be mercilessly exposed and reexposed by
the Gonzales gazette. If any corruption or official wrong-
doing should be perpetrated by the followers of the agricultural Moses, it was certain to be revealed and portrayed in its
darkest aspects by *The State*. If any disaffection should develop in Tillman ranks, the paper could be counted on to
gloatingly publicize and magnify it. If Tillmanism introduced any innovation completely innocuous, *The State* also

was likely to condemn it for its source, if for no other reason. Worse still for Tillman's administration, many of the country weeklies around the state followed and imitated the recognized leader of the not-so-loyal opposition, *The State*.

In his first inaugural address, the new governor presented a long list of suggested reforms. He declared that his election was a revolution—a "triumph of democracy and white supremacy over mongrelism and anarchy, of civilization over barbarism."[1] Denying that Negroes had any political rights, this spiritual stepson of Mart Gary promised a strong defense of white supremacy while at the same time calling on the two races to live together in peace. He demanded reforms in higher education: a less ambitious South Carolina College and a stronger Clemson. He also advocated a number of other reforms with the stress on centralization and better law enforcement.[2]

During Tillman's first administration (1890–1892), many things were accomplished despite a recalcitrant legislature. The South Carolina College was reorganized, and Clemson and Winthrop colleges were promoted; representation in the legislature was reapportioned; tax assessments on corporate wealth were increased; and the Tillmanites enjoyed success in dealing with the phosphate interests and the lunatic asylum, and in filling public offices. On the other hand, many rebelled against Tillman's methods and some aspects of his program were not adopted: no new constitutional convention met; no new railroad laws were passed; no revision was

[1] Simkins, *Tillman*, p. 171. No effort is made in this study to treat the Tillman movement and South Carolina history of the period except insofar as to show the Gonzales role. The Simkins biography, reprinted in 1967, is still the best source. The present writer has also done a brief coverage of his movement in "The Pitchfork," chap. 18 of *South Carolina: A Synoptic History for Laymen* (Columbia: Sandlapper Press, 1971), pp. 205–17. Since preparation of this Gonzales study, the Tillman story has been thoughtfully reexamined in William J. Cooper, Jr., *Conservative Regime*, chaps. 5, 6.

[2] Speech in South Carolina *House Journal* (1890), pp. 130–54.

made of congressional districts; and no reorganization of county government was accomplished.[3]

Viewed from a point fifty years later, Tillman can undoubtedly be classed as a liberal or progressive despite his defense of many of the most reactionary prejudices of South Carolina. His methods drove away many who might have endorsed his aims, and his dictatorial, abrupt, and profane actions and language alienated many of his own followers; and yet his very demagoguery and appeal to the prejudices of the masses elicited the popular support necessary to keep him in office long enough to make many of his reforms a permanent part of the South Carolina body politic. Unfortunately, the demagoguery survived.

Among the most vocal critics of Tillman's methods was the South Carolina press. A few small country papers, called "organettes" by Gonzales, supported Ben, but generally he had the backing of only one city "organ," the first being the Charleston *World*. *The State* constantly chided the *News and Courier*, "wholly governed by its pocket," of being at best "semi-hostile" to the administration: "If the *News and Courier* would withdraw its fire from David B. Hill, whom it cannot hit a thousand miles away, and turn it against Benjamin R. Tillman, who is within range, it might inspire more respect for its courage."[4] Actually, Hemphill's editorial policy opposed Tillman in general and his extreme stands in particular, while in Columbia, August Kohn maintained cordial relations with the governor and thus could generally get the news.[5] In contrast, the reporters of the less circumspect *State* were banned from the Mansion and office.[6]

---

[3] Simkins, *Tillman*, pp. 190–91; Wallace, *History of S. C.*, III, 354–56. For an appraisal of the good and bad of Tillman, see the latter, III, 366.

[4] *The State*, January 12; March 22, 1892.

[5] August Kohn to J. C. Hemphill, May 19, 1893, in Letterbook, 1893–96, of Kohn Papers. Also see Helen K. Hennig, *August Kohn*, pp. 96, 97, 102.

[6] *The State*, January 17, 1892.

It was hardly surprising that Tillman took such action against a paper that never rested and never showed restraint in its attacks. The following is typical of the daily blasts of *The State* and came after the governor had suffered a minor political reverse:

> We have as Chief Executive . . . an individual . . . budding into a dictator. Serene in his appreciation of his own capacities, secure in his assumption that he and he only, had been chosen to rule South Carolina, contemptuous of precedent, holding himself above those whom he had led into office, he came naturally to think that . . . he was the State. He is as promising a tyrant as was ever bred by a free republic.[7]

Scorning suggestions to be less rabid, Gonzales constantly attacked this "usurper" who came to power by "bitter and unjust assaults upon the men who administered the State government, . . . by introduction of discord into a previously peaceful and harmonious society," and by a victory which "made possible the supremacy of the Stokeses and Talberts and other gnats of political life."[8] Frequently and outspokenly, Tillman paid his respects to his antagonist, whereupon the editor retorted, "Governor Tillman is still advertising The State. We pay him nothing for doing it. It is a service of love."[9] Even the Tillmanites were reputed to read the paper; N. G. Gonzales said they should do so since its "purifying ozone" gave the best news coverage in the state, and "It will be a mental tonic to them, a stimulant to righteous living, and an unfailing monitor of the fact that 'public office is a public trust.' "[10]

Plagued by such an adversary, the administration sought a

[7] *Ibid.*, July 3, 1891.
[8] *Ibid.*, September 8, 1891.
[9] *Ibid.*, June 8, 1892.
[10] *Ibid.*, March 19, 1891.

voice with which to reply. After the end of the Charleston
World, with whose management he had quarreled, Tillman
had no daily to support his cause. To fill this need, the
Columbia Register was the obvious choice after Tillman's
plans to start a new Columbia paper in 1891 had failed.[11]
Ruin now confronted the weak *Register,* which had supported the Conservatives in 1890, and the lucrative state
printing contract was an enticing lure to Charles A. Calvo,
Jr., the publisher. In April 1891 Colonel John W. R. Pope,
editor since 1877, had resigned as editor, and it was generally
agreed that the new Tillmanite voice in the paper was that of
Dr. Sampson Pope.[12] Still the paper floundered, and in early
1892 cuddled closer to Tillman. Actually, administration
leaders never bought out the paper, as some Conservatives
believed. Ben Tillman explained the new relations to Irby:
"Calvo is all right now & will make the Register a strong paper in a few weeks. I told him we would subscribe for the paper and distribute them rather than lend him money or take
stock in his paper. [George] Koester told me today he had engaged Larry Gant [*sic*] as Editor."[13] The governor had already given his ultimatum to Calvo, warning him that "unless the course that I have indicated be pursued 'The Register' will certainly be driven to the wall." Ben admitted his
paper would have to be alert to compete with *The State.*
Calvo was ordered to build his paper up and "in an honorable, and manly and strong way 'fight the devil with fire.' "[14]

T. Larry Gantt, the prejudiced, spirited, direct, typical
agrarian agitator imported from Athens, Georgia, was a good
man for fighting the devil with fire. Born in South Carolina,
he tried farming briefly and then turned to newspapering.

---

[11] B. R. Tillman to W. T. Crews, June 20, 1891, in Simkins Notes.
[12] *The State,* April 21; May 6, 7, 1891; December 2, 1897.
[13] B. R. Tillman to J. L. M. Irby, February 8, 1892, in Simkins Notes.
[14] B. R. Tillman to C. A. Calvo, Jr., January 30, 1892, in Simkins Notes.

Although he was the fastest typesetter on the Chicago *Tribune* in the late 1860s, he spent most of his early unsettled journalistic career in migrating from one small Georgia paper to another. He was both an editor and a printer—and sometimes combined the two trades by setting his thoughts in type without first composing them on paper. In 1880 his *Banner-Watchman* had been the only Georgia daily to espouse the Farmers' Alliance cause.[15]

This new editor of Gonzales' nemesis was a formidable antagonist for the redoubtable N. G. As Francis B. Simkins says, Gantt was a beacon which undoubtedly would soon burn out, but "He had humor and an unaffected plainness in contrast with Gonzales's unimaginative earnestness."[16] Exceedingly eccentric, this colorful and earthy editor made no pretense to be anything that he was not. Violently partisan, he was never bitter, but frankly warned the South Carolinians, "If I leave South Carolina before my mission is ended, it will be in a casket with feet foremost."[17] A bundle of restless, surging energy, an inveterate reader of history, conscientious objector to any formal proceedings, he generally wore a coarse woolen shirt, a soft collar, and a remnant of a tie. His trousers always stopped well above his brogans. The tobacco in his long pipe was always supplemented by another wad in his cheek. When he arrived, he announced, "There's no use for you fellows to begin telling lies in this thing, now, for I give you fair warning that I kin beat any man in South Carolina in the lying business."[18]

And according to Gonzales, he could. Although he edited

[15] For a biographical sketch, see Athens *Banner-Herald*, August 30, 31, 1931; *Greenville Piedmont*, August 31, 1931.

[16] Simkins, *Tillman*, p. 203.

[17] *Register*, April 10, 1892, as cited in Simkins, *Tillman*, p. 162.

[18] Zach McGhee, "Tillman, Smasher of Traditions," in *World's Work*, XIII (September 1906), 8019.

Calvo's sheet only from late February to December, 1892,[19]
Gantt almost obfuscated N. G. Gonzales, editor of what "Tillman's salaried prevaricator" now called the "old-ring organ"
and supporter of "old moss-back office holders." One can
peruse both roaring dailies of 1892 and hardly realize that he
is reading about the same events. Each called the other an
"organ," one's "assemblage" became the other's "mob," and
one's "noble gentleman" might also be described as "a poor
little 'me-too'." Even N. G. became exasperated with "the
most brazen and unconscionable liar which ever disgraced
journalism," "the paterfamiliar of prevarication."[20] After six
weeks of "T. Liar Gantt's" presence *The State* tried to dis-
miss the needling organ:

The State had for a long time previous to the engagement of
Mr. Larry Gantt as editorial writer for the local Tillman organ,
treated that paper with the contemptuous indifference it had deserved as a truckler to power and a willing beneficiary of fraud.
. . . [But since his advent,] as fast as one false statement or assumption was exposed and crushed a couple of new ones sprung
[sic] up. We confess to fatigue after these forays into the mazes
of mendacity. . . . It has exposed its own unscrupulousness. It
has demonstrated . . . that it is working only for its master, Tillman. It addresses itself to the meanest prejudices of the most ig-
noble minds. It can't be induced to acknowledge its own prevarication and demagogism.[21]

The unruffled Gantt merely retorted that N. G. was one of
the most even-tempered men in the Carolinas because he was
mad as a blind adder all the time.[22]

Gonzales constantly hammered away at "Tillman's salaried

[19] *The State*, February 28; December 24, 1892.
[20] *Ibid.*, December 8, 1892; January 14, 1893.
[21] *Ibid.*, April 4, 1892.
[22] *Register*, April 5, 1892.

prevaricator" for being a hack writer interested only in his salary. The disarmingly frank editor admitted his salary and his position in replying to *The State,* "organ of the Sheppard's Sheep."[23] The anti-Tillman press in general stressed the fact that Gantt was an imported product (today the catch phrase is "outside agitator") and gleefully pounced on such comments from Georgia papers as "For goodness' sake burn the bridges behind him so he can't come back to Georgia."[24] Ben's "chief trumpeter" dared to point out that Dawson also had been an immigrant, to which Gonzales replied, "He [Dawson] was not imported to sling mud for money. He was not a flitting bat of journalism. And while he may ultimately have been a dictator, he never was a puppet with any governor's string tied to him."[25] The *Spartanburg Herald* joined in by calling the editor of the "Tillrodgerster" " 'a dirty mendicant' who admits he tells 'whoppers' because he is paid $7 a day to do it"; *The State* disagreed, saying he was dirty but no mendicant—not at $7 a day.[26]

In 1892 *The State* plunged into its first election campaign. Early in the year it set the tone for its opposition to Tillman's second term:

> The *pro tempore* organ of Governor Tillman . . . has "come out" in favor of his re-election, on the broad principle that it is unsafe to "swap horses crossing stream." . . . As to the horse argument, South Carolina has been bound, in Mazeppa fashion, to the back of a wild ass in the desert. . . . It is the wild ass, and not South Carolina, which has plunged into the torrent. The State, if it can succeed in cutting its bonds, will be only too happy to swim ashore, without insisting upon another mount.[27]

23 *Ibid.,* March 29, 1892.
24 Cited by *The State,* March 31, 1892.
25 *Ibid.,* May 14, 1892.
26 *Ibid.,* July 29, 1892.
27 *Ibid.,* January 3, 1892.

Many anti-Tillmanites wanted to follow Hampton's advice
and hold a Conservative preconvention like the farmers'
March Convention of 1890. When a committee ("The Thirteen") called such a state meeting for March 24, *The State*
said their plans were too compromising since they recognized
the Irby organization as the Democratic party whereas only
the Straightouts were Democrats. Unbending Gonzales asserted that "the compromisers"—the *News and Courier,* the
Greenville News, Edward McCrady, Johnson Hagood, J. C.
Sheppard, *et al.*—would "have a high old time conducting an
anti-Tillman campaign on a Tillman platform."[28] At least,
he admitted he was alarmed by the split in Conservative
ranks but irritated at the *Greenville News,* "whose ability we
admire, but whose political immorality we utterly condemn."[29] After Hampton had urged the Straightouts to support "The Thirteen" and after A. B. Williams had written
him that he could no more fight Tillman successfully outside
the party than he could make the Wando River run over
Caesar's Head, N. G. relented and was even elected a Richland delegate to the March 24 meeting of Conservatives.[30]

The State insisted on calling this session of anti-Tillmanites the "State Democratic Convention" and optimistically
headlined its meeting as the "DOOM OF THE DESPOT."
The news reporter said: "It was the general verdict that
never had a finer body of men, or one more thoroughly
representative of South Carolina and her best citizens, been
gathered within four walls." Besides drawing up a platform,
the meeting sponsored a state ticket headed by J. C. Sheppard and James L. Orr. Thirty newspapers at once supported
the platform.[31]

[28] *Ibid.,* February 23, 1892.
[29] *Ibid.,* February 24, 1892.
[30] *Ibid.,* March 7, 8, 17, 24, 1892.
[31] *Ibid.,* March 25; April 1, 1892.

The Democrats moved toward a full primary system for nominations in this election by having a popular vote for choosing the county delegates who would go to the state Democratic convention which in turn selected the party nominees. During "the speakings," *The State* admittedly dropped all of its other interests. Its strategy was to tie the third-party label to the Tillman movement and to take advantage of any splits among the Reformers. All along Gonzales had been attacking Jasper Talbert, Tillmanite and Allianceman, who was superintendent of the state penitentiary. The editor forecast that "such vicious blatherskites as many undertake to carry out his program will be dumped into the horsepond of disgraceful retirement" because the farmers "are not the monumental fools which this infernal charlatan takes them to be."[32]

In this 1892 campaign *The State* first unleashed a new weapon, a series of satires in Biblical language which ridiculed the Tillmanites' foibles off and on for a number of years. Never signed, these chronicles by the "Prophet Zerrachaboam" were written by W. G. Chafee of Aiken, who later became editor of the Greenwood *Index*. The first of these parodies appeared August 15, 1892, and the second "chapter" about a fortnight later. In his first chapter, "Zerrachaboam" thus began recording history:

1. Now in the fullness of time arose one Benjamin, a man haughty of spirit and subtile [*sic*] of heart, who greatly deceived the people. The same was spoken by the Prophet, saying "a one-eyed man shall be king among the blind."
2. He feared not God, neither regarded man, and had his raiment of coarse cloth, and covered his head with a hat of wool, and his nether garment was held up by one gallus.
3. Being desirous of ruling over all the people, he lifted up his

---

[32] *Ibid.*, April 7, 1892.

voice against the scribes, and the rulers and the judges of the people, and hardened his face against those who were weavers of cloth, and went about to overthrow the tables of the money changers and destroy those who carried travellers and merchandise for hire.

This latter-day prophet gave the same interpretation of history that "N. G. G." did, however, for his first chapter seemed to prophesy the downfall of "Benjamin the Tillmanite":

12. Now, no sooner had this Benjamin begun to rule among the people than he hardened his heart . . . and did go from place to place with carriers of travelers without paying his pence therefor . . . and clothed himself in costly raiment and fine linen and two galluses withal, and fared sumptuously every day. 13. Now the people were moved greatly, saying one to another, we accounted our ancient rulers as devils, but surely we have cast them out by Beelzebub, the Prince of the Devils. 14. So they called unto them one John, surnamed the Sheppard, to do battle against Benjamin who had so grievously deceived them. . . .

During the campaign J. Wilson Gibbes covered the stump meetings for *The State* and imitated N. G. Gonzales' habit of heckling the speakers. The meetings were, if possible, more tempestuous than those of 1890. To convince potential delegates to the state convention of the popularity of his cause, Tillman frequently called for "a show of hands" (thereafter called "the hand primary"). More conducive to disorder were efforts to "howl down" the Conservative candidates—a practice that produced fireworks and often near bloodshed. (This trick dated back to Mart Gary and his "Edgefield Plan"; it was used by his faction and entourage in the campaign of 1876 to squelch, intimidate, or silence the opposition.) To keep up his followers' hopes lest they get apathetic, Gonzales ran frequently such headlines as "OLD FAIRFIELD IS SAFE" (which did not mean it had been saved from a natural calamity but was safely Conservative) or "GLORIOUS DAY IN MARION" (which meant the Conservatives had outshouted the Tillmanites at a rally, or so a *State* reporter judged the noise). The condition of the holiday crowds added to the tenseness and threatened serious incidents. A rowdy day in Walterboro was reported in *The State* under the headline, "Tillman Toughs, Fired by Mean Firewater, Continually Interrupt." The editor apologized for his native county, but added: "Colleton is not half bad, and Walterborough whiskey is not wholly bad, but the company of Tillmanism and whiskey is too much for any county. The old county will be in line for the Conservatives in August. Just now it is suffering from fermentation."[33]

Always *The State* tried to build up Conservative determination by creating confidence in its side and by belittling Tillman strength; no devotee of *The State* was permitted to think he would be "throwing away his vote" on Sheppard. For example, from "news" stories: "The most herculean efforts were put forth to make a show of Tillmanite strength . . . , but they resulted in a dismal and palpable failure"; "Tillman and Irby are very, very small fry here"; "Where the Tillmanites know they are few and far between, they import their howlers and try to drown free speech."[34] The same tactic was used in headlines: "TILLMAN ON THE DOWN GRADE"; "WATERLOO FOR THE WHALE | Tillman Drowned in Aiken Political Sea"; "NO TRUTH IN BEN TILLMAN"; "WATERLOO AT WALHALLA | For Tillman and His Coattail Swingers."[35]

[33] *Ibid.*, June 11, 1892.
[34] *Ibid.*, June 15, 22; July 5, 1892.
[35] *Ibid.*, July 3, 7, 13; August 12, 1892.

Column after column was employed in the attack. For example, the issue of July 5—selected at random—contained twenty-four columns exclusive of advertising; eighteen of these dealt with politics. Therein, *The State* gave flavor as well as colored and colorful facts in its portrayal of flowery oratory, profane speeches, coatless orators, men "wind-milling" as they stood on their chairs, the air "lurid with Tillmanites' curses," ladies "with lips pursed," and the only calm moment of the meetings—the invocation. Nearly always in the "hand primary," *The State* accorded victory to the Conservatives; when they failed, imported Tillmanites were blamed. Always the "Refawmers" were portrayed as "unhorsed at every shock of the political battle by the onslaught of the Conservative knights, whose weapons combined the keen scimetar [*sic*] of Saladin and the ponderous battle axes of Richard Coeur de Lion."[36]

But these must have been the wrong armaments for achieving the "defeat of the State wreckers," because the county primaries picked Tillmanite delegates to the state convention, or as *The State* put it, "Tuesday was a great day for the coat-tail swinger. . . ." Although in the course of the campaign, "Pitchfork Ben" had spoken of "N. G. Gonzales and his *State* paper, the essence of Haskellism, and rattle-snakeism and skunks,"[37] the editor wrote that he could not complain of the outcome as he did not think that the reputation of South Carolina could be any more tarnished or besmirched than it had been by the first term and hence he announced that he would hold his nose and bear up in defeat.[38] According to Tillman's biographer, Gonzales himself contributed unwittingly to the 1892 outcome because he was "too opin-

---

[36] *Ibid.*, August 13, 1892.
[37] Cited in *ibid.*, June 9, 1892.
[38] *Ibid.*, September 1, 1892. In the race, Jasper W. Talbert defeated George D. Tillman for Congress.

ionated to develop the realistic tactics through which voters are won . . . ; by raising issues he gave Tillman opportunity to strike back; and by his vehemence he foolishly accentuated the division between businessman and farmer."[39]

During the second Tillman administration, *The State* was only slightly more restrained. With a more friendly legislature and a strong spoils system now in operation, Tillman had more absolute control than ever. Those who crossed him risked his wrath, and August Kohn reminded Hemphill that in Columbia he had to work tactfully since "I am on the brink of a volcano up here."[40]

During N. G. Gonzales' efforts to get a consular plum in 1893, Governor Tillman dropped his pitchfork long enough to urge President Cleveland not to appoint either Gonzales or Hemphill to any offices "by reason of their malignant and outrageous assaults on my personal and political character."[41] More extreme was the governor's wish that somebody would lynch one or more editors who "slander and misrepresent men and distort facts."[42]

Various accomplishments were made during Tillman's second term, and when he left office he pointed with pride to these reforms.[43] But Gonzales did not consider them "reforms" and fired broadsides constantly at the "Refawmers," promising to continue until *The State* should "rid South Carolina of the domination of hatred, tyranny and greed."[44] Favorite and suitable target for the editor's gibes was Senator John L. M. Irby, whose replacement of Senator Wade Hampton in 1890 had been considered by *The State* as the greatest

[39] Simkins, *Tillman*, p. 202.

[40] August Kohn to J. C. Hemphill, January 30, 1894, in Hemphill Papers.

[41] B. R. Tillman to Grover Cleveland, March 8, 1893, in Simkins Notes.

[42] B. R. Tillman to F. H. Richardson, January 15, 1894, as cited in Simkins, *Tillman*, p. 217.

[43] Summarized in Simkins, *Tillman*, p. 233, and in Wallace, *History of S. C.*, III, 358.

[44] *The State*, February 17, 1894.

indignity which the Tillmanites had inflicted on South Carolina. As Simkins understates it, Irby's sensational vices over-
shadowed his virtues; offensive and dangerous when drunk,
demagogic when sober, he cut a melodramatic and stormy
trail through the South Carolina of the 1890s. His selection
for the Senate added insult to injury, and *The State* never
relented while working to widen the wedge that inevitably
developed between the ambitious governor and the senator.
Particularly vulnerable was Irby's susceptibility to Populism,
as can be seen in the paper in one of its "grapeshot" editorials: " 'We have come to the fork of the roads.'—Senator
Irby. So The State told you. Take the left hand trail for the
Populist swamp, and kindly oblige us by not turning back."[45]

Against Irby, *The State* brought into effective play "The
Book of Zerrachaboam." The prophet had a fine subject for
his chronicles when Senator Irby arrived by train in Columbia—roaring drunk, firing pistols into the air, scaring
Negroes, and finally going to the Governor's Mansion in a
hack. "Zerrachaboam" concluded his chapter on the episode
as follows:

14. But when a deep sleep had come upon him [Irby], the
driver of the chariot, notwithstanding his fear, did convey him
unto the house of Benjamin, his master.

15. When he arrived at the house of Benjamin, the Tillmanite,
John did salute his brother, saying, "All is lost. I bring unto you
bad news, even ill tidings."

16. Nevertheless, being cast down by much wine, he disclosed
not the tidings which so sorely did rend his soul.

17. When Benjamin, the Tillmanite, had beheld him stretched
out upon the chariot, and the driver thereof stricken with great
fear, he was much troubled in spirit, and lamented heavily.

18. And when Benjamin had delivered unto him a bottle of
strong drink he straightway dismissed him from his own house.

[45] *The State*, October 21, 1893.

19. Then were the Tillmanites much troubled, and reasoned one with another, while many repented them that they had despitefully treated Wade, the just, and set an evil man in his stead to rule over them.[46]

The single act of the second Tillman administration which most enraged Gonzales was the creation of the Dispensary in 1892. For some time, prohibition forces led by Lysander D. Childs had gained strength; in 1890 a prohibition bill had passed the House only to fail in the Senate, and in 1892 an unofficial referendum in the state primary showed 40,338 for prohibition and 30,197 against; many, however, did not vote in "the side-box," and Tillmanites as a rule were not drys. With this mandate, a dry law again passed the House in the fall of 1892 and went to the Senate, where Ben Tillman then took over.

Temperate himself, the governor was known to oppose the bill because he did not think it enforceable. With the prohibitionists pointing to the referendum and talking loudly of the will of the people but with the Tillmanites inclined to be imbibers, Ben was on the horns of a dilemma. Larry Gantt then suggested the system of state ownership and strict control of liquor dispensing—the system which was first tried in Gothenburg, Sweden, in 1865 and which Larry had seen in operation in Athens, Georgia. Converted by his editor, Tillman endorsed the scheme as one that would minimize the evils of drink and bring in profits as state government went into the liquor business. In the Senate, the prohibition bill was "bob-tailed" by John Gary Evans with an amendment providing for a State Dispensary, and within three days the bill was enacted into law by the legislators un-

[46] *Ibid.*, September 23, 1893. A clue as to Chafee's authorship is to be found in *ibid.*, November 14, 1897.

der terrific pressure from the executive and in their own rush
to get home for Christmas.[47]

The State at once began a fourteen-year campaign to do
the Dispensary to death. In a story headlined "THE ABOR-
TION PASSES," the newspaper said that "the orders from
the lower regions of the capitol [governor's office] were
obeyed to the letter and the Evans 'blind' saddled itself on
the two houses." The news item also predicted the result:
"More offices for the obsequeous [*sic*], great profit for a few
favorites, inconveniences for the public at large, special privileges for the elect."[48]

The new system was to operate under a Dispensary State
Board of Control, which supervised county boards, which in
turn governed the one dispenser assigned to each county
who did business at the county seat—not unlike modern
ABC stores. The state commissioner bought all the whiskey
for the state in bulk and sold it to the dispensers. Various
regulations were aimed at the promotion of temperance—
such as no liquor to be consumed at the dispensaries, none to
be sold to minors or to drunks, and so forth. To enforce the
law by locating "blind tigers" and by ferreting out illegal
whiskey, many new constables were appointed by the governor—men to be quickly resented as his "spies." The state
made its own bottles with the state seal on them—considered
a sacrilege by the anti-Tillmanites—and followed the X, XX,
and XXX grading system with the number of Xs indicating
in years the age of the liquid.[49]

---

[47] The literature on the subject is voluminous, and even more is still being
produced. One account is John E. Eubanks, *Ben Tillman's Baby: The Dispensary System of South Carolina* (Augusta, Georgia: published by the author,
1950) . More satisfactory and more scholarly is Ellen A. Hendricks, "South
Carolina Dispensary System," in *North Carolina Historical Review*, XXII
(1945) , 176–97, 320–49. Also good is Simkins, *Tillman*, chaps. XVI, XVII, and
XXV.

[48] *The State*, December 24, 1892.

[49] Hendricks, "S. C. Dispensary System," 183–89.

The governor took an active part in getting the supplies on hand for the opening by July 1, 1893, of what *The State* called "the device of despotism." Columbia and Charleston were both as determined to frustrate the new "socialism" and the constables as was *The State,* which warned of the opportunity for graft and corruption by the officials entrusted with the large enterprise. The "Chronicles of Zerrachaboam" also reported the opening of the new system:

2. Being exceeding wise in his own conceit, he [Benjamin the Tillmanite] exclaimed, Verily! I am he of whom the prophet has spoke. Behold! I shall become the Chief Tapster unto the people.

7. And straightway did Benjamin establish shrines throughout all the land, where the *tired* might receive dispensations to imbibe strong drink.

8. Moreover, Benjamin did appoint many vagabonds, who clung to his garments, as spies to go . . . through all the land, by means of lies and cunning devices to entrap their neighbors who might sell strong drink.

12. And Benjamin did place upon his bottles the emblem and seal of his country, which, being translated, means "Always prepared to take a drink."

13. Then was Benjamin much exalted in spirit and reckoned upon a profit of many shekels by making his neighbors drunk.[50]

The Gonzales' paper condemned the new monopoly as a bad revenue act, as did the *News and Courier* and the *Greenville News.* Many other arguments were utilized—some valid and some far-fetched—but in general, opinion was divided strictly along Tillman and anti-Tillman lines.[51] *The State*

[50] *The State,* July 24, 1893.
[51] Arguments on both sides are summarized in Hendricks, "S. C. Dispensary System," 191–92. In theory, the proponents were probably right, but in practice many of the evils prophesied by the opponents developed. The writer is inclined to question that there was anything basically wrong in the system;

was at its harshest when berating the special constables, the "spies" and "sneaks," and expounded: "The people will know that if the Governor's armed spies enter their homes [to seek illegal whiskey], insult their women, and shoot down their sons or brothers, they will be promptly pardoned."[52] The news columns gave much space to every drunk arrested and constantly reiterated that drinking had increased rather than decreased, as Tillman had prophesied to the Prohibitionists. Most papers avowed that the system had failed in Athens, Georgia, and would fail in South Carolina. The only consolation *The State* got was in frequent forecasts that it would drag Tillmanism down with it; meanwhile, it could only gloat over much publicity to such stories as that of a constable who "FILLS UP ON DISPENSARY BOOZE, PAINTS THE TOWN RED."[53]

Out of such an atmosphere came the "Whiskey Rebellion" or the "Darlington Riot" in 1894. In that anti-Dispensary town, rumors that twenty-three special constables were to search private homes without warrants caused a number of citizens to gather menacingly. After a company of militia came to Darlington and spent one night there, the tense atmosphere abated. But not so in *The State*. It said blood had "not yet" been shed but the "worthy descendants of the men who fought and suffered with Marion for the cause of liberty" were determined to "resist a threatened invasion" launched by "the will of a petty despot, drunken with vanity and power."[54] That same day, as the constables were leaving town, a quarrel between one of them and a couple of tense local citizens led to harsh words, a skirmish, and a few shots.

---

after all, the alleged graft, corruption, and biased enforcement must be blamed on the shortcomings of men, not the system. But such, unhappily, can be said of most failures recorded in history.

52 *The State*, January 28, 1894.

53 *Ibid.*, November 18, 1893.

54 *Ibid.*, March 30, 1894.

The clash ended with two citizens and one constable dead, the other constables in the woods, and aroused citizens forming an armed posse, whereupon Tillman ordered three militia companies to Darlington and declared a state of insurrection. Governor Tillman said, "People . . . had been stirred to fury by the inflammatory bulletins of *The State*," but that paper pointed to Mayor W. F. Dargan's assertion that conditions were misrepresented by Tillman and that no troops were needed.[55]

Tillman's call to the militia of Columbia, Sumter, and Manning went unanswered. In effect, mutiny reigned and was cheered by Gonzales in what Tillman called "the organ founded by the Haskellites to keep alive prejudice and malice."[56] At this stage, Gonzales was doing some of his most acrimonious writing: "The lifeblood of gallant men, shed in defense of the liberties of South Carolina, stains, yet glorifies, the bosom of their native state. . . . The grotesque vanity of our mimic dictator has borne the fruit of death."[57] March 30 was the "most exciting night in Columbia in years" as the anti-Tillman mob went wild and the local militia companies threw down their arms rather than go to the aid of "the spies." N. G. Gonzales showed one note of restraint as he mounted a box and pleaded with the mob not to pursue their plans to burn "the State gin mill," telling them "that they had already gained a great victory and should not spoil it by going into such a thing as this."[58]

Tillman then ordered every militia company in the state

[55] Quotation from Simkins, *Tillman Movement* (Durham: Duke University Press, 1926), p. 194; *News and Courier*, January 30, 1909; *The State*, March 30, 1894.

[56] Simkins, *Tillman Movement*, p. 163. Five militia companies were called: three in Columbia and one each in Manning and Sumter. Hendricks, "S. C. Dispensary System," 195.

[57] *The State*, March 31, 1894.

[58] *Ibid.* Later, *The State* defended N. G. as having been the voice of calmness during the riot. *Ibid.*, February 1, 1909.

to prepare to march to Columbia. Thirteen companies and the Fourth Brigade of Charleston refused, but within two days hundreds of soldiers and volunteer "wool hat boys" were there, with headquarters in the secure penitentiary.[59] Several hundred men were sent to Darlington, but Tillman, according to *The State,* "bully that he is," preferred to stay in the capital and conduct his campaign by telegraph. While *The State* for the first time carried its columns draped in mourning black, the governor accused the editors of the *Greenville News,* the *News and Courier,* and *The State* of having stirred the people up with false ideas about a man's house being his castle: "The editors of these papers . . . are the murderers of those who have been shot down over yonder."[60]

Actually, A. B. Williams had come to Columbia with the Greenville troops on April 1, saying that if, as Tillman charged, he had caused all this trouble, "he thought it but proper that he should come to quell it."[61] He found that Tillman was planning to declare martial law in Columbia on the following day and to suppress *The State* "on the ground that its editorial utterances were incendiary and dangerous to the public peace." Without telling the Columbia editor of Tillman's design, at a conference at Wade Hampton's home Williams subtly calmed Gonzales' mood and then persuaded Tillman to agree not to implement his threat. Later Gonzales furiously said he had been hoodwinked "into a course he would not have adopted with his eyes open."[62]

Tillman added fuel to the flames by unearthing an old statute of "Radical times" by which press censorship was

[59] Hendricks, "S. C. Dispensary System," 195.
[60] *The State,* March 31, 1894.
[61] *Ibid.,* April 2, 1894.
[62] *Ibid.,* April 8, 1894—in an anti-Williams editorial, four columns long. Tillman's account of his threat is in a letter to Hemphill printed in the *News and Courier,* January 30, 1909.

established over the Darlington area. Soldiers were placed in all offices of the telegraph companies—although some were too illiterate to serve as censors. Ambrose Gonzales, old-time telegrapher now turned publisher-reporter, tapped the wires at Floyds, three miles from Darlington, and, without writing his story out first, sent his own dispatches to *The State* office where N. G. Gonzales, old-time telegrapher now turned editor, took them down and sent them to the composing room.[63] "Mr. Ambrose" also helped August Kohn with his reports although the latter soon hired another wire tapper and had his own "blind tiger telegraph office."[64] Terming the news embargo "the Czar's censorship of the telegraph," *The State* gloatingly printed its "scoop" under the following head:

SECOND EDITION
IT RAN THE BLOCKADE!
This News Has Outwitted Tillman.
The Truth Is Here.[65]

The Tillman followers were just as bitter, since Gonzales commented dryly, "We forgot yesterday to ask Governor Tillman to declare Chester county in a state of insurrection because of the threats of the Tillmanites against the life of the editor of The State."[66] In a very bitter speech, Governor Tillman gave his explanation of the troubles:

Simply because the minority will not let the majority govern. . . . Why? Because in this city and in Charleston the papers have

---

[63] Ball, *The State That Forgot*, p. 251; John K. Aull's reminiscences in *The State*, November 2, 1930. The latter ran a series of articles on the riot in *ibid*. at intervals between October 12 and November 9, 1930.

[64] J. C. Hemphill to Patrick Walsh, April 13, 1894, in Letterbook, 1887–1894, of Hemphill Papers.

[65] *The State*, April 2, 1894.

[66] *Ibid.*, April 4, 1894.

taken to their bosoms a viper in the shape of a newspaper, which distills day by day poison into their system, and will not let the fever subside. They give me credit for nothing. . . . They try to sting me by abuse, slander, and misrepresentation. . . .

These men would destroy the state in their bitterness and anger, if thereby they could destroy me and through me the rule of the majority.[67]

Even while Editor Hemphill was urging Hampton to try to allay the excitement, the fire began to go out for lack of fuel—despite the fanning breezes.[68] Ambrose Gonzales' reports all along had stressed the fact that the sleepy streets of Darlington hardly resembled a besieged fortress, and the editor saw no reason for the governor's "prolonging the agony" unless he enjoyed helping *The State* sell 3,000 extra papers daily. The loyal militia obviously not being needed, it was almost immediately disbanded. *The State* almost as rapidly assumed a more conservative tone, although it continued to claim that the events in the whole ugly episode had been a great defeat for the governor. Tillman, on the other hand, declared, "We are in the saddle more firmly than ever."[69] His political antagonist, A. B. Williams, admitted that the governor's acts had been "sensible, conciliatory, and in all respects proper."[70] The writer agrees with Professor D. D. Wallace in his view of the unpleasant affair:

[67] *Ibid.*

[68] J. C. Hemphill to Wade Hampton, April 3, 1894, in Letterbook, 1887–1894, in Hemphill Papers.

[69] B. R. Tillman to J. L. M. Irby, April 13, 1894, in Simkins Notes.

[70] *Greenville News,* April 8, 1894, as cited in Simkins, *Tillman,* p. 257. The *Spartanburg Herald,* anti-Tillmanite paper, had all along urged calmness and said the troops should obey orders. (*Herald,* April 1, 1894, as cited by *Register,* April 3, 1894.) The *Columbia Register* had been about as unrestrained as *The State,* although, of course, on the other side. Gonzales was becoming increasingly irritated with Williams and spoke of "The Greenville News, whose position day after tomorrow affords the people . . . a continuous problem of greater charm than a beans and bottle guessing contest." (*The State,* June 1, 1894.)

It was one of the ugliest manifestations of defiance to authority in South Carolina history, and left in a poor light our two leading journals, habitual denouncers of lynchers and rapists, now loosing their own passions against the officers of the law in sympathy with a property-destroying mob of man-hunters.[71]

In less than a month, the South Carolina Supreme Court declared the Dispensary unconstitutional.[72] Even though this action created an accidental state of prohibition, it was temporary, for during the summer of 1894 Tillman was able to swing the balance of the court in his favor after the election of Eugene B. Gary, Tillmanite, to the bench in place of Samuel McGown, Conservative.

The reconstituted court at once performed as predicted and upheld the Dispensary on the basis of an 1893 statute rather than the original one of 1892.[73] Amid its screams of anguish, the Gonzales gazette printed the following proclamation, labeled "THE IMPERIAL UKASE":

In the name of the Czar, Rum!

Whereas, it hath been made known to Us, by divers communications from Our loyal subjects, that there lingers in Our realm a taste for "that good, honest whiskey" which We did lately dispense to them; and whereas it pleaseth Us to minister to the desires of Our subjects, the more especially when . . . We can promote the cause of temperance and religion and turn a penny for Our private purse; Now therefore,

We, by the grace of Fraud, of Little Russia, Emperor, Defender of the Faith, and so forth, do publish and announce to Our dutiful subjects Our most gracious intention to reopen . . . Our large and varied assortment of choice Whiskies . . . which will

[71] Wallace, *History of S. C.*, III, 362. For Tillman's analysis of his censure of *The State*, see S. C. *Senate Journal* (1894) , pp. 18–40. Simkins says the outcome was a triumph for Tillman; see his *Tillman*, pp. 255–57.

[72] *McCullough* v. *Brown*, 41 S. C. 220, as discussed in full in Hendricks, "S. C. Dispensary System," 196–97. Also, cf. *The State*, April 20, 1894.

[73] *State* v. *Aiken*, 42 S. C. 222, as discussed by Hendricks, "S. C. Dispensary System," 320–21.

be sold . . . for spot cash, in the high and holy interest of sobriety, religion, and profit.

We further make known to Our loving subjects the appointment, upon Our Imperial nomination, of Our good and faithful servant, Eugene B. Gary . . . to sustain by the terms of Our gracious law Our Imperial pleasure. Call early and avoid the rush.

Done at our palace of Trickem, in Our City of Columbia, this twenty-third day of July, in the Fourth Year of Our Imperial Reign.

Benjamin I, Imperator

By the Czar:
Jagary Evans, Lord High Lackey[74]

The incensed Gonzales fulminated about Tillman's "vanity, his disposition to tyranny, his wish to scourge his enemies" by "this unique outrage upon law and decency. . . . Convinced of his invincibility, he begins his march to Moscow. We shall take note of his grand army upon its return." When even the *Register* questioned Ben's action, Gonzales saw it was "the beginning of the end."[75]

Although not invincible, Tillman and his followers did manage to lug their pet experiment through a welter of legal tangles over the years. Always the Dispensary emerged, but each time it suffered severely as popular suspicions began to arise concerning its honesty and its efficiency. A host of enemies sprang up against it with the passage of the Tillmanite Metropolitan Police Act, which authorized "the head barkeeper" to take over the police force of Charleston in order to see that the law was enforced in that independent city. The loud cries that Charleston had been deprived of local self-government were as excessive as most of the partisanship of the time.

---

[74] *The State,* July 23, 1894.
[75] *Ibid.,* July 23, 26, 1894.

By 1895 *The State* had moderated its attacks on the Dispensary—perhaps because the editor saw the discontent and suspicion spreading among the Tillmanites. Even Larry Gantt had joined in the attack on the administration of a system which he had introduced to South Carolina. "T. Liar Gantt" departed from Calvo's *Register* late in 1892 after rendering yeoman service for Ben Tillman, who denied the extent of his influence.[76] When his rival departed, N. G. was almost sad and regretted the loss of his "whoppers," adding that he had often committed offenses against the ninth commandment but had never sought to break the sixth. Almost wistfully, N. G. confided how the two editors had been personally friendly. However, he warned Editors Garlington and Petty of the Spartanburg papers to seek the prayers of their respective churches for Larry was

to be unloaded from its [*Register's*] editorial tripod and quietly inflicted upon a helpless, unconscious—and as yet unborn—Alliance weekly in Spartanburg. . . . Spartanburg deserves a better fate. . . . At least, . . . while they are inflicted in personal propinquity they will suffer from the prevarications of print only once a week. When they consider that they might have had doses of L'Arioso diurnally instead of hebdomadally they will conclude that, after all, Providence is pitiful. . . .[77]

Gonzales soon dutifully reported the birth of the *Piedmont Headlight* and observed, "As the *Piedmont Lighthead* the paper undoubtedly will secure a large circulation in the strongholds of the featherbrain population." "L'Arioso" retorted: "*The Columbia State,* better known as the 'sorehead,' says our paper should be called 'The Piedmont Lighthead.'

[76] Ben avowed, "I cannot & never have controlled the *Register*. Calvo is against us at heart & he dislikes me personally." B. R. Tillman to J. L. M. Irby, December 15, 1892, in Simkins Notes.

[77] *The State,* July 13, 1893.

We can inflate a toy balloon with feathers, and it will be heavy enough and possess brains enough to answer any editorial that may appear in *The State*."[78]

Gantt was unswerving in his support of the agrarian movement but not always of Tillmanism. In 1894 Ben accused Gantt of being a traitor because of his criticism and threatened "to open up the whole subject and tell all I know."[79] Gonzales even gleefully took up for Gantt when "no less than seven Refawm Joabs [were] whetting their blades on the polished phrases of the Piedmont Headlight" and warned them that the word *lying* was to be reprehended and should not be used on "those whose enthusiasm in the great Cause of truth compels them to go a step beyond the limits of proof."[80] But the stuffy Major Hemphill never relented, still sanctimoniously referring privately to Gantt and his paper as "such utterly contemptible and disgusting incidents."[81]

In 1894 Tillman's plans called for him to run for the United States Senate against the incumbent, M. C. Butler, and for his faithful lieutenant-governor, John Gary Evans, to succeed him as chief executive. Gonzales wanted the Conservative press to give Ben as little free advertising as possible and to stop distributing his campaign thunder.[82] No strategy would have been adequate while Tillman was so popular with his followers, and Butler tried to conceal his Bourbon policies by masquerading under a Populistic phi-

[78] *Ibid.*, January 25; February 5, 1893. Also, see Charles Petty, "A Look into the Past of South Carolina Journalism," in S. C. State Press Association *Proceedings* (1912), p. 26.

[79] B. R. Tillman to T. L. Gantt, July 15, 1894, in Simkins Notes. Also, Tillman to Stanyarne Wilson, July 21, 1894, in *ibid.*, shows that Gantt would not be intimidated.

[80] *The State*, March 28, 27, 1894.

[81] J. C. Hemphill to August Kohn, October 12, 1895, in Letterbook, 1894–1896, in Hemphill Papers.

[82] August Kohn to J. C. Hemphill, August 30, 1894, in Hemphill Papers. A good background of the race is in Simkins, *Tillman*, pp. 264–65. Evans was nephew of Tillman's patron saint, Mart W. Gary.

losophy—a role which he was not qualified to fill. "Zer-rachaboam" surveyed the situation:

4. And there came another John, called the Squedunk [Evans], who held strong grasp upon the nether garment of Benjamin, and did earnestly hope to wear the worn sandals of Benjamin when he should be minded to cast them aside.

5. Now, as of old, Benjamin did open his mouth in profaneness before the people and sought to set them one against another.

6. And John the Squedunk did squint with his eye and utter blasphemies, hoping that they who beheld him would liken him unto Benjamin his master.

7. But he was held in scorn by as many as heard him, and with one accord they cried out that an ass could not be hidden by the skin of a lion.

11. And when Benjamin had made an end of speaking unto the people at Tirzah, Calbraith [Butler] arose and smote him sore and showed that he was infamous among just men, while, moreover, the greatest liar among his countrymen.

12. Now did the bystanders make loud acclaim and commended Calbraith that he had spoken wisely in discovering the wickedness of Benjamin the Tillmanite.[83]

"Zerrachaboam" was a poor prophet. "Benjamin the Tillmanite" won the senatorship by a five-to-one majority.

Five of Tillman's disciples were in the race for governor, and *The State* was in a quandary. Repeatedly, it tried to inveigle George D. Tillman to make the race but failed, and hence watched the contest from the sidelines, urging the Conservatives at least to attend the meetings so that they might "witness a variety performance more entertaining than the sort they usually pay a dollar to see."[84] Although Gon-

---

[83] *The State,* June 24, 1894.
[84] *Ibid.,* July 25, 1894. The writer is making no effort to rewrite the history of this race; see Simkins, *Tillman,* chap. XIX.

zales and Hampton were inclined to make a fight, the
majority of Conservatives preferred to offer no candidates
but to let dissension wreck the Reform Movement.[85]

During the race "Johngaryevans" (as *The State* spelled
him) and William H. Ellerbe became the leading candidates.
Gonzales exploited the Reformers' feuds for all they were
worth. The paper jumped with glee on Irby's calling Evans
a "squedunk" (origin of "Zerrachaboam's" name for the
small and luckless lieutenant-governor). With tongue in
cheek, *The State* called him "absolutely angelic," and when
some suggested that Evans had overimbibed, the paper
righteously defended him as "Peter the Hermit of a great
temperance crusade." The paper swooped down on him when
Evans made an admission about the *Register* that "We had
to buy it out." Chortled the editor: "Bought! Ye Ariels
of Refawm, that minister to noble 'wool-hat' boys who
hate 'a venal and subsidized press,' mark the words and
spread the confession! 'We had to buy it out!' . . . Dear!
dear!"[86]

Ellerbe, less repugnant to Gonzales than Evans, lost his
chance when Irby and others devised the "Colleton Plan" of
holding an *ad hoc* convention of Tillmanites to "suggest" a
candidate for the support of the agrarian faithful.

Evans was always a particular anathema to *The State*. One
reason that he may have been a frustrating foe for the anti-
Tillmanites was that he did not personally fit into the Tillmanite stereotype—those "horny-handed sons of the soil"
about whom Ben talked or the "one-gallus farmers" whom
N. G. G. ridiculed. Dapper lawyer, a bit of a dandy, a man

[85] J. C. Hemphill to Wade Hampton, March 10, 1894, and Hampton to
Hemphill, March 13, 29; April 9, 25; May 11, 1894, in Letterbook, 1887–1894,
in Hemphill Papers.
[86] *The State*, June 30, 1894.

delicate in appearance and blessed with some erudition and taste, John Gary Evans hardly seemed the typical Tillmanite. True, his uncle was Mart Gary and that was enough to endear him to the "Pitchfork." The truth was that the Reform stereotype was false, for the Tillmanites were a heterogeneous group, not by any means all "dirt farmers." In an analysis of twenty-five leading Tillmanites, William J. Cooper, Jr., found that 44 percent of them were lawyers; 28 percent, planters; 16 percent, farmers; and 12 percent, professional men. Of the leaders, 62.5 percent had attended college, and 16.7 percent also a professional school (law or medicine).[87] As the biographer of Evans puts it, the new class was little different from the one it had replaced; in short it "had less elegance and less refinement and was no longer reluctant to ride into office upon the vote of the common man."[88] Evans, however, had both elegance and refinement, either of which was hardly a characteristic of his mentor, "Pitchfork Ben."

In the August preconvention of the Tillmanites, Evans was overwhelmingly "suggested" and Ellerbe agreed to support the winner on promise of the governorship at a later date. This highhanded method of ring rule stirred a furor among Conservatives—especially Gonzales, who, now again a Straightout, demanded a fight to the finish "against Populism and Tillman mongrelism."[89] There was again talk of a new bolt, but in the September nominating convention the Tillman-controlled Democracy abolished such conventions for the future and provided that all nominations thereafter for state offices should be made by direct primary. Such

[87] Cooper, *Conservative Regime*, pp. 212–13.
[88] Carlanna L. Hendrick, "John Gary Evans, a Political Biography" (Ph.D. diss., University of South Carolina, 1966), p. 25.
[89] *The State*, September 5, 1894.

tactics cut the ground out from under the Conservatives and Straightouts although Gonzales threatened to have *The State* continue the fight.[90]

The Irby committee warned that such a bolt could only mean an appeal by a minority clique to the Negroes.[91] In late September a convention of Conservatives did meet, but *The State* regretfully headlined the meeting, "FARCE, NOT FIGHT | Confusion Rampant | No Platform—No Nominations—No Anything." Gonzales put the direct responsibility for Evans' election by default on the *News and Courier*.[92] "John the Squedunk" was in, "Zerrachaboam's" prophecies notwithstanding. At the time of his inauguration, he was still only thirty-one.

The State continued to suffer from Tillmania during the rule of Ben's heir (1894–1896). This aristocrat and lawyer, whose background, dress, and training made him a somewhat unorthodox Tillmanite, received only condescension from the paper. Satirically, it referred to Evans as "our candidate" and in horrified tones assured the farmers that he was *not* an aristocrat, never gambled on Sundays, had not been seen on trains drunk, was not a railroad lawyer, and had never worn a cutaway coat, tight pants, and toothpick shoes. Since "he is only following the example of his political pastor and master," Gonzales expressed no surprise that his speeches were "characteristic outbursts of inveracious gasconade."[93]

During most of Evans' term, *The State* was less rampant in its attacks than it had been during Governor Tillman's regime. Never, however, did it treat the rival *Register* with

[90] Among the reasons he gave was the fact that it would bring business to the paper. See August Kohn to J. C. Hemphill, September 2, 1894, in Hemphill Papers.
[91] A poster, "Address to the State Democratic Committee of South Carolina," dated October 9, 1894, and signed by J. L. M. Irby, in Hemphill Papers.
[92] *The State*, September 26, 27, 1894.
[93] *Ibid.*, January 15, 1896.

respect or restraint, saying that it merely served as "a congenial channel for all the dirty things said about The State. The only objection to its use is that it contaminates even the sewerage that passes through it."[94] Outstanding event of the Evans administration was the Constitutional Convention of 1895. *The State* had opposed this "reform" of Tillman's, having early said it was better to "bear the ills we have, than fly to others we know not of." Worse, the paper feared the "Till-Pops" would incorporate into fundamental law some of their acts which would 'go further, perhaps, in the direction of communism.'[95] Other dailies agreed that a time of factionalism was no time for rewriting a constitution, but in an 1894 referendum the Tillman strength provided for a convention—although the vote, according to *The State,* was fraudulent. The chief objective of the new instrument was the elimination of the Negro vote by more certain methods than such devious subterfuges as the "eight-box law." Wrote "Zerrachaboam":

2. Being little in mind, he [John the Squedunk] was in no wise able to see in what contempt he was held by all just men.

3. He did wickedly seek by counting of ballots to change the great tablets of the law so that the Sons of Ethiopia might no longer vote, and that he and his followers might reign forever.[96]

During 1895 Gonzales became more involved in political intrigue than ever before. Both Conservatives and Reformers early saw that some compromise would be needed; otherwise they feared their division would permit the Negro Republicans to win the general election of delegates to the Convention. In December 1894 a group of conservative Reformers,

94 *Ibid.,* July 27, 1895.
95 *Ibid.,* December 23, 1891; and September 14, 1894.
96 *Ibid.,* May 16, 1895.

"The Forty," issued a manifesto calling for a conference on March 27, 1895, to provide means of choosing a nonpartisan convention. Uncompromisingly *The State* at once spurned the proposal as putting the Conservatives in the position of surrendering or depending on the magnanimity of the Tillmanites. The paper further noted that the only honest means of disfranchising Negroes would involve education and property requirements which would also disfranchise whites. This *The State* nevertheless advocated, even at the expense of permitting some Negroes to vote, in preference to the adoption of a dishonest scheme or subterfuge in which the polls managers would be dictators of the suffrage. "The only enduring safety is in honesty and straightforwardness."[97] At times, Gonzales was a wondrous mixture of William Elliott's conservatism, the best of ante-bellum principles, and his own latent liberalism.

Tillman, stage manager of the coming convention, was inclined to compromise since he knew that he needed Conservative help to eliminate the Negro from politics; furthermore, he would need legal wisdom and many of the most influential and leading lawyers were Conservatives. J. C. Hemphill and Joseph W. Barnwell summoned leading Conservatives to a secret meeting in Columbia on February 14 to confer with Tillman and try to devise a coalition plan.[98] Gonzales was not invited to attend but, to the horror of Hemphill, was able to print the decisions reached at the secret session.[99] Tillman and Hemphill agreed that Conservatives should get half of the delegates and that they

---

[97] *Ibid.*, December 6, 1894.

[98] J. C. Hemphill to T. M. Gilland, February 8, 1895, in Hemphill Papers; Hemphill to August Kohn, January 18, 1895, in Letterbook, 1894–1896, of Hemphill Papers; August Kohn to J. C. Hemphill, February 12, 1895, in Letterbook, 1893–1896, in Kohn Papers.

[99] *The State*, February 15, 20, 1895; J. C. Hemphill to H. J. Haynesworth, February 20, 1895, in Letterbook, 1894–1896, in Hemphill Papers.

would support the "Mississippi Plan" of disfranchising Negroes. This plan provided for a suffrage test requiring voters to be able to read the constitution, or, in lieu of that, be able to "give a reasonable interpretation thereof" when it was read to them; the interpretation of "reasonable" rested with election officials. According to N. G., putting such discriminatory authority into the hands of election officials was a greater danger than the Negro vote and would lead to wholesale fraud.[100]

In taking such a stand, Gonzales showed perhaps more principle than he did statesmanship; Hemphill irritably said he showed an utter lack of common sense. When approached by a committee of Conservatives, he would only "snarl and snap as we go along."[101] But Gonzales was not the only extreme dissenter: John Irby at once kicked over the traces and led N. G. to prophesy that Tillman would back out of his agreement when he found his followers would not acquiesce in his contract. Gonzales admitted that he himself was open to suggestions as to how to get an honest, liberal, just constitution, but he did not think the way was yet open to one.[102]

The bipartisan conference suggested by "The Forty" met on March 27 as scheduled. Although the Tillman-Hemphill meeting made this one an anticlimax, Gonzales endorsed it because its proposals were not binding in advance and had no further strings attached—such as the "Mississippi Plan." Resolutions called for equal Conservative-Reformer representation in the Constitutional Convention and for white supremacy by fair and constitutional means. Kohn said A. B. Williams and Gonzales were pleased but would have pre-

[100] *The State*, February 20, 1895.
[101] J. C. Hemphill to T. M. Raysor, March 2, 8, 1895, in Letterbook, 1894–1896, in Hemphill Papers.
[102] J. L. M. Irby to N. G. Gonzales, in *The State*, February 25, 1895; also, see *The State*, February 28, 1895.

ferred more fire in the resolutions.[103] Hemphill was also satisfied since he carelessly thought that this conference virtually endorsed what his earlier agreement had provided.[104] Some of "The Forty," including Editor Louis Appelt, did not welcome Gonzales' blessing, and the "ultra-Conservatives" optimistically continued their plans for implementing their February agreement with Tillman.[105] They should have listened to N. G.'s prophecy that Irby's political influence was so powerful that Tillman would have to renege on his promise. "Zerrachaboam" said "The Forty" had sought "peace and unity among the people" and that "John the Squedunk" and "Benjamin the Tillmanite" were willing to agree. He chronicled the outcome of these plans as follows:

6. But it came to pass that John the Senator [Irby] did have a secret hold upon John the Squedunk and Benjamin the Tillmanite, or as they say in vulgar language, "a string tied to them."

7. And when he had commanded them to appear before him at the Chief City of the land, they obeyed him with much fear and trembling.

8. When they had come into the presence of John the Senator, he did frown upon them so that their hearts sank within them, and their teeth did gnash one against another.

9. And when they had prostrated themselves upon the earth and made obeisance before John the Senator, he did speak harshly unto them so that they were overcome with dread, and were at their wits end.

11. When they had again returned unto their homes, John the Squedunk and Benjamin the Tillmanite did then wickedly

---

[103] August Kohn to J. C. Hemphill, March 29, 1895, in Hemphill Papers; also, see *The State,* March 28, 29, 1895.

[104] J. C. Hemphill to H. J. Haynesworth, March 13, 1895; to August Kohn, March 29, 1895; to D. H. Chamberlain, April 17, 1895; all in Letterbook, 1894–1896, in Hemphill Papers.

[105] August Kohn to J. C. Hemphill, n.d., in Kohn Papers; John F. Sloan, Jr., to J. C. Hemphill, April 1, 1895, in Hemphill Papers.

deny that they had agreed that peace should dwell in the land, and would in no wise follow the promises they had made.[106]

After this debacle, Conservatives tried to salvage their strength. Hemphill complained that Gonzales was only an obstructionist interested primarily in magnifying his own importance.[107] The latter could not refrain from enjoying the discomfort of the trusting Conservatives: "The old lady of Broad Street so long ago reached the age of consent that we doubt whether a jury would award her heavy damages on the ground of youthful innocence and trust; but it is clear that she has a good prima facie case for breach of promise and desertion against that gay Lothario, Ben Tillman."[108] A Straightout conference failed to provide a solution for the Conservatives,[109] and Gonzales urged that Conservatives boycott "the Irby Primary" of July 30 and try to elect a good slate in the general election later. His advice was snubbed, and he was attacked for "independentism." Without a formal agreement, concessions were made with substantial representation granted to the Conservative minority. Had the delegates been chosen on a strictly partisan basis, the Conservatives would have carried only Richland and Charleston counties; as it was, the Convention contained 43 Conservatives, 113 Tillmanites, and 6 Republicans.[110]

[106] The State, May 16, 1895. Also, see ibid., June 16, 17, 1895; and J. C. Hemphill to T. M. Rogers, July 16, 1895, in Letterbook, 1894–1896, in Hemphill Papers.

[107] J. C. Hemphill to August Kohn, May 22, 1895, in Letterbook, 1894–1896, in Hemphill Papers.

[108] The State, June 17, 1895. Gonzales' utter independence during this period annoyed many Conservatives. See August Kohn to J. C. Hemphill, May 21, 1895, in Hemphill Papers.

[109] J. C. Hemphill to T. M. Rogers, June 22, 1895, in Letterbook, 1894–96, of Hemphill Papers.

[110] Simkins, Tillman, p. 289; leaders are listed in George B. Tindall, "South Carolina Constitutional Convention of 1895" (M.A. thesis, University of North Carolina, 1948), pp. 56 et seq.

The Reformers' internal divisions led T. Larry Gantt to try to arrange a conference of himself, Tillman, and Evans to avert a split in the movement and to have "a definite line of policy mapped out, and the hatchet buried." As "T. Liar" piously interpreted their situation, "all of you are hot-headed and impetuous. I have no axe to grind, but I don't want to see our movement wrecked by such senseless wrangles."[111]

During the Convention which met throughout the fall of 1895, Gonzales did not deviate from his advocacy of a fair and honest constitution. Always he stood for white supremacy —but not at the expense of fraud, intimidation, or the raising of a race issue; he urged straightforward provisions which would permit qualified Negroes to vote but which by their very nature would give the whites a majority.[112]

Tillman, on the other hand, favored the "Mississippi Plan"—a permanent educational qualification with a temporary optional "understanding" test. Although he said he wanted to save the state from the "rule of ignorance," Gonzales noted that to Ben "ignorance . . . is only dangerous when it is black ignorance."[113] In the course of the discussions, *The State* praised the rational speeches of Negro delegates Thomas E. Miller and W. J. Whipper, although admitting that the whites could not accede to their plans. The suffrage qualification as adopted—and it was the prime reason for writing a new constitution—was a modification of the "Mississippi Plan": the alternative "understanding" clause (to enfranchise illiterate whites) would create lifetime voters until 1898, after which time the " 'or' clause" (to be used in lieu of literacy qualifications) provided for payment of

[111] T. L. Gantt to John Gary Evans, August 3, 1895, in John Gary Evans Papers.

[112] *The State*, May 11, 1895.

[113] William A. Mabry, "Ben Tillman Disfranchised the Negro," in *South Atlantic Quarterly*, XXXVII (1938), 178.

taxes on property assessed at $300.[114] Negroes would find it virtually impossible to convince even an ignorant election official that they understood the constitution, and of course they would have no recourse for appeal.

Although not a delegate, N. G. became an issue during the proceedings of the Convention. The Irby-Tillman friction came to the fore as Irby supported George Tillman in getting a new county named Butler, an act intended as a direct slap at Butler's last opponent. At the time Ben was absent, but upon his return he exerted pressure to get the name of the county changed back to Saluda. A motion was made to defer action until the Irby supporters could be rallied; the outcome of the maneuver, according to an editorial by Gonzales, was: "The president [Evans] openly and defiantly misstated the returns of the tellers, subtracting two announced votes from Irby's side in order that he might show a majority of one against postponement."[115] Thus, the county became Saluda once again. Gonzales added: "Senator Tillman brought into the Constitutional convention an utter ignorance of parliamentary law and usages, an abnormal vanity, a habit of absolute dictation, a ready sneer and a bitter tongue."

Two days later a resolution was introduced branding the Gonzales editorial about Evans' action "a malicious falsehood," but this was watered down to "an abuse of the privilege granted the Press in admitting its members to the floor of this convention."[116] Tillman was not satisfied; he said Gonzales should be "sued for libel or flayed with a stick" and that he had "dished out more malice and hatred than any other man in the State except myself." At the latter re-

[114] *Journal of the Constitutional Convention of South Carolina, 1895*, pp. 297–98. Also, see Wallace, *History of S. C.*, III, 369–73, and Simkins, *Tillman*, pp. 295–303.
[115] *The State*, September 17, 1895.
[116] *Journal of the Constitutional Convention*, pp. 156–58.

mark on the floor, Gonzales bowed ironically to Ben.[117] A vote was forced and the resolution of censure passed, 123-23. Gonzales was not suppressed; in an editorial, "The King Can Do No Wrong," he defiantly refused to be intimidated and added that "we are invulnerable to compulsory or perfunctory resolutions."[118] He also pointed out that Evans had never denied his charge of misstating the vote.

At the close of the Convention, *The State* admitted pleasure that such a partisan body had done as much good and as little harm as it had. In the editor's opinion, "bossism" had not been the controlling factor that he had feared—perhaps because "familiarity with their idol reduced greatly the awe with which he had been held." Greatest weakness was the failure to provide real safeguards for the ballot, but "We . . . may take a long breath and congratulate ourselves that things are no worse."[119] Maybe a great change was at work, for once during the sessions Gonzales had broken over long enough to write, "Senator Tillman . . . is perceptibly broadening in his policy, and, we hope, in his mind."[120]

Such mollification was not extensive, but it did presage a slight shift in the policy of *The State*. During 1896 the paper referred to the "Democratic Convention," instead of the "Irby Convention" as previously. During the campaign for Senator Irby's seat that year, its venom was directed primarily at the sycophant, "Johngaryevans," and the paper regretted that Irby withdrew from the race.

The State continued to show no charity to Evans. In 1896 his message to the legislature was widely applauded, even by

---

[117] Tindall, "S. C. Constitutional Convention," p. 87; Simkins, *Tillman*, p. 295; *The State*, September 19, 1895; Kohn's account in *News and Courier*, September 20, 1895.

[118] *The State*, September 20, 1895.

[119] *Ibid.*, November 26, 1895. The Constitution was published in full in *The State*, December 6, 1895.

[120] *Ibid.*, November 15, 1895.

the *News and Courier*, but the Gonzales gazette merely noted that the message began and ended "with characteristic outbursts of inveracious gasconade" and was even "crude in composition." Early in 1897 it called him "unworthy" as well as "small and cheap and mean."[121]

Such severe condemnation indicates why Gonzales the reporter had made Dawson the editor uncomfortable when fourteen years earlier that Charleston journalist had besought his testy writer to seek reform and root out abuse but to beware of a "bad-tempered or querulous" style and "the sort of controversial writing which is the delight of half-baked Western journalism." In the 1890s, Gonzales still was not following Dawson's advice: to say what he thought but to say it "in a good-natured and dignified way, and you should avoid, besides, as far as possible, any imputation upon the motive . . . of those whom you criticize, or who differ from you in opinion."[122] In later years, William Watts Ball, who considered N. G. G. the greatest journalist that South Carolina had produced, conceded that he had a "tendency to harshness of expression and partisanship" but that because of his style and strength *The State* attracted the devoted (and almost fanatical) following which it had from 1891 to 1897, without which the paper never would have gotten established. After that, Gonzales mellowed a bit and developed more judgment but what had "made" him was his "fervency, an intensity, a tenacity and a pugnacity."[123]

In reporting the 1896 senatorial canvass, Willie Gonzales reincarnated the spirit of N. G. Gonzales when the latter had been the *News and Courier* political reporter, writing stories under such headlines as "FLAT AS A FLOUNDER | The Meeting at Camden Too Dull to Mention." (He then

121 *Ibid.*, January 18, 1897.
122 F. W. Dawson to N. G. Gonzales, July 23, 1883, in Dawson Papers.
123 W. W. Ball, Diary, III, 190, in Ball Papers.

proceeded to mention it for three and a half columns.) [124]
Later, when Judge Joseph H. Earle struck his opponent,
Evans, the same reporter told of "A VERY SAD SPECTA-
CLE," but editorialized in his news story: "Perhaps if a
dozen people had been killed today it would have been a
blessing to the State. It might have so shocked her people as
to awaken them fully to a realization of the degeneration of
public men."[125] Willie increasingly sounded like N. G. as he
wrote, "I expected . . . to see many men reach down and
get their specimens of Smith and Wesson's latest work on
how to perforate the human form. . . . There was a small
cyclone of excitement. . . . Some say they had gotten hold
of some of the 'breakage' at the local dispensary." At the
end of the campaign, his "news story" closed with a series of
pointed and loaded questions, concluding with, "Alas, that
there should be doubt as to the issue!"[126]

In this Senate race of 1896, the Gonzales gazette supported
no candidate. It enjoyed the discomfort of Evans at the hands
of Irby and a perennial candidate, John T. Duncan. The editor of *The State* even proclaimed that he would vote for his
archenemy, Tillman himself, if he were running against
Evans, for "It is not a question of politics but of personal
and official dignity."[127] The prophet, "Zerrachaboam,"
viewed the situation as follows:

10. Now it came to pass in the fullness of time that the term of
office of John the Senator did draw to a close. . . .
11. But Benjamin the Tillmanite . . . wishing to have his servant John the Squedunk always near him, did go from place to
place and set all men of authority against John the Senator, so

124 *The State*, July 15, 1896.
125 *Ibid.*, July 24, 1896.
126 *Ibid.*, August 5, 20, 1896.
127 *Ibid.*, August 21, 1896.

that John . . . was stricken in heart and dared not stand before the wrath of Benjamin.

13. But at the eleventh hour came two men [Earle and Duncan], bold of heart, to do battle against John the Squedunk. . . .

14. And they did show how John the Squedunk had made unlawful profit of many shekels among the money changers [by the floating of state bonds on Wall Street] and he was speechless and could in no wise explain it to . . . the people so that they set their faces against him.

16. Then went John the Squedunk straightway to Benjamin, his master, and showed unto him what things Duncan had brought to light before the people and their hearts sank within them while their spirits were in sore bitterness.

17. And straightway did they send a swift messenger unto Rhind [involved in the alleged bond fraud], saying unto him arise, saddle thine ass and depart quickly into a far country, and there abide until we send thee further word, for there be many who seek to mark thy words concerning the doings of money changers.[128]

Despite such revelations, Evans led the ticket in the first race and was pitted against Earle in the second primary; Tillman climbed off the fence and supported Evans, while Gonzales—using practically his whole paper daily—successfully endorsed Earle. At the end, under a huge headline, "SHAKE!" *The State* reported "a political revolution," a victory over the "hosts of darkness," because "The freemen of South Carolina recognize no King Canute. . . . Boss Rule is over in South Carolina!"[129] For days, Gonzales used his press to exult over his first notable state victory.

[128] *Ibid.*, October 22, 1896.
[129] *Ibid.*, September 9, 1896. Wallace, *History of S. C.*, III, 384, says that the Conservatives, who had been unorganized and dispirited during the first race, beat Evans in the second.

The joy and claims of *The State* were perhaps premature and too optimistic, but the old smooth machine of Tillmanism was definitely beginning to develop serious weaknesses and fissures. Even so, during this same campaign, a pro-Tillman governor, William H. Ellerbe, and a pro-Tillman legislature were elected, but the Gonzaleses had been too busy fighting "Johngaryevans" to be very worried about the state race.

Readers of *The State* got no respite from politics, however, since the new Senator Earle promptly died and a new race had to be run in 1897. To the vacant seat, Governor Ellerbe had appointed John L. McLaurin—some believed at the behest of N. G. Gonzales. Many Reformers were alarmed anyhow at the role of kingmaker which they now believed it possible for him to play.[130]

In the 1897 primary that followed, McLaurin, Irby, Evans, Duncan, and S. G. Mayfield ran. Because of his influence, Gonzales was a favorite target with both Irby and Evans. Both *The State* and the *News and Courier* supported McLaurin—a Reformer, but one not guilty of the worst excesses, according to Gonzales. These two papers also combined forces to cover the hustings and thereby saved expenses as August Kohn, Willie Gonzales, William Banks, and others wrote the reports for both papers.[131] Candidates at once complained that they did not get fair play.

The State resumed its blistering methods of 1892. Irby, "a man . . . so abandoned to honor," "known as a wilful and malicious traducer," received a telling back-handed attack after he made one of several personal attacks on Gonzales. The latter declared that although "we said nothing of

---

[130] J. Y. Jones, "Open Letter to the Governor of South Carolina" (1897), and August Kohn to J. C. Hemphill, January 26, 1897, in Hemphill Papers.

[131] August Kohn to J. C. Hemphill, June 23, 24, July 15, 1897, in Letterbook, 1896–1897, in Kohn Papers.

his drunken orgies in Washington, his other disreputable
conduct there, nor of . . . [his] trying to kill a hack driver
in his maudlin rage," he did not "care to go into the details
of his personal record. The subject is too malodorous and
we shall not stir it unless forced to do so."[132] As for "Johngaryevans," the paper all but ignored him "because The
State does not believe in wasting shot on dead ducks."[133]

For its support of Tillmanite McLaurin, *The State* was
needled and taunted by some of its "eminent contemporaries." Naturally, it replied in kind. With A. B. Williams away
and its editorial page graced by young Billy Ball, the *Greenville News* received abrupt treatment from Gonzales as "a
rubber ball, constantly full of resilience, soft all over and full
of beautiful, harmless, limpid air."[134] After the race in which
its candidate, John McLaurin, won on the first ballot, *The
State* returned to normal.

This "normality" involved more restraint than had typi-
fied *The State* of a few years before. Although steadfastly
claiming to be the "last to make its Pickett's charges against
'Reform,'" the paper wearied of its own tactics and started
supporting men or measures good in themselves, regardless
of the Tillman stamp. Such tactics paid dividends because
even his enemies recognized N. G. Gonzales' intelligence.
The State never underrated the ability of Ben—unless it was
to predict that he would never be re-elected to the Senate.[135]
Even "Pitchfork Ben" gave the devil his due, saying in 1895,
"I have always given Gonzales credit for being honest and
straightforward and a man with backbone and principle,
though he is my enemy."[136] Tillman also made friends with

[132] *The State,* August 27, 1897.
[133] *Ibid.,* July 13, 1897.
[134] *Ibid.,* July 10, 1897.
[135] *Ibid.,* February 1, 1896.
[136] In an interview with Richard Carroll, published in the *Greenville News,*
n.d. [July 2, 1895?], and reprinted in *The State,* July 3, 1895.

Judge A. C. Haskell and no longer used "Haskellite" as an epithet.[137]

A few kind words did not mean that *The State* had changed sides. Although his denunciation of measures no longer was based on his finding the answer to a simple question, "Is Tillman for it?" Gonzales never really spared Tillman and seemed to take nefarious joy in such gibes as publishing a group of thirty-seven terms that had been applied by others to "our Chesterfieldian junior senator," including such choice names as "a blackguard, a buffoon, a baboon, . . . a dangerous blatherskite, . . . an intemperate and demagogic accident, . . . clown, . . . an obscene corruption, . . . the product of a freak brain, . . . a pot house polemic." Smugly the editor commented: "Those who live by the pitchfork shall fall under the harrow."[138]

Although the paper became somewhat more rational in its attacks on Tillman, the Dispensary and the corruption which allegedly flourished within it furnished constant targets for attack. In this crusade, Gonzales had the pungent aid of Larry Gantt, who regularly launched into "the gin mill," to the annoyance of his former patron now ensconced in distant Washington.[139] Ben said Gantt "merely dips his syringe in the gutter of filth and slime" coming from the Conservative dailies but that his "affrontery . . . gives out so much smoke and so little fire."[140]

Some papers relented, but *The State* never let up on the Dispensary and often demanded a thorough investigation. The editor wrote that the only way to reform it was to reform it out of existence since it "was conceived in trickery, brought forth in crime and nourished on partisan hatred and human

137 B. R. Tillman to C. L. Blease, August[?], 1912, in Simkins Notes.
138 *The State*, February 4, 1896.
139 George W. Thorpe to B. R. Tillman, May 31, 1897, in Tillman Manuscripts, Duke University Library.
140 B. R. Tillman to M. B. McSweeney, March 14, 1897, in Simkins Notes.

blood."[141] To remove it, the paper proposed a referendum by counties ("local option") in which the people would have an opportunity to vote for county dispensaries, prohibition, or high license. Of these alternatives, the editor favored the latter as the best encouragement to law enforcement and temperance.

The Dispensary was weakened in 1895 when a federal court held that the state could not interfere with interstate shipments of whiskey to individuals for private use. In 1897 a federal judge also sanctioned "original package stores" for the state. Such court decrees and the revelations of suspicious dealings in the administration of the Dispensary gave much glee to "Zerrachaboam," who intoned, "Weep, oh, ye spies. . . . Prepare ye for your return to the plow and workshop, for the day of rewards from blind tigers is past and tribulation compasseth you round about."[142] These inroads on the Dispensary were removed in 1898, however, when that institution got a new lease on life from the United States Supreme Court, which declared that the state, in the exercise of its police powers, could take complete control of the sale of liquors.

The state election in 1898 again raised the fever of *The State*. In the race for governor were Governor Ellerbe, Dispensary candidate; C. C. Featherstone, Prohibitionist; and George D. Tillman, advocate of county option. When Ben Tillman said he would stump the state if necessary in behalf of the dispensary law, regardless of the candidates, the *Spartanburg Herald* accused him of "fiendish," unbrotherly conduct. Gonzales, however, said Ben's hatred for George was selfishness and not fiendishness.[143] Infuriated, Ben wrote a

[141] *The State*, October 24, 1904.
[142] *Ibid.*, June 7, 1897. This was one of the "Prophet's" longest chapters.
[143] *Spartanburg Herald*, December 30, 1897, as related in *The State*, January 2, 1898.

letter from Washington saying that Gonzales and Hemphill were the authors of factionalism in the state and that "the treacherous Spaniard who makes the charge of betrayal and unbrotherly conduct against me, only advertises his own depravity and blackness of heart."[144] Since *The State* had recently been accused of truckling, N. G. was not overly angered by the insult, although he did rise to pay his respects to "this sham and charlatan statesman." "We have never known Ben to attempt to purge himself of one lie without hatching half a dozen others. The cotton caterpillar doesn't approach him in fecundity."[145]

After George Tillman was eliminated in the first primary in 1898, Ellerbe sought and obtained the support of *The State* for the second primary. In return, he agreed, in writing, to support local option.[146] If N. G.'s support influenced as many as 2,600 votes, he was responsible for Ellerbe's subsequent victory; but later, verbally, Ellerbe denied ever having made any agreement with Gonzales and supported the continuation of the Dispensary. Eventually he did admit writing an equivocating but incriminating agreement with F. H. Weston before the election, but he alleged that it was not supposed to have been shown to N. G. Gonzales or to have bound him to the editor or to any plan. Blaming the pressure of Tillman for this outcome, the editor admitted, "I am fair game; I have been buncoed."[147]

In the 1900 state elections, Gonzales and Tillman were again in opposite camps. Ben supported M. B. McSweeney

[144] *The State*, January 2, 1898 (under the headline, "WILL WE PRINT IT? WHY, CERTAINLY!"). Also, Letter to Press, December 21, 1897, in Simkins Notes.

[145] *The State*, January 4, 1898.

[146] W. H. Ellerbe to F. H. Weston, September 8, 1898, as cited in *The State*, January 11, 1899; also, see *The State*, September 10, 1898.

[147] N. G. G. in *The State*, January 11, 1899. Also, see *ibid.*, January 12, June 3, 1899; Wallace, *History of S. C.*, III, 392; Hendricks, "S. C. Dispensary System," *loc. cit.*, pp. 330–32.

for governor—a well-intentioned man who favored keeping the Dispensary but reforming it. Gonzales vigorously supported Colonel James A. Hoyt, Prohibitionist editor, because—according to *The State*—there was no local optionist in the race, because he was the best man in the race, and because he could not be bossed by Senator Tillman.[148] Tillman's active opposition to Hoyt pitted the senator against the preachers, and Gonzales warned him that he was "fast getting out of the preachers' vocabulary" and that they would have to get special dispensation to tilt with him verbally.[149] It made no difference, however, as McSweeney was elected. At the same time, the formidable "Pitchfork," whom no candidate had dared to oppose, returned to the Senate for his second term.

During the first decade of the twentieth century, *The State* continued its war of attrition against the faltering Dispensary.[150] As it seemed apparently impossible to purify it even under the determined Governor D. C. Heyward (1903–1907), many came to favor local option and steps were taken toward that solution. In 1905 the legislature established an investigating committee, which, led by Niels Christenson, Jr., and J. Fraser Lyon, uncovered a statewide system of graft and rebates.[151] In 1906 Martin F. Ansel, local optionist, and an anti-Dispensary legislature were elected—with the blessings of *The State*. In 1907 the state system which had re-

---

[148] J. A. Hoyt, Jr., to Col. J. A. Hoyt, May 17, 1900, in Hoyt Papers (and photostat in Wofford College Library). Also, see *The State*, July 26, 1900; and for a biography of Hoyt, *ibid.*, August 11, 1900. Gonzales tried unsuccessfully to get J. C. Sheppard or some other local optionist to run.

[149] *The State*, August 10, 1900. Hoyt was a longtime editor of the *Baptist Courier*.

[150] Obviously, no effort is being made to give a history of that complicated subject here except insofar as necessary to show reactions of *The State*.

[151] Hendricks, "S. C. Dispensary System," 338 *et seq.*; Niels Christensen, Jr., "State Dispensaries in South Carolina," in *Annals of the Academy of Political and Social Sciences*, XXXII (1908), 545–52.

ceived so many verbal brickbats from Gonzales was at long last abolished. Thereafter, counties were to choose between prohibition and county dispensaries.[152] The rejoicing in *The State* was what one might have expected.

Despite the demise of the Dispensary, *The State* could obtain only faint consolation from subsequent events. The first investigating committee did its work well and exposed so much corruption that it reported fumigation was necessary even to approach the subject with comfort. At every hand, it found its efforts frustrated and thwarted, and later Governor Cole L. Blease—loyal friend of the Dispensary—began investigations of the investigating committee and even tried to indict T. B. Felder, Atlanta attorney who had helped Fraser Lyon unearth the legal proof of corruption, fraud, and graft. As W. W. Ball said, "South Carolina had experienced no more than a spasm of virtue."[153] Professor Simkins defensively states: "That it [the Dispensary] did not . . . become a permanent South Carolina institution was due not to lack of statesmanship on the part of the creator but to the development of religious and moral opposition over which Ben Tillman had no control."[154] He might have added immorality and graft over which he apparently had no control, as well as Gonzales.

During all of this period, *The State's* delirium over Tillmanism had continued to dissipate. In 1901 came the famous and unique controversy and fistfight between the two South Carolina senators, Tillman and McLaurin. At first, the paper was downright enchanted at the spectacle: "Here's a pretty kettle of fish! Ben Tillman accusing Johnnie McLaurin of

[152] *Acts of S. C.* (1907), pp. 463–81, especially pp. 464–65. Also, *The State*, February 13, 14, 1907.

[153] Ball, *The State That Forgot*, p. 258. For details, authenticated by primary sources, see Hendricks, "S. C. Dispensary System," 342–48.

[154] Simkins, *Tillman*, p. 234. Nevertheless, the same writer says (p. 460) that Ben favored its abolition if its administration could not be reformed.

political heterodoxy and political treachery! What a spectacle, ye gods and minnows!"[155] Soon the paper was also strongly opposing McLaurin as a pseudo-Republican who was supporting "the party of plutocracy, monopoly and subsidies." Over and over the paper refused to accept McLaurin's claim that his movement was anti-Tillmanite, not anti-Democratic: "There is room in South Carolina for a decent white Republican party, but there is no room in it for a Hermaphrodite party—and for hypocrisy and treachery in politics there shall be no tolerance."[156] The dissenter was eventually read out of the party.

As *The State* moderated its attacks on Tillmanism and ceased using that *ism* as a criterion for testing the good and evil in all things, it inevitably had to fend off other papers accusing it of losing its virtue, spirit, or courage. Even Columbia in 1899 received Tillman as an honor guest at a banquet, "her heart melted to gentleness by the touch of a Federal appropriation for the Congaree River."[157]

In 1899 the paper frankly stated its policy toward Ben: to ignore him as much as possible since the paper always refused free advertising to quacks, whether medical or political.[158] Nevertheless, in 1900 the senator listed N. G. Gonzales, J. C. Hemphill, J. C. Carlington, and A. B. Williams as "paid agents of the Whiskey Trust" that opposed the Dispensary. This charge forced *The State* to notice Ben, only to say that it was not disconcerted by the "brazen front and blushless cheek" of this "veteran of 15 years of false charges." N. G. wrote that he would not have been surprised to be called a horse thief, but the charges were unfair to the other three editors. After listing some of their acts of submission

[155] *The State*, April 22, 1901. For details of the controversy, see Simkins, *Tillman*, pp. 8–12, 383–90.
[156] *The State*, October 5, 1901.
[157] Simkins, *Tillman*, pp. 371–72. Gonzales tactfully absented himself.
[158] *The State*, August 11, 1899.

to Ben, he concluded: " 'Ingratitude, thou marble hearted fiend.' We do not mind what Benjamin says about us, but our heart bleeds for our poor contemporaries."[159] But, in general, silence on Ben was the new rule.

Frequently *The State* rebuked the lukewarmness of the *News and Courier* and its disinclination to rush loudly into every fray. Evidently Major Hemphill was trying to avoid clashes with the increasingly conservative Tillman, but often his increasing friendliness or familiarity was ignored; after he was presumptuous enough in his correspondence to seek patronage favors, the "Pitchfork" replied very briefly: "If you want to help this woman get her a job in Charleston, and do not undertake to dump your office-seeking friends on me. I have enough troubles of my own."[160] Later, he irritably added a postscript to a letter: "Be a Tillmanite or be an anti—I will not have you play off both roles on me."[161] This last advice was the substance of what Gonzales kept telling the Major.

The *Spartanburg Herald* gave a reasonably accurate appraisal of "the new *State*" in 1901: "It has laid aside much of the bitterness and narrowness, the personal animosity and spite that once characterized it."[162] Others, however, were accusing it of inconsistency or insincerity—charges which it vigorously denied by saying that it was the voice that had adhered to its principles regardless of state factions and partisanship. Most annoying of the carping critics was the 1897 *Greenville News,* then edited by W. W. Ball, once of the *Columbia Journal* but now "on the fence, casting sheep's-

[159] *Ibid.,* August 25, 1900.
[160] B. R. Tillman to J. C. Hemphill, January 28, 1903, in Hemphill Papers.
[161] Same to same, January 24, 1906, in Hemphill Papers. Hemphill replied (January 26, 1906): "I shall be obliged if you will explain to me what it is to be a Tillmanite."
[162] *Spartanburg Herald,* February 18, 1901, as cited in *The State,* February 21, 1901.

eyes at John Gary Evans" and accusing *The State* of non-combativeness.[163] Reactionary but reasonable Ball had said that the political atmosphere was one of conciliation and that Tillman represented about the only "positive and aggressive idea in politics, bad as that idea is." In reply, Gonzales said there was no fight left in the Conservatives, and "Politics in South Carolina today is individualistic, not aggregational."[164] Ball wrote similarly discouraged opinions to the New York *Evening Post,* and *The State* commented that its old friend perhaps needed "Dr. Strait's Tomato-Fig Syrup" since it was good "for that 'languid and tired feeling,' and also . . . cures biliousness and nausea."[165]

Latent Tillmania continued to manifest itself occasionally, almost as if N. G. were trying to keep in practice. With his old antagonist in Washington, there were fewer clear-cut and easily discernible issues and events about which the average Carolinian could be readily aroused. Most frequent subjects of condemnation were Ben's crudeness, profanity, and tactlessness, which Gonzales frequently marked as sources of embarrassment to South Carolina and a disgrace to the Senate. An example of this was a political speech in Wisconsin by the Edgefield farmer in which he "displayed the characteristic brutality and his usual disregard for facts" as he ranted and roared and boastfully sanctioned lynching. Of this display, the editor wrote as follows:

Since Ben histed the tune at an Edgefield Baptist meeting last summer The State had entertained great hopes of his spiritual regeneration. Along with . . . the News and Courier, . . . of the Seceder persuasion [Hemphill was a famous Associate Reformed Presbyterian], The State, unorthodox though it may be, is

[163] *The State,* May 17, 1897.
[164] *Ibid.,* May 15, 1897; also, Wallace, *History of S. C.,* III, 385.
[165] *The State,* October 4, 1897. A. B. Williams did not finally break all of his connections with the *News* until 1900. See *The State,* May 7, 1900.

rejoiced to learn that Senator Tillman would not deign to dese-
crate the Sabbath by telling Wisconsin people how southerners
lynch "niggers" and shoot them to keep the darkeys from voting.
If he lives long enough Ben Tillman may yet become so good and
pious that he would not only refuse to lead a lynching bee but
would even disdain to use a stronger cuss word than "dog-gone
it." But we really do not expect Tillman to be a second Methuse-
lah.[166]

And so the "new calmness" went, with Ben toned down to
the point of only calling *The State* "that rattlesnake down on
Main Street."[167]

Most original critic during this period was "Zarracha-
boam" with his less venomous animosity. This chronicler
specialized in assailing Tillmanism through the shortcomings of the Dispensary that were so frequently aired until its
demise in 1907. An 1899 sample follows:

1. Now when Zerrachaboam was returned from the tents of
Uncle Sam he did journey into his own country, even the land
called Tillmania.

2. But as he journeyed he was oppressed by a great thirst. . . .

3. And the scribe spake to the prophet, saying, Hail! Zerrachaboam, . . . whither goest thou? . . .

4. Whereupon the prophet answered and said, I . . . journey
unto a servant of Benjamin the Tillmanite, even a dispenser of
strong drink.

5. And the scribe said . . . , whither thou goest, I will go, for
it has been many years since mine eyes hath beheld thee and I
do treasure in my heart the words of a former ruler of our people
which he spake unto a ruler of the people which abideth to the
north of Tillmania.

6. Then was the heart of the prophet glad within him and he
answered, . . . hasten my footsteps . . . , for hath not Benjamin

---

166 *Ibid.*, August 16, 1901.
167 *Ibid.*, September 5, 1900.

inscribed upon the bottles of strong drink the words in the Latin tongue "Animis Opibusque Parati," which being interpreted means "always ready to take a drink"?

7. Having come unto a vendor of strong drink they did pay into his bosom a shekel of silver for a bottle bearing the three mystic signs of Benjamin. . . .

8. Now when they had retired into a back lot . . . they did imbibe . . . , whereupon their souls were disquieted within them . . . , for though it beareth the symbol of refreshing drink it hath the taste of the lightning of the land called Jersey.

9. And it came to pass that many of the servants of Benjamin . . . waxed exceedingly evil, taking unto themselves many pieces of silver and gold and would then cry aloud that robbers had entered into their places of business, carrying away strong drink of great value, but no man even to this day hath beheld the face of such a robber. . . .[168]

The State also eventually ceased its forays against Larry Gantt. Occasionally he provided subject matter, as in an editorial, "Larry and Liquids," in which the Spartanburg editor was upbraided at length for having dared to write about the impurities of Columbia water, a subject on which he was not considered an expert, never having touched it while at the capital—or so said *The State*.[169] After the hectic nineties, Gantt was less susceptible to attack since he was also assailing activities of the Tillmanites and said that all of their roseate promises had ended as "but ashes in the mouths of the people."[170] In 1899 "T. Liar," who had added the Spartanburg *Evening Star* to his *Piedmont Headlight*, sold his papers and retired to a farm near Inman. After several brief flings at a return to newspapering in the area, he finally

[168] *Ibid.*, December 1, 1899.
[169] *Ibid.*, February 17, 1896.
[170] Gantt in the *Observer*, June 27, 1901, as cited by Wallace, *History of S. C.*, III, 412.

left the state and in 1910 was comparatively well settled (for him) with the Whiteville (N. C.) *News,* where he no longer was within range of *The State.*[171]

Another favorite target, John L. M. Irby, also departed during this period of declining Tillmania. In 1900 at the age of forty-six, this reprobate "went to his reward." Editorially, *The State* did not relent at the time and expressed one of the central themes of Gonzales' political philosophy: "No qualities of person, however amicable, can compensate the people for faults which, deemed venial in the private citizen, they forbid to the public officer. . . . The measure of success is not what we get out of life but what we leave after it."[172]

A remarkable facet of Tillmania was the fact that out of all the harsh words, which have been only briefly sampled in this chapter, neither Tillman nor Gonzales had developed any personal antipathy toward each other. No physical or personal clash was ever threatened or discussed after the Blackville difficulty in 1888. The Gonzales brothers frequently said this in their paper and admitted that Ben was a man of ability and intelligence—as well as "an exceptionally able leader and finished student of human nature."[173]

Tillman reciprocated this respect. Even during the 1888 campaign he had confessed that N. G.'s reports were "scrupulously fair" and the best of any paper. In 1897 he advised a Reformer to read *The State* instead of the *Register* because the latter "is so unreliable that you can never tell where it stands, and while Gonzales is as bitter as gall, you can always tell just where to put your finger on him."[174] Years

171 Athens *Banner-Herald,* August 31, 1931; *The State,* December 7, 1898; March 2, 1899; January 28, 1902; June 14, 1915.

172 *The State,* December 10, 1900.

173 *Ibid.,* May 9, 1912.

174 *Yorkville Enquirer,* September 1, 1897, as cited in *The State,* September 3, 1897.

later Ben said he had never had any personal ill will toward any of the brothers, of whom he said N. G. was decidedly the most brilliant. "I always felt that those men were not altogether bad. They allowed their malignancy, however, to get the better of their judgment, and used to enjoy hating me. I certainly reciprocated in kind."[175]

As D. D. Wallace wisely says, it is impossible for a fair-minded man to be the unequivocating champion today of either side. Much in South Carolina government before 1890 needed change, and those in control stubbornly resisted any change while those who forced the changes did so with unscrupulous violence and without careful wisdom. In the bitterness of the partisanship that ensued, "prejudice was so rampant on both sides as to make a humiliating story." Acts and measures were accepted or rejected for no other reason than that they were associated with certain factional leaders.[176]

In the early twentieth century, as has been seen in the last few pages, some changes in this blind partisanship became manifest. Tillman became more conservative in his acting and even in his thinking. Gonzales used his brilliance more judiciously to appraise measures strictly on their merits and on the basis of principle. As he did so, his influence became greater than it had been in more unrestrained days when his flamboyant writing conveyed his greatest acidity. After about 1897 readers could know that his brilliant prose was a product of conscience that was more independent than it had been since 1890.

[175] B. R. Tillman to J. A. Banks, March 4, 1916; also, see Tillman to D. W. McLaurin, February 22, 1916, both in Simkins Notes.
[176] Wallace, *History of S. C.*, III, 366.

CHAPTER VII

The State *Achieves*
Success and Stability

DESPITE ITS CONCENTRATION ON THE TILLMAN FIGHT, THE Gonzales gazette did not devote all of its energy and attention to that subject. As Tillmanism became less revolutionary, *The State* relaxed its obsession and at the same time became more stabilized financially and more restrained editorially. By 1903 a new *State* was evolving.

Better times helped to dissipate the financial instability which had dogged *The State* in 1893 and 1894, and by 1896 it was making a small surplus for the first time and boasting that a Columbia paper could prosper without dependence on the state treasury or public officials.[1] Proof of prosperity was the fact that when it was three years old (1894) its circulation among state papers was second only to the ninety-year-old *News and Courier* and already was double that of the *Columbia Register.*[2] By June 1900 average daily circulation was 4,542. Such increases in subscription lists received healthy boosts from numerous circulation contests, free

[1] *The State*, November 8, 1896; February 18, 1897.
[2] *Rowell's American Newspaper Directory* (1894), pp. 713–14.

prizes, and sprightly advertisements which incessantly sought new readers.

Further evidence of the prosperity was the erection in 1897 of a three-story building to house the paper on Main Street near the State Capitol. In it, Ambrose Gonzales installed a new flat-bed press which printed up to 6,000 eight-page papers per hour. Also there was a relatively large job printing department.[3]

Events at the rival *Columbia Register* also helped the Gonzaleses. The two papers continued to conduct editorial, circulation, and advertising wars,[4] but the faltering "Till-rodgerster" lacked the resiliency necessary to survive such combat. Even Editor George Koester, like his predecessor Gantt, wearied of the *Register* and parted company with it. In June 1897 Charles Calvo himself abandoned it when he lost his mind and had to go to a Baltimore sanitarium.[5] In January 1898 the paper was sold at auction to W. A. Hatfield of New York. *The State* concluded its news story of the transaction, "'Here endeth the first lesson.'" Within a month, the new owner tried unsuccessfully to sell his paper to Gonzales, even threatening that a million dollars of Northern capital would be used to bolster the *Register*. By July the new owner had converted the limping organ into an afternoon paper and was paying *The State* to print it for him. On December 3, 1898, the 23-year-old *Register* published its last issue when Northern men withdrew their support. *The State* thus never had to buy out this competitor which was estimated to have lost $110,000 during the 1890s.[6]

---

[3] *The State*, December 23, 1897; August Kohn to J. C. Hemphill, July 6, 1901, in Kohn Papers. This remained the home of *The State* until 1955.

[4] August Kohn to J. C. Hemphill, November 3, 1896, in Hemphill Papers.

[5] August Kohn to "My dear Walter," June 17, 1897, in Letterbook, 1897–1898, of Kohn Papers.

[6] *The State*, December 14, 24, 1897; January 15, 1898; December 6, 1898; February 17, 1901; C. A. Calvo, Jr., to R. R. Hemphill, July 6, 1903, in Hemphill Papers. The latter was written after Calvo had mental problems.

Other papers were also collapsing. In 1897 the Charleston *Sun* was eclipsed when it was merged with the Charleston *Critic,* which, according to N. G., was aptly named since it would be "critical high and low, horizontally, perpendicularly, latitudinally and longitudinally, of everything in the heavens above, the earth beneath and the waters under the earth." Even so, he estimated that such "a carboy acid" would be good for the "local molases-spreading [*sic*] of the other Charleston papers."[7]

In Columbia the Gonzales brothers never had a newspaper monopoly. In 1895 the Columbia *Evening News,* heir to the old *Journal,* was launched with James Henry Rice, Jr., as editor. In 1897 its end came, but it was replaced by a new Columbia *Evening Record* edited by George R. Koester, who had just departed from the *Register* with a few final salvoes at Calvo.[8]

In 1901 *The State* received new financial nourishment from what it had heretofore treated as a tainted source: public printing. State contracts for this lucrative work had always been granted not to printing establishments but to individuals who were then responsible for getting the job done. Since 1892 Tillmanite Charles A. Calvo, Jr., had been public printer for the state and naturally had done the work with the equipment of his *Register.* When he lost his mind in 1897, some state politicos connived to give the contract to J. T. Parks, a reporter for the *Register,* and thereby hold the editorial support of that paper and its Northern owners.[9] At the time, N. G. Gonzales opposed Ambrose Gonzales' efforts to get the state printing contract since his paper had become a lukewarm supporter of Governor Ellerbe and he feared it would be accused of having been "bought." The bid

[7] *The State,* June 12, 1897.
[8] *Ibid.,* January 25, 1895; March 15, 19, April 28, 1897.
[9] August Kohn to J. C. Hemphill, January 26, 1898, in Hemphill Papers.

finally went to C. B. Calvo, son of C. A. Calvo, Jr., who then split the printing job with the *State* office since his relations with his father's old paper were "the reverse of cordial." Those whom Kohn called "the boys" found technical irregularities in his election, however, and succeeded in nullifying Calvo's contract and in giving it to J. T. Parks for the remainder of that session. *The State* expressed no regrets, however, since all of the maneuvers and accompanying publicity had facilitated passage of a new printing law which provided for letting contracts thereafter to the lowest bidder. In 1900 the paper won the first of many state printing contracts. Actually, since the work was too big for one plant to handle efficiently, The State Company and the R. L. Bryan Company made joint bids and then subdivided the work between them.[10]

Strength which stabilized *The State* also came from its spreading influence and fame. As August Kohn said, the country papers always seemed to be throwing bouquets at *The State*,[11] and every year at February 18, scores of papers always joined in extravagant birthday felicitations to the Columbia paper. N. G.'s literary polemics seemed to be popular, and by 1900 his paper was frequently quoted in New York, Atlanta, and other distant cities. In 1901 the Springfield (Mass.) *Republican* said it was "one of the few provincial papers in the country that possess an individual quality and ability distinguishing it as far as it can be seen."[12]

Although a fire-eater in many of his pungent pieces, N. G. wrote calmly and carefully as well as vigorously. His prose flowed with incredible speed. One observer told of seeing

[10] The lengthy efforts to get state printing can be traced in *The State,* December 11, 14, 16, 1897; January 14, 28, 29, 1898; February 17, 1898; May 10, 11, 1901; October 14, 15, 1905. On the Bryan firm, which claims to have the oldest bookstore in the South, see *ibid.,* March 3, 1915.

[11] August Kohn to J. C. Hemphill, May 17, 1901, in Kohn Papers.

[12] Cited in *The State,* February 25, 1901.

him enter his office at midnight, pick up a message of the governor, read it, and then before the paper went to press write a three-column review and analysis which cogently touched every point of it.[13] Often editorials appeared in the morning paper commenting on news stories which did not "break" until after midnight. In his early days, he wrote in longhand at a big table in the old office; later, his editorials were dictated to his stenographer, Robert Lathan (who later won a Pulitzer Prize for editorial writing). Underlying these outpourings were much careful study and research which almost wore out the *Encyclopedia Britannica* in his office.[14]

Many times the editor gave his own conception of his own acidity. While the Springfield *Republican* said that he was "the best force for intelligent progress in the state," it also lamented his faults of hot temperament which made him use a bitterness that blistered.[15] Aware of this strong style, he felt it was a useful—but nevertheless unpleasant—weapon of his arsenal. In the second year of his editorship, he had admitted that perhaps his language was too strong or even personal, "but it must be pleaded in extenuation that it [the paper] has had very strong convictions, an unruly tendency to frankness, a plain political course, . . . and a strong disposition to hit every hostile head as it showed itself." Indeed, with so much provocation, he said that at times he marveled at his own moderation.[16] Ten years later

13 E. H. Aull, "Newspapermen I Have Known Since I Have Been President of the Association," in S. C. State Press Association *Proceedings* (1910), p. 57.
14 Reminiscences of Howard A. Banks (of the staff) in *Charlotte Observer*, January 25, 1902.
15 Clipping of Springfield *Republican*, n.d., in scrapbooks of the N. G. Gonzales murder and the Tillman trial, in South Caroliniana Library. There are three of these unnumbered volumes, containing clippings from scores of newspapers. Hereinafter they will be referred to as Gonzales Scrapbooks.
16 *The State*, December 26, 1892.

he still lamented that "public wrongs cannot be righted and abuses removed without much effort and vigorous language"; nevertheless, he again confessed that, in the eyes of many, he had perhaps spoken with greater vigor than circumstances had required and thus offended some, but he felt that he should speak as duty demanded.[17] He once told Professor R. Means Davis of the University of South Carolina that he had sought to run a Davis letter as an editorial but had to add a few lines since "It was too temperate and judicial . . . to pass as my own production. . . ."[18]

W. W. Ball, longtime fixture in South Carolina journalism, judged that others were more brilliant and original but less effective because "N. G. G." "genuinely believed that a newspaperman's mission is to elevate the people . . . and to do that he usefully employed his newspaper. . . . He was ambitious and he had his share of egotism but to make himself a conspicuous success he *chose* the improvement of the people as the way."[19] Gonzales said somewhat the same thing when in 1901 he described the purpose of the paper to be to "strive to serve the broader and greater interests of the public and only through these to advance the personal interest of its owners."[20] N. G. G. believed that in a democracy an editor was as much a public official and servant as an elected officer—with many of the same responsibilities to his constituents for good and enlightened government. Because of that concept, this otherwise timid person could in language vehement and vivid "roast" those whom he considered dangerous to the public welfare. Contrary to the idea of many, he never really enjoyed this. Some of his associates insisted that such writing to him was actually a pain-

[17] *Ibid.*, January 16, 1901.
[18] N. G. Gonzales to R. Means Davis, May 9, 1894, in Davis Manuscripts.
[19] W. W. Ball, Diary, III, 191, in Ball Papers.
[20] *The State*, February 17, 1901.

ful, onerous duty that was one of the unpleasant responsibilities of an honest editor of deep convictions.[21]

The president of The State Company, Ambrose Gonzales,
may have been the best writer of the family, and certainly
showed marked similarities to his grandfather, William Elliott. Sometimes he contributed something, but "Billy Ball"
confided to his diary that for such work "Mr. Ambrose" was
"too emotional and impulsive by far." But apparently Ambrose frequently nudged the younger but fiery brother whom
he still called "Nanno." In later years he criticized Ball's
editorial work, writing, "An editor's mind should be like a
hawk on the wing,—hovering here, striking there, and quest-
ing everywhere, and his interests should be limited only by
the far horizon."[22] Maybe it was his experience with N. G. G.
that caused him to warn Ball to avoid gloom:

Abate, if you can, your predisposition to gloom. There are pessi-
mists on every street corner, loaded to the gunwales with dire
forebodings, who will cheerfully spin you funereal yarns and
weave you a tale of woe, but at a time like this, the only helpful
note is the hopeful one, and The State, always helpful, *must be*
hopeful.[23]

Although N. G. Gonzales is best remembered for his part
in weakening and dividing the Tillman forces, he was perhaps even more significant for various less flamboyant concerns. A study of his newspaper is a study of an evolving
South Carolina entering the twentieth century while merg-

[21] *Ibid.*, April 5, 1901. This opinion has been confirmed by all of the
acquaintances of N. G. with whom the writer has talked, and also by printed
reminiscences of others. He rarely discussed or showed his vitriolic pieces to
others before they were published—hardly the trait of an egotist who took
much glee in such "roasting"—which was the conception some of his antago-
nists had of him.

[22] A. E. Gonzales to W. W. Ball, June 1, 1922, in Ball Papers.

[23] *Ibid.*

ing Bourbonism and Tillman-Reformism. The two really never coalesced, but South Carolina has benefited from its ability to preserve some of the Bourbons' concern for "style," *noblesse oblige,* and good manners along with the flexibility of those who sought changes, reforms, and greater democracy. The Gonzales brothers appeared able to make this adjustment, or synthesis, since their personalities seemed always to have been a combination of respect for tradition and a willingness to accept innovations. The new era had some of the flavor of the contemporary Progressivism usually associated with Bob La Follette, Theodore Roosevelt, and Woodrow Wilson—but it was always Progressivism, South Carolina style.

When working for the *News and Courier,* N. G. Gonzales had launched crusades in behalf of his adopted town, and when he controlled his own paper there, he redoubled his efforts. In season and out of season, he hammered away on the idea of a great future for Columbia. Within four months after the paper was born, it beat the drums loudly to stress the centennial celebration of the city. When the paper moved into its new building in 1897, it put out a special issue giving a full survey of the city and its assets. By 1900 it was regularly reporting plans for great enterprises; or as the editor quipped; "This is survey time for Columbia, the proceedings covering two railway routes and a dam site besides."[24] Enormous amounts of publicity were given even to vague rumors of new businesses, and by 1899 both the *News and Courier* and the Greenwood *Index* were moved to attribute the phenomenal recent growth of Columbia to *The State.*[25] In 1902 the New York *Sun* reported on Columbia at length, averring:

[24] *The State,* April 7, 1900.
[25] *Ibid.,* August 4, 1899.

It is only fair to repeat the universal opinion expressed here [Columbia] that one of the great factors in Columbia's progress has been the influence of The State, taking upon itself as it has from the first, labors which elsewhere often fall to chambers of commerce and boards of trade, and working incessantly and wisely toward the promotion of Columbia's best interests. In all the country there is not to be found a more striking instance of what a good newspaper can do toward the making of a town. . . .[26]

Another crusade that was pursued by the editor with all the fervor of an evangelist was the advocation of industrialization. Unlike many New South editors who constantly clamored for new industry, Gonzales recognized that there were problems inherent in such change, sociological as well as economic. Financiers who came to Columbia in their private cars and on chartered trains received a warm welcome, both editorially and personally, from the Gonzales brothers. In his efforts to woo such builders, Tillmania still cropped up in the editorials, for the editor constantly warned that the political turbulence of the state was not conducive to economic stability because "the belief prevails in the North that South Carolina is in the hands of the Socialists and therefore a dangerous place for investment."[27] The paper also warned the legislature against passing laws which would "tamper" with the creations of capital. The editor underscored and supported the idea of community cooperative undertakings to raise local capital for new mills.

Although in mid-1895 the paper was pursuing "Columbia's fifth cotton mill—the fourth of this year!" the editor noted the danger of such lack of diversification and frequently

[26] New York *Sun,* November 30, 1902. Both N. G. and A. E. Gonzales were among the twenty-three charter members of the Commercial Club, organized to boost Columbia and promote its industrial possibilities; see *The State,* December 3, 1895.
[27] *The State,* April 14, 1895. Also, see *ibid.,* January 25, 1893; October 5, 1894; and November 29, 1892.

tried in vain to stir Columbians to seek furniture factories.[28] Gonzales was also farseeing enough to know that the new mills were not a panacea for all troubles nor devoid of brand new problems. Like his grandfather, he bitterly opposed tariffs, arguing that "without this artificial protection they [cotton mills] would move to the point of cheapest production, which is the South."[29] Another problem he faced was that of Negro labor in the mills, and on this he took a reactionary stand. Contending that the South needed a white "mechanic class," he warned that it would be impossible for whites to work in the mills if Negroes were also hired, as "they cannot live down to the level of negro living which will be the standard and will fix the standard of wages."[30] It never seemed to occur to this refugee from Oak Lawn that the Negroes' standard might or should be raised.

Along with endorsement of industry went encouragement of new means of transportation, and on this perennial subject the enthusiasm of the paper outran its judgment. Railroads seemed to be springing up monthly, with many more planned and publicized. Most of them had ambitious names —including "Chicago," "Ohio," or "Memphis" in the designation of lines that never extended beyond two South Carolina counties. If one road was good, then to the enthusiasts of that age two or three seemed better; hence *The State* blessed as wise the duplication of roads from Columbia to Charleston, Charlotte, Savannah, Greenville, or Spartanburg. (For example, there were two rail routes to Spartanburg, but the paper later sought a third.) The Gonzales brothers went along enthusiastically on the specials that made the first run over new lines, and the joy and optimism of their reports knew no bounds. By 1902 they were able to note with pride

[28] *Ibid.*, April 30, 1895.
[29] *Ibid.*, June 15, 1894.
[30] *Ibid.*, June 14, 1897; also, *ibid.*, June 19, 1897.

that forty-four passenger trains used the new Union Station—not even including the trains of the Seaboard.[31]

N. G. Gonzales also publicized another transportation craze which he had become enamored of as a *News and Courier* reporter: riverboats. Immodestly he claimed to have first imported the idea to Columbia; the riverboats were later boosted even more optimistically by his brother Ambrose.[32] The idea of improving the Congaree and operating steamers to Columbia from a deep water port (Georgetown) was a complement to the industrial theme since it was hoped that such a line would lower rail freight rates, thus making Columbia an inviting locale for industries.

Even while espousing the new industrial era, Gonzales acknowledged that employer-employee relations needed to be faced wisely. In this area, he showed himself more liberal and humane (by 1890 standards) than the Bourbon factory masters of the New South. Different from many editors of the time, he defended labor unions and said that each should be judged on its own merits. *The State* policy was to oppose "tyrannies of which labor unions are capable, but we shall not be guilty of the injustice of opposing such organizations merely because they can be made instruments of wrong."[33] Columbia typographical unions in turn upheld N. G. G. and his fairness, pointing to harmonious working conditions in *The State* plant, which was always a union shop. In labor strife in Columbia factories the paper sought to judge the issues in each case; and the new mill owners, often personal friends of the Gonzales brothers, became righteously indignant with the paper for not condemning all strikes and union activities *per se*. In 1901, for example, N. G. Gonzales worked actively with a union leader to help avert a serious

[31] *Ibid.*, February 10, 1902.
[32] *Ibid.*, December 21, 1895.
[33] *Ibid.*, January 23, 1901.

strike only to have the intransigent owners instigate a lock-
out followed by discrimination against union members.
Using documentary evidence, the paper blasted the owners
for all it was worth and condemned their stubbornness,
broken promises, and duplicity.[34] That same year the editor
just as definitely sided against a union in local railway shops
because the workers had resorted to violence.[35] For the same
reason, the paper always commended John Mitchell, president of the United Mine Workers, a group which successfully avoided violent acts in an era of much strife. In the
famed Pullman strike of 1894, it called a plague on both
houses for "unwarranted aggression." Said *The State:* "But
the best remedy of all, and the only one which can be permanent, is such a reform of the laws as will check monopoly,
distribute more fairly the burdens of taxation and decen-
tralize the money power. We need less government, not more;
equity, not force."[36]

On the matter of labor legislation, *The State* was not consistent. Always it opposed state laws to compel reduction of
the hours of work in cotton mills because such laws "did not
really help the factory operatives . . . and will retard the
progress and development of the State." At the time, most
workers were in mills sixty-six hours a week. The editor
warned that the advantages that the South had in attracting
industry from the North were being rapidly offset by tech-
nological improvements and that such legislation would ruin
the two remaining advantages of the South: namely, longer
working hours, which he justified because of a milder climate;
and lower wages, which he justified by the cheapness of living costs in the South.[37]

[34] *Ibid.,* August 30, September 2–6, 1901.
[35] *Ibid.,* June 25, 1901.
[36] *Ibid.,* July 10, 1894; also, July 7, 1894, and October 1, 1900.
[37] *Ibid.,* January 26, 1897.

In direct contrast with this attitude was the liberal and forthright stand which the paper took on child labor legislation. Here it welcomed state statutes and saw nothing socialistic about such controls—as it did about hours (and, later, wages) laws. The thorny path of child labor legislation had begun in South Carolina in 1884. Strategy of the mill owners in opposition was to tie compulsory school attendance laws (which had little chance to pass) to child labor laws, saying that the latter would not then be necessary since the children would be at school anyway. In such efforts, the *News and Courier* supported the owners against "the agitators."[38] Until a child labor law was again rejected in 1900, Gonzales stayed quiet, but on January 29, 1900, appeared the first of scores of editorials on the subject. It was not timid.

The State had said nothing, according to the editor (who had no children), because the cotton mill owners themselves had promised that they were going to abandon the use of child labor as soon as they could get their competitors in North Carolina to promise to do likewise. *The State* said the public had been hoodwinked by dilatory owners who should be compelled to do what apparently they would not do themselves. Pulling aside the curtain which had concealed the wretched conditions under which ten-year-old children worked sixty-six hours a week in cotton mills, the editor said: "The joyousness of childhood is not theirs; its freedom they do not know; they are dwarfed in mind, stunted in soul." To its friends and to the lobbyists for the industry, *The State* thundered: "We are its friends while it keeps its place. But its place is not in the legislative body making laws for South Carolina or defeating them. . . . Corporations must be the servants of the people, not their masters." The editor probably did not add to their joy with the following:

[38] *News and Courier*, January 27, 1900. See Elizabeth H. Davidson, *Child Labor Legislation in the Southern Textile States* (Chapel Hill: University of North Carolina Press, 1939), pp. 89–91.

Let us have done with the pretense that cotton manufacturing here is an infant industry, too tender to be touched. . . . For more than ten years every proposal to change by legislation any of the conditions of this industry has been met by appeals for more time. . . .

An industry . . . does not need coddling at the expense of degrading our citizenship when it is strong enough to control both senate and house. . . . It is not weak when it controls a large part of the press . . . to prevent legislation for humanity. Rather it is too strong in ways that it should not be.[39]

Mill owners and the *News and Courier* stormed when the South Carolina Federation of Labor endorsed a child labor law under consideration. Even though such endorsement was the kiss of death, *The State* blessed the Federation. It also prophesied that the mills would not be ruined without their cheap child workers; but even if they were injured, it would be "infinitely better to forego a small percentage of profit than to allow tens of thousands of white children . . . to be dwarfed in mind and body."[40]

In this fight, Gonzales frequently tangled with the *Manufacturers' Record,* constant champion of Southern industry. In 1902 he was busy exposing what he interpreted as the twisted arguments and biased reasoning of such mill owners as James L. Orr, Jr., Ellison Smythe, John H. Montgomery, John B. Cleveland, and Lewis W. Parker. When a child labor law failed by two votes, N. G. Gonzales said that the legislature had been too impressed "by the claptrap of cotton mill attorneys and stockholders about the violation of personal and parental rights. Parental rights! The parent is the guardian of the child, not its owner."[41] N. G. G. noted that the state had a statute for the prevention of cruelty to animals but not

[39] *The State,* January 29, 1900.
[40] *Ibid.,* September 4, 1900; Davidson, *Child Labor Legislation,* p. 92, citing *News and Courier,* January 21, 22, 1901.
[41] *The State,* January 9, 1902.

for children. Mrs. Irene Ashby-Macfadyen, a leading spirit in the fight and a representative of the Federation of Labor, said N. G. Gonzales "would do more than any man in the state to bring success to the cause."[42] Others recognized him as the most zealous advocate of child labor legislation, and certainly none could have been more persistent than he was in the uphill fight.[43]

On the subject of education, the Gonzales paper was equally tireless. Hardly an issue appeared without one of its journalistic weapons in this campaign: a hard-hitting editorial, an exhaustive news story, or a long feature article. They obviously were planted with a purpose of inciting action. Many were designed to stir the conscience, others to stir pride. No other single issue received so much "free advertising." For legislative action, the chief goal was a compulsory attendance law, just as it was with W. E. Gonzales later.

Among the colleges, N. G. showed no partiality unless it was to South Carolina College. He even endorsed Ben Tillman's favorite, the new Clemson, and called on the state to eliminate causes of weaknesses and to make it more effective in fulfilling its agricultural and mechanical goals. He also defended the state colleges against the unfriendliness of certain narrow sectarians and insisted that, although not under denominational influence, state schools were nevertheless under Christian influence.[44]

In setting policy toward the racial problem—"the central theme" in Southern history and an obsession in South Carolina history—Gonzales was tugged in several directions. His

[42] Davidson, *Child Labor Legislation,* p. 99, quoting Mrs. Macfadyen to Samuel Gompers, n.d.

[43] *Ibid.,* p. 100.

[44] Summarized in *The State,* September 28, 1899. In his paper, November 13, 1899, Gonzales pointed out that the leading critic, editor of *The Baptist,* entrusted the education of his children to a state college which he had said was not Christian. (If he meant *Baptist Courier,* Gonzales gave the wrong title.)

thinking was decidedly colored by his plantation and family background. Furthermore, like most people of his generation in South Carolina, his distrust and disgust had been aroused by the excesses of Reconstruction which he had witnessed. Offsetting these conservative influences were his sense of justice, his faith in education, and his determination that the law be impartial and respected. In brief, his policy became one of justice, but not equality, for the Negroes.

His views on the subject sound today quite reactionary, and they were; only the environment and customs of the 1890s can be offered in extenuation. For example, when Queen Liliuokalani of Hawaii was "pushed aside by civilization" in 1893 and a government of "Americans" was established, he said the change was "for the benefit of humanity, however selfish or unjust the motives influencing it. The white race is to have dominion of the world, for the world's good." He predicted that within a century white men would be the only rulers on the globe.[45] Blaming much of the retardation of the South on the backwardness of the Negroes, Gonzales wrote more strongly for exporting them than for improving them. Forgetting his state rights phobia (as Southerners are wont to do when convenience dictates), he advocated an appropriation by the federal government for Negro emigration, thereby "removing an issue which offers no sound solution" and thus "giving the South a homogeneous population and making it the garden spot of the country." He did not worry about the destination of the Negroes—"Massachusetts or Africa or somewhere else where they can attain their best racial development"—but he benignly added, "A kindly and liberal feeling toward the negro is not incompatible with a desire, for mutual benefit, to bid him bon voyage!" The same year, he was urging a "broader spirit of toleration" as a means of

45 *The State*, November 13, 1893.

encouraging newcomers to the state![46] This last-named suggestion always complemented his scheme for Negro emigration: that white immigrants should be found and encouraged to come to South Carolina to make it a "garden spot of the country," a dream that N. G. Gonzales had nourished in his youth and which he had inherited from both William Elliott and General A. J. Gonzales.

As has been noted, N. G. hoped that public opinion would force mill owners "to leave negro labor alone and import white labor from other States when South Carolina's supply is exhausted. . . . The greatest industrial need of this state is a white majority. . . ."[47] To his generation, Gonzales' suggestion perhaps did not seem ungenerous, since others, like him, were convinced "that the negro laborer in the Southern States can . . . earn more money in proportion to his necessary expenses of living, than can the peasant of any other country on the face of the earth."[48] And it never occurred to many of that generation, apparently, that God or the Negro had any interest in the latter's being anything other than a peasant.

In a journalistic habit not yet abandoned in the South, *The State* gave much attention to the news of racial unpleasantness in the North. On these occasions, it preached to Yankee papers that racial tension and feeling was not a sectional monopoly. On the other hand, *The State* never welcomed advice from fellow sufferers on the outside: "The race question cannot be settled by theorists. It must be worked out by ourselves, with judgment, foresight, and charity."[49] Actually, the editor did not worry much about the effect of

[46] *Ibid.*, March 20, October 18, 1895.

[47] *Ibid.*, January 13, 1900. In 1900 South Carolina had 557,807 whites and 782,321 blacks (58.4 percent).

[48] *Ibid.*, August 23, 1891.

[49] *Ibid.*, March 31, 1891. Of course, it was to be worked out to a predetermined solution.

outsiders. "The southern white man intends that the negro shall 'keep his place.' . . . As long as unmolested by ignorant agitators the darkey was, and is and will be content to 'keep his place.' "[50]

Strangely enough, Gonzales did not fear the Negro as a political influence. Constantly he berated Tillman for using the threat of "Negro rule." The fear of a white schism in a one-party state made many Democrats "slaves of our former slaves" because "we dare not indulge our consciences, lest the whites should divide." This belief, said Gonzales, did not mean that he was abandoning white supremacy but that he was merely taking issue with such people as the editor of the *Greenville News* who would vote for a Democratic scoundrel in preference to a non-Democratic saint."[51] Always A. B. Williams' paper had feared that too strenuous opposition to Tillman would so split the whites as to restore "Negro rule." Hence, according to Gonzales, the *News* kept "its particular make of Pandora's box on hand, and whenever there are indications of revolt against outrages committed by what it in courtesy styles the 'Democratic organization,' our friend opens its box, and the horrid figure of a Jack with a ballot in his hands jumps up to affright the naughty Caucasian rebel."[52]

On the subject of Negro education, N. G. also suffered from a remarkable case of schizophrenia. Claiming that the Negro had not yet earned the right to an education paid for by the white man, nevertheless the editor felt that such an expense was in the interest of the white people. Ante-bellum Negroes had been effectively controlled by the system of slavery, said the editor, but now Negroes could be reached

---

[50] *Ibid.*, October 27, 1901.

[51] *Ibid.*, November 9, 1893. While still a reporter, he had proved his partisanship was not blind, saying that efforts to do anything other than putting "capable and honest men in office" would be a betrayal of the party's sole mission. N. G. G. to R. M. Davis, March 30, 1888, in Davis Papers.

[52] *Ibid.*, January 20, 1892.

only through their minds. Observing that the worst Negro criminals were always uneducated, *The State* said that South Carolina could advance only in relation to the capacity of all of its people. Still, the editor's plan of education would hardly have altered drastically the Negro's economic status, for he called for only one school in each county where town Negroes could be taught trades by local "colored workmen of average capacity"; and as for those on the farms—the peasants— "What more than the 'three R's' does the average country negro need to know?"[53]

In contrast, on the more liberal side was an N. G. Gonzales who opposed Jim Crow laws as "cheap demagogy [sic] at the expense of the convenient butt, the negro." Prompted by one law which applied segregation to railroad coaches and which had been passed by a Tillmanite legislature, *The State* rose enough above its racial prejudice to say, "The negroes who pay for passage in first-class coaches are almost invariably of the better class, quiet, orderly, cleanly. There are exceptions, as there are among white men, but not enough to create a real disturbance."[54] On another occasion, this enigmatic editor pleaded for justice for a Negro militia company, "If we are to justify our supremacy and prove our civilization we must not have one code of equity for the helpless negro and another for the white man who can retaliate and punish."[55]

On one aspect of racial problems, however, there was never any question where N. G. Gonzales stood: his steadfast opposition to lynching. In that day an unequivocating denunciation of "Judge Lynch" was a stand that took boldness; many "respectable" Southerners condoned such vicious vengeance

---

[53] *Ibid.*, February 20, 1898.

[54] *Ibid.*, December 13, 1894. This belated effort to achieve legal segregation and the opposition to it is treated in C. Vann Woodward, *Strange Career of Jim Crow* (New York: Oxford University Press, 1955; 1966).

[55] *The State*, September 8, 1900.

for certain crimes. With such sanction, eighty-five successful "lynching bees" took place in South Carolina from 1889 to 1903.[56] Enraged over "the unmentionable crime" (rape) and stimulated by race hatred, Southerners given to violence pursued a lawless road which, if unchecked, could have led to anarchy.

The paramount reason behind Gonzales' strong and not-always-popular stand was his strong detestation of lawlessness. He was deeply convinced that men taking the law into their own hands—regardless of how well justified they considered their actions—tore down respect for law and the courts and could lead only to chaos. He also recognized that some of the alleged "attacks" were not rape at all but rather acts of "voluntary depravity" which the "victim" "covered up or condoned by murder."[57] A third factor behind his position was the knowledge that aroused mobs could, and did, make mistakes: "No mob is reasonable. Once admit the righteousness of mob judgments and we give up the case of the law."[58] And last but not least, he observed that both the lynchers and those who sanctioned their deeds had adopted "an attitude which is unworthy of a moral newspaper and a moral man."[59]

[56] Monroe N. Work, ed., *Negro Year Book* (1925–26), pp. 400–401. Of those lynched, three were white. From *ibid.* (1937–38), p. 156: During the period 1891–1903, the score for the whole United States was 502 whites and 1,406 Negroes lynched. According to the *World Almanac* (1951), p. 438, there were 156 Negroes and 4 whites lynched in South Carolina during 1882–1949; in contrast, only three persons (all Negroes) were lynched in the United States in 1949. According to Thomas D. Clark (*Southern Country Editor*, p. 227), there were over 2,500 "lynching bees" in the South during 1885–1903, but apparently he included many in which the victims survived.

[57] *The State*, March 2, 1896. In this issue, Gonzales discussed a miscarriage of justice in which he had all but proved that such was the case. A close associate of his, who asks not to be quoted, has told the writer of N. G.'s conversations in which he deplored certain events that were not "rape" until the act was discovered or regretted.

[58] *Ibid.*, June 4, 1894.

[59] *Ibid.*, August 8, 1901. Even justice-supporting Dawson of the *News and Courier* had sanctioned lynching for one crime, feeling that swift retaliation

A less admirable explanation of Gonzales' opposition to lynching was that Tillman at times seemed to favor it. As governor, Tillman made extreme statements in regard to his creed of unvarnished white supremacy. He constantly talked of better law enforcement and even sought a law which would give him power to remove sheriffs who failed to protect prisoners from mobs—a request that failed because his opponents did not want to give him any more power. On the other hand, "Pitchfork Ben" put white supremacy above strict law enforcement. During his first administration, his private secretary wrote, "Governor Tillman directs me to say that he thinks any man, of any color, should be lynched who commits a criminal assault on a virtuous woman of any color."[60] The following year, he again expressed the traditional attitude of many Carolinians: "There is only one crime that warrants lynching, and Governor as I am, I would lead a mob to lynch the negro who ravishes the white woman."[61] In a campaign speech in 1892, he had said practically the same thing.[62] Such statements made Tillman fine prey for Gonzales.

The two personalities clashed in 1893 over a Negro, John Peterson. This man was suspected of the crime of rape and Tillman ordered his captors to carry him to the town of Denmark, where the crime had occurred. *The State* warned that he was sent without proper guard and would probably be lynched. The prophecy came true. The headline then in *The State* read, "AN INNOCENT MAN LYNCHED | Gov. Tillman an Accessory Before the Fact," and an editorial bluntly indicted the governor for murder. Ebbie Watson's verbatim report of the hearing proved there was at least a

was the most effective means of preventing other violations. Logan, "Dawson," p. 320.

[60] D. H. Tompkins to William J. McPherson, July 1, 1892, in Simkins Notes.

[61] *News and Courier*, April 27, 1893.

[62] *The State*, June 8, 1892.

reasonable doubt of Peterson's guilt, if not a strong likelihood that he was innocent. Gonzales outdid himself for several days as he bitterly censured both Tillman and the mob. A resentful group of five hundred people promptly held a mass meeting at Denmark and passed a resolution condemning the editor and commending the lynchers. According to these resolutions, Gonzales had "sought to besmirch and befoul the people of this community, and . . . to arouse the passions of the negro race against the white people and incite the negro men to attack and rape white women to avenge the punishment of John Peterson." N. G. was further accused of acting only to vent his hostility against Tillman, and his editorial ire was condemned as "unworthy of a pure journalist and emanating from the heart of one blacker than the one assaulting Miss Baxter and deserving the same fate as John Peterson."[63] At the same time, a similar mass meeting in Barnwell condemned Gonzales and hanged him in effigy.[64] Even though the Denmark crowd urged all to "hold aloof from one so destitute of virtue and truth as N. G. Gonzales," his reply in an editorial, "Moral Murderousness," reaffirmed his judgment: "To the editor of The State as a man this day is the proudest of his life; as a citizen it is the most humiliating."[65]

In 1897, after an Orangeburg mob had lynched a Negro suspected of burning a barn, Gonzales put his theme in question form: "Property, then, in the enlightened judgment of these barbarians, is more sacred than life. . . . How can lawlessness rebuke lawlessness, or crime discourage crime?"[66] Two days later, *The State* recorded another bloody lynching, this time at Sumter: "Human nature threw off all the trammels of civilization . . . yesterday, and primitive passions wrought primitive justice. . . . It was gruesome enough to

[63] Columbia *Weekly Register,* May 2, 1893.
[64] *The State,* May 2, 1893; April 2, 1902.
[65] *Ibid.,* May 2, 1893. On the whole affair, see *ibid.,* April 24–May 2, 1893.
[66] *Ibid.,* January 7, 1897.

last it [Sumter] a long time. . . . It was a shameful deed, for which the people of Sumter will blush when they come to their second thought." Some of them did not blush, however, but instead held a mass meeting to condemn the editor of *The State*.[67]

The strategy of *The State* involved not only such editorial statements but also lengthy news stories which spared none of the repulsive and sickening details of the affairs. Presumably readers were to be horrified and ashamed by knowing the bestiality of humans, and even if the mobs did not read *The State,* the editor could hope his readers might support better law enforcement and less lax juries. He also warned Negro leaders that their race could do much to improve public sentiment and influence white juries by showing that Negroes were as actively opposed to the "unspeakable" crime that provoked lynching as were the whites themselves.

N. G. G.'s attitude toward lynching was but one facet of his near obsession that led to many editorial crusades: his concern for the elimination of lawlessness and violence in general. He condemned a state which did occasionally hang a white man but never for their most frequent offense: "shooting down their enemies 'on sight' in alleged defense." The trouble with the state, he said, was a "perverted sentiment against hanging men who kill in hot blood. . . . We need a quickening of the public conscience which will make the juries consider the dead as sympathetically as the living."[68] The problem of juries he pinpointed over and over again, stressing that no basic change was needed in the state judiciary system, simply required an awakening of the citizens (i.e., the jurors) to a sense of their responsibilities. Noting how many exemptions to jury duty were permitted, he insisted

[67] *Ibid.*, January 9, 10, 1897.
[68] *Ibid.*, October 8, 1892.

that men of "above average intelligence" were needed to handle matters of life and death: "The ignorant and the shiftless, the men to whom a juror's per diem is an attraction, do not ask to be excused. That is one reason for bad verdicts."[69]

Another crusade which N. G. continued from his *News and Courier* days was that to abolish the convict-lease system of the state penitentiary. Since Reconstruction, this system had been a blight on the humanity of South Carolina and other states. Under it, state convicts were rented out to greedy and sometimes cruel lessors to be worked and abused until they served out their sentences—or died, as a shocking number did. Those who rented the convicts were responsible for their charges whom they got so cheaply, but many felt little concern about their health or their treatment. Blood-curdling and nauseating exposures of mistreatment were published to arouse the public conscience against this crime of inhumanity. By 1901 the legislators were moved to prohibit leasing convicts out for farming work but they authorized leasing them to counties for work on highways; after new revelations, Gonzales was soon urging outlawing the system entirely.[70]

In the matter of political reforms not peculiar to South Carolina, N. G. Gonzales often was quite progressive and even endorsed some reforms demanded by the Populists. Although the Australian ballot was not adopted for general elections in South Carolina until nearly a half century after his death, N. G. G. called for this voting tool from the first year of his paper. Likewise revolutionary was his advocacy

[69] *Ibid.*, July 29, 1891. Many editorials appeared on this subject; a good summary is January 7, 1897.

[70] In South Carolina, prisoners were used primarily in phosphate mining, railroad construction, and farming. On this system, see Fletcher M. Green, "Some Aspects of the Convict Lease System in the Southern States"; also, George B. Tindall, "Crime and Convict Leasing," chap. 13 in *South Carolina Negroes*.

of women's suffrage in 1895.[71] The editor was wary, however, of direct election of U.S. senators as a threat to state rights "in these times [1892] when centralization and communism go hand in hand."[72] Gonzales also embraced the unceasing campaign for reform of the civil service, but he shied away from pensions for government employees because "persons who for any length of time feed upon public pap, soon become the most improvident of wage earners. The certainty of income begets a satisfaction which frequently degenerates into shiftlessness."[73] Gonzales also supported more home rule in a state dominated by power centralized in the legislature, noting that much time was wasted with basically local affairs:

As the case stands, if a stray steer jumps into Representative Blank's cabbage patch the whole State is called upon to consider an amendment to the fence law; and if Senator Dash's cousin loses a hog suit which he ought to have won, the legislature is asked to amend the jury law.[74]

In national political affairs, *The State* generated much less heat than it did about South Carolina problems. When Grover Cleveland ran for president in 1892, the editorials of the paper gave him strong support. Things soon changed, and the paper that claimed to be Democratic in all things began subjecting the president to frequent fire. This must have caused some dilemma when Senator Tillman also was trying to "jab his pitchfork" into the president's side, and certainly "Zerrachaboam" enjoyed giving a full account of the patron-

---

[71] *The State*, October 29, 1895. It was not adopted. Among the reasons the editor gave for his endorsement: a means to white supremacy and the elimination of rowdyism at the polls.
[72] *Ibid.*, May 31, 1892.
[73] *Ibid.*, August 13, 1891.
[74] *Ibid.*, March 4, 1897.

age clash between the Democratic Administration and the Tillmanites:

1. Now when it had come to pass that Grover did reign in the room of Benjamin, surnamed Harrison, John the Senator [Irby], and those that were with him, were exceedingly troubled in mind, and secretly did gnash their teeth.

4. [They visited him for patronage], But Grover was unmoved, at their much speaking; nevertheless he commanded them to be brought before him; and when he had beheld them, in the wisdom of his heart he discovered their hypocrisy, and exclaimed, "Truly it is the hand of Tillman, but the voice of Weaver" [James B. Weaver, Populist leader].

5. And straightway he dismissed them; and when he had taken a scroll, upon which were the names of the unfaithful, he also placed their names upon it and did turn their likenesses to the wall, and great fear came upon them all.

6. But when they had girded up, each man his own gallus, They came again to Grover saying, Master, we have borne the burden and the heat of the day. Lo! we will serve thee always. But he knew them not.

8. Now Grover . . . sought out one Wade [Hampton], a man just and upright, of good report among the brethren and mighty in battle, who, on account of his uprightness, was despised of Benjamin. . . .

9. And . . . Grover called him unto himself and made him a ruler over the carriers of travelers [U.S. Commissioner of Pacific Railways].

10. Now when John the Senator knew these things he rent his garments and was exceeding wrath. . . .

11. And . . . Benjamin . . . was stricken as it were with a grievous murrain and the joints of his spine shook together with a great chill. . . .

12. And he called unto him Daniel [Tompkins] his scribe [private secretary], and said unto him: Write! . . . Give me, I pray

thee, if it be but the crumbs from thy table wherewith to stay the bellies of my disciples, for they are become as ravening wolves and will devour me should I feed them not.

13. Turn, oh Grover, thine ear from one Benjamin, who is called Perry, and let not the voice of Gonzales come unto thee. For I am sore displeased with Benjamin, and Gonzales is more terrible unto me than an army with banners, for he slayeth my followers and smiteth my captains.

14. But when this writing had come unto Grover he marked and considered it well and caused it to be placed in a place called in our tongue "the waste basket" and was not deceived, for in the uprightness of his heart he knew the false prophets when they came unto him in sheep's clothing, and could in no wise be taken in the snare of the Weaverites.[75]

All through the 1890s *The State* proclaimed itself an exponent of "true Jeffersonian Democracy." This stand pitted it against all Republicans, violently against all Populists, and often against many Democrats. On the pressing matter of the currency, the editor professed to be alarmed by both "gold bugs" and extreme silverites but said, "Silver will come out all right in time if it can only be delivered from some of its fool friends." As for such Populistic panaceas as the subtreasury scheme (not unlike the Commodity Credit Corporation of federal farm programs that later began in the 1930s), he had only the most bitter scorn. The Populists he accused of being lined up with socialists or—even worse—Tillmanites.

In the field of foreign affairs, N. G. Gonzales engaged in paradoxical pursuits of widely different objectives. His flag-waving, impetuous patriotism endorsed some of the objectives of contemporary jingoists, and yet sometimes he wrote calm editorials that were downright isolationist. He violently opposed imperialism and yet demanded the annexation of

[75] *Ibid.,* April 7, 1893.

Hawaii. He believed that the United States should carefully avoid meddling, but he was willing to ignore borders and sovereignty for America to avenge "an insult."

The anti-imperialism was evident in a number of instances. After Dewey's victory at Manila in 1898, the paper urged that the Philippines be bought by Japan; later N. G. G. vigorously opposed American acquisition of the islands. As for considering our acquisition a "purchase" from Spain, he said, "It is a question of buying an extinct title and subjugating a people who had already won their independence." With regard to conquering the Filipino rebel leader Aguinaldo, he said America was "shooting down men who strive for their liberties as we in the last century strove for ours." Bluntly and boldly, N. G. G. wrote: "We need to get rid of our scandals and establish the rule of law and equity before even Americans can with decency attempt to reform others."[76]

Enigmatically, when aroused, this sometime isolationist could openly wish that America had a Napoleon Bonaparte to conduct its foreign policy. When a "half-civilized race," the Japanese, protested United States' designs on Hawaii, *The State* screamed that it was an insult: "Fling talk to the winds and take the islands at once! That would be acting like a nation."[77] Only a few years later when many Chileans resented high-handed actions by the United States and its ambassador there, Patrick Egan, Gonzales condemned the diplomat—a "dynamiter blatherskike who, by meddling with Chile's domestic affairs, has made himself obnoxious" and had almost brought a dishonorable war "for the glorification of Mr. [Secretary of State] Blaine's 'vigorous foreign policy.' "[78]

Despite its comments at the time of the Hawaiian crisis,

[76] *Ibid.*, May 6, 1898, July 10, September 11, 23, 1899.
[77] *Ibid.*, July 30, 1897.
[78] *Ibid.*, October 31, 1891.

The State was generally a friend of Japan. In 1895 she was encouraged to attain a thorough victory in the Sino-Japanese War, for "Chinese vanity is such that as long as their government is free to issue proclamations of imaginary victories . . . there will be no peace. The illusions of the Flowery Empire must be dispelled."[79] To Gonzales, Japan should serve as a stabilizing influence in the Orient where Russia constantly threatened the equilibrium. The Russian bear always alarmed *The State,* which, as early as 1894, pontificated: "It would be better for civilization and for humanity if the Russian empire could be dismembered. . . . The only hope for the lifting of Russia to a civilized power lies in the revolt of her own people against the tyranny under which they suffer."[80]

Although the colorful editor's name had become a household word in South Carolina before 1900, *The State* was not a one-man production. As in its first early and struggling days, it leaned heavily on a staff that must have had a great deal of hustle and *esprit de corps.*

By 1900 the staff had grown rapidly. E. J. Watson was assisted in the local work now by William Banks and James Williams; the former almost rivaled Watson in his ability to produce a prodigious amount of prose daily, and Williams soon showed his ability by moving on to become editor of the *Boston Transcript.* As for Ebbie Watson himself, he had found his duties as city editor too easy, and by the turn of the century he managed the Columbia Chamber of Commerce by day and worked at *The State* by night.[81] Least known and most retiring of the Gonzales brothers, Willie

79 *Ibid.,* January 9, 1895.
80 *Ibid.,* October 7, 1895.
81 August Kohn to J. C. Hemphill, July 6, 1901, in Kohn Papers; *The State,* February 18, 1916.

Gonzales was given the post of news editor in 1901, having been earlier telegraph and state editor.[82]

In early 1899 James A. Hoyt, Jr., heretofore Greenville correspondent for the paper and now twenty-two years old, joined the editorial staff in Columbia. In 1900 he left the paper temporarily to edit the Greenville *Mountaineer* while his father campaigned unsuccessfully for governor. Returning to Columbia that fall and moving into the home of W. E. Gonzales, he went back to the paper as an assistant editor. Besides helping N. G. Gonzales daily, he wrote the editorials for the Sunday edition, the paper following a policy of avoiding political and controversial subjects on the Sabbath.[83] In 1900 the young man wrote his father that N. G. Gonzales told him that he had selected him as his successor.[84]

In 1900 Robert Lathan—age nineteen—began his three years of service on the staff where he wrote routine news and acted as secretary and stenographer for N. G. Gonzales. Respecting his vocation as a minister should his, Lathan early showed the promise of a future that would include the editorship of both the *News and Courier* and the *Asheville Citizen,* as well as a Pulitzer Prize.[85]

The State also acquired the services of a man listed in *Who's Who* as naturalist but whose widespread interests might classify him as a literary gadfly: James Henry Rice, Jr.

[82] *The State,* June 18, 1901.
[83] Many churchmen even objected to the paper's being published on that day.
[84] J. A. Hoyt, Jr., to Colonel J. A. Hoyt, May 17, 1900, in Hoyt Papers, and photostat in Wofford College Library. Hoyt later had a very varied career. His copious papers in the South Caroliniana Library reflect an apparent resentment that he never had been fully appreciated by N. G.'s successors at *The State* and hence never achieved his desire to be its editor—an ambition he held in later decades.
[85] J. C. Hemphill to August Kohn, January 30, 1906, and Robert Lathan to J. C. Hemphill, February 10, 1906, in Hemphill Papers; *The State,* September 28, 1937.

On the staff a couple of years in the 1890s, he was to continue until 1935 to write articles on every conceivable topic, doing most of his work on his plantation on Cheeha Creek, which made him a spiritual neighbor of Ambrose Gonzales.

In contrast with the erudition of such writers as Professor R. Means Davis, *The State* treated its readers to the literary gems allegedly written by one M. D. Pitts, self-styled "The State's Colard Porter." He purportedly submitted outpourings occasionally on civic or national matters, war or peace; his greatest rarity would have been a sentence correctly punctuated or a phrase with all the words correctly spelled. The following is the conclusion of one of his essays:

Let us have street cars for the white people and street cars for the colard people. and dont let inny mix up be on eather of theas cars. Please see to it, my friend. if you dont there will be trobel in columbia shure.

wrote BY M D Pitts,
the State Colard Porter[86]

Some hinted darkly that a Caucasian hand lay behind the published wisdom of Pitts' pen, but the editor rose to defend him: "The genius of Pitts is never sullied by plagiarism. We do not believe that he could be tempted to work off a passage from the Rubaiyat, a limpid thought from Browning or even one of Gen. Otis's reports as original with himself. This . . . shows Pitts to be a person of complete literary propriety."[87] A year later a headline told the sad story of Pitts' downfall: "THE 'COLARD PORTER' IS NOW A 'COLLARED PORTER.'" The *littérateur* was reported to have swapped his porter's uniform "for a zebra suit, several sizes too small, and a spade. . . . Heretofore Pitts has not given any of his

[86] *The State*, June 27, 1900.
[87] *Ibid.*, September 2, 1899.

attention to modern roadbuilding; now he will take quite a course." The black Simeon Stylites of *The State* had let ambition run away with him and had long been using his mailbag for surreptitiously moving part of a drug store—as well as a sizeable library from The State Company.[88]

One episode flared up with such intensity that it temporarily became a veritable obsession with both *The State* and N. G. Gonzales; hence a digression in the narrative of both the newspaper and man is properly called for. The topic—Cuba—during a specific period attracted the same total and emotional attention that Tillman once had.

Throughout the 1890s *The State* had understandably given considerable space to the Cuban independence movement. With the outbreak of revolution in 1895, the press campaign was intensified tremendously. A. J. Gonzales would have shared his son's optimism: "[A]utonomy will be granted; that will lead to independence; independence will result in annexation. Cuba will yet be a State in the American Union; it is her manifest destiny."[89] Coverage was not objective: Grover Cleveland's commitment to United States neutrality was headlined "A COLD-BLOODED CUBA POLICY." Constantly urging the recognition of the belligerency of the Cuban rebels, *The State* surfeited its readers with a plethora of atrocity stories and "shocking outrages."

In the first four months of 1898, *The State* rivaled the Hearst and Pulitzer papers in its partisanship. Never in its history has the paper so completely "lost its journalistic head," its sense of proportion. Interested though the population probably was, it is difficult to believe that South Carolina wanted to have its attention riveted on Cuba and Cuba alone,

[88] *Ibid.*, June 17, 1900.
[89] *Ibid.*, March 1, 1895. N. G. painted his boyhood memories of Cuba in *The State*, April 10, 1895.

but *The State* seems to have made that assumption. Every angle, rumor, and suspicion of the sinking of the *Maine* was exploited, and the editor said that Spain had at last fallen into President McKinley's hands by supplying an issue "which none but a poltroon people could fail to sustain him in." Historians later have not been so kind about American reaction and judgment in the *Maine* mystery.

Gonzales so lost himself as to note that war would bring a grand economic boom. Furthermore, it would release government money, and, "We say that this money would be better in the pockets of the people than lying idle in the treasury."[90] Repeatedly he observed how the South in particular would benefit from the war which he advocated. As the frenzy of the paper increased, the editor prophesied how glorious such a conflict would be and how utterly dishonored the United States would be if somehow it managed to avoid this war. Whereas the front page of *The State* had heretofore always exhibited the most conservative typography (single-column heads, all side by side), now it blossomed forth with "screamer heads" in "millenium type" spelling out wild rumors, scores of exclamation points, romantic pictures of speeding navy ships, maps of Cuba, and such headlines as "CRAWFISHING BY THE SPANISH," "HORRORS OF CUBA," "TIME TO BE KILLED WHILE CUBANS PERISH," "NATION'S HONOR IS DROPPED," and "WHILE THOUSANDS ARE DYING THE SENATE RUNS A WINDMILL." Pandemonium reigned in banner type.

In contrast, the rival *News and Courier* took a different position. The editor, Major J. C. Hemphill, said he opposed the war as being unnecessary and held that such a stand was not "evidence of a Pro-Spanish or Anti-Cuban sentiment,"[91]

[90] *Ibid.*, February 28, March 8, 1898.
[91] J. C. Hemphill to W. F. Rhame, April 23, 1898, in Letterbook, 1897–1898, of Hemphill Papers. Also, see D. Hemphill to J. C. Hemphill, April 18, 1898, in Hemphill Papers.

but the furious Gonzales charged that Charleston "Tory paper" with being "a disgrace to South Carolina" and with trying "to chill patriotism and sneer down courage."[92] When, to the delight of *The State,* war finally came in April 1898, N. G. Gonzales got his chance to prove his sincerity. For some time he had been keeping in close contact with Cuban insurgents, including Gonzalo de Quesada, a friend of General A. J. Gonzales, and with the Cuban junta in New York.[93] He had also been in negotiation with the state militia, but the hawkish N. G. G. said this was too tame since he was "hankering for the front."[94] On May 9 he left Columbia for Tampa "to prove his faith by his works."[95] Having no success there as he sought to convince American generals that he would be useful as a guide, some of his father's friends managed to get him a position as a lieutenant on the staff of Cuban General Emilio Nuñez, who for some time had been landing filibustering expeditions on the island and now was preparing to lead a force of Cuban patriots which included many Cubans from Tampa cigar factories. Pleased at his successful coup, N. G. demonstrated that he was as much an Elliott as a Gonzales as he wrote to reassure his class-conscious, Old South aristocratic aunt: "He [Nuñez] is a gentleman, and all of his staff seem to be also of good social standing."[96] Aunt Anne probably then became reconciled to the martial spirit—and not before.

During his six weeks in Tampa, N. G. sent back to his paper a series of letters, including some humorous "Character Studies at the Front." At long last, General Nuñez sailed with his force to relieve General Maximo Gomez in central

[92] *The State,* April 21, 1898. The Columbia editor also said the Spanish would find Charleston harbor "a friendly port."
[93] Reminiscences of J. H. Rice, Jr., in *The State,* December 3, 1922.
[94] N. G. Gonzales to Miss Anne Elliott, April 3, 1898, in E.G.P.
[95] J. H. Rice, Jr., in *The State,* May 13, 1898.
[96] N. G. Gonzales to Miss Anne Elliott, May 12, 1898, in E.G.P. This is a long, detailed letter.

Cuba. After being repulsed at two points, they finally landed at Palo Alto on the south coast on July 3 and on the next day reached General Gomez.

N. G. Gonzales' war record has been thoroughly preserved. During his time in service, he kept a detailed journal. Occasionally parts of it appeared in *The State* while he was in Cuba, and after he returned he printed it in the newspaper in fifty-one installments from September 8 through December 7, 1898. Years later, Ambrose Gonzales published it as a book, *In Darkest Cuba*.

In his foreword to the book, Ambrose said it was "a simple record of hardships borne with philosophical cheerfulness and fortitude." Here Ambrose exaggerated, for his brother Nanno was now no more cheerful than he had been in his youthful lamentations from Varnville, Savannah, Valdosta, or Washington. He was correct in saying, however, "There were few exciting incidents; little to stir the blood, but— under constant privations—much to try the spirit, to test the moral and physical fibre of the man."[97]

After landing, the newcomers with Nuñez were resented by the veterans with Gomez who viewed the expeditionaries from Tampa as having come at the last minute simply to reap the spoils. This friction became well-nigh unbearable during the six weeks while this combined force pushed its way through the jungle and along the *trocha*. Although the hardships were no more severe than in other wars, N. G. and his companions did undergo arduous difficulties. His book is primarily a detailed journal of his troubles and is filled with lengthy jeremiads interspersed with many boasts about how stoical and uncomplaining he was. When his horse was stolen, for example, he carried the tragedy straight to General Gomez himself, and, when his plight failed to arouse any action,

[97] A. E. Gonzales in the foreword to N. G. Gonzales, *In Darkest Cuba*, p. 31.

he delivered a virtual stump speech in the camp on generals who "did not have the decency to extend even temporary aid to an American who had come to offer his life in the service of Cuba."[98] He also became a grand critic of American strategy. Despite his earlier editorial predictions of the glories of the war, he now bitterly attacked what he called powerful interests nefariously trying to prolong the war; among these, he listed the Republican Party, contractors, "the bulls generally," a host of army officers, mobilization ports, favored railroads, and other beneficiaries.

Deploring the fact that he had come to Cuba "for a fighting campaign and had had a starving campaign,"[99] he finally was involved in some limited gunfire in an attack on the town of Moron on August 12. Learning on August 17 that the war was over, he promptly procured his discharge, trudged out to the north coast, and boarded a schooner which, after various adventures, landed him at Key West on September 1.

Had he been living, General Gonzales would have been pleased to know that three of his sons served in a war considered a war for Cuban independence. In May 1898 Ambrose Gonzales was given a captain's commission in the U.S. Army quartermaster corps and served at Santiago. The youngest brother, William E. Gonzales, enrolled in the state militia on May 21, received a commission, and throughout the rest of his life in title-conscious South Carolina was known as "Captain Gonzales."

Actually, William Gonzales served the longest of the brothers but never was in hostile action. Once mustered into service, his Second South Carolina Infantry Regiment spent seven weeks of "war" in Columbia and did not leave the state until after the conflict was over. The group went to

[98] Gonzales, *In Darkest Cuba*, p. 141.
[99] *Ibid.*, p. 277.

Cuba early in 1899 as occupation troops. William T. Sherman's classic description of war hardly provides a description of the campaign waged by this South Carolina group at their station, "Camp Columbia," five miles from Havana. The wives of four of the officers—including "Mrs. Capt. Gonzales" —came down and set up housekeeping in a comfortable settlement of tents. The militia troops bore up for about eleven weeks of occupation duty which was enlivened by regular band concerts and horse racing.[100] Their colonel, Wylie Jones of Columbia, was hardly a martinet in his restrictions, and in his narrative of their arduous experience, wrote: "A few days before we sailed from Havana, I called on the General and asked him please to give us a good ship to go home on, as we had such an awful old ship to carry us there."[101] The regiment was finally mustered out of federal service on April 19, 1899. During these travels, Willie Gonzales, like N. G., sent vividly descriptive articles back for publication in *The State*.[102]

While all the Gonzales brothers were away fighting for the independence of their father's native land, the devotedly loyal staff kept the paper going. Taking over as news editor and virtually managing the whole organization was the indefatigable E. J. Watson. The editorial page was prepared by James Henry Rice, Jr., and John S. Reynolds. Captain Ralph Elliott described the former as "a walking encyclopedia of useless information," and "Mr. Ambrose" described

[100] Mrs. Mary Elliott Johnstone to Miss Anne Elliott, May 14, 1898, in E.G.P. Also, see *The State*, May 20, 1898. *The State*, July 30, 1898.
[101] Colonel Wylie Jones in J. W. Floyd, *Historical Roster and Itinerary of South Carolina Volunteer Troops Who Served in the Late War between the United States and Spain, 1898, Coupled with Brief Sketches of their Movements from the Beginning to the Ending of the Conflict* (Columbia: R. L. Bryan Company, 1901), p. 137.
[102] Published at irregular intervals in *The State*, beginning January 11, 1899. Also, see Henry T. Thompson, "Historical Sketch of the Independent Battalion, S. C. V. I.," in Floyd, *Historical Roster and Itinerary of South Carolina Volunteer Troops . . .*, pp. 146-48. For detailed but condensed itinerary of Company "I," see *ibid.*, p. 153.

the latter as "the most brilliant conversationalist and the dullest writer I ever saw." Acting president of the company was Christopher Fitzsimmons, close friend of Ambrose Gonzales and a founder of the Southern Cotton Oil Company.[103]

As so often happened for *The State,* the financial road was not a smooth one. The *News and Courier* even lent paper to the interim management and had difficulty collecting for it.[104] On one occasion, money was needed badly, and the staff found that the newspaper did not have enough credit at the bank to get a loan; the funds were procured by the staff members' borrowing the needed cash and giving their personal notes for it.[105]

During the war, the paper changed little the frothy appearance which it had so flamboyantly acquired in 1898. Much of the time the whole front page was divided into only three wide columns which related one heroic, romantic exploit after another about "the splendid little war." To *The State,* every soldier was a knightly hero undergoing privations hitherto unknown in military annals. Headlines showed more passionate patriotism than good journalistic practice; the following "banner head," typical of dozens, appeared July 15:

THE FLAG "WHOSE HUES WERE BORN IN HEAVEN"—
AMERICA'S BANNER, FLOATS OVER EASTERN CUBA.

Military censorship was unknown: troop and ship movements past, present, and future were reported in full. Wil-

---

[103] Reminiscences of J. H. Rice, Jr. (who received $15 a week as editor) , in *The State,* December 3, 1922; Ambrose Gonzales to W. W. Ball, May 15, 1922, in the Ball Papers; interview with J. A. Hoyt, April 7, 1951; reminiscences of W. W. Watson in *The State,* February 18, 1931; N. G. G. in *ibid.,* September 19, 1898; *The State,* October 8, 1925.

[104] News and Courier Company to August Kohn, July 31, 1898, in Kohn Papers.

[105] Reminiscences of W. W. Watson in *The State,* February 18, 1931.

liam Banks, formerly city editor of the *Register*, came to *The State* as a war correspondent sending full and glorifying minutiae of everything that befell the South Carolina First Regiment as it went to war—or, at least went as far as Chickamauga.[106] *The State* also retold Cuban history, in which A. J. Gonzales was made to appear in a not inconsiderable role.[107]

The war and Cuba, however, did not monopolize all the space in the papers, and loyal readers of 1898 still got their daily diet of violence under such tried-and-trusted captions as "PISTOLS AT THE WEDDING," "BATTERED, BENT AND BROKEN," "DIED IN THE DEN OF A DUSKY DAMSEL," and "BAGGED A BIG BOA BY USE OF A BARREL."

The war interlude over, *The State* returned to normalcy as quickly as it had gone wild. The veteran N. G. G. soon became disillusioned with American policy toward Cuba, fearing increasingly that Cubans "will have liberty, but the Americans will make the money."[108] After a press association excursion there, he attacked critical South Carolina editors as not knowing enough about Cuba to write on the subject; to help them out, he published a series of "Notes on Cuba."[109] Bitterly he viewed the island as being virtually annexed to the United States and branded the famous Platt Amendment of 1901 as an act of faithlessness, a mortifying pistol pointed at the head of a trustworthy friend.[110]

---

[106] Floyd, *Historical Roster and Itinerary*, p. 35, describes his reports as "brilliant and pathetic letters."

[107] For example, *The State*, June 28, 1898, republished an old account of the López expeditions by W. L. Trask which had originally appeared in the Memphis *Commercial-Appeal*. N. G.'s propaganda for Cuba before war came managed to involve his father prominently and manifested much pride in him—in contrast to his private correspondence.

[108] Gonzales, *In Darkest Cuba*, p. 52.

[109] Appeared in *The State* in the spring of 1900.

[110] *The State*, March 1, 1901.

From 1898 to 1903 the more stable *State* showed strength as it passed beyond its awkward and feverish adolescent period. The physical makeup of the paper returned to its normal conservatism. More attention now went to events far away—the Dreyfus trial, the Boer War, the death of Queen Victoria, international sailing races (especially whenever a sloop named *Columbia* participated), or the McKinley assassination. Minute details of the death and funeral of Wade Hampton occupied the paper for days in April 1902, and for a long time thereafter the paper was filled with eulogies and resolutions about one of its favorite heroes.[111] That same year *The State* had to chronicle sadly the death of another inveterate Confederate, Captain Ralph E. Elliott—"Uncle Rafe."[112]

The regular series of Dr. Thomas De Witt Talmadge's sermons finally ended with the death of that divine in 1902, but there was no shortage of syndicated features. Numerous local columns and columnists appeared as regular features in the paper over the years: "Rail and Crosstie," one devoted to railroad developments and personnel in a day when a conductor was a widely known public personage; "Where Women's Eyes May Wander," a chatty listing of social events; "S. C. News and Gossip," a daily caption allocated to the gleanings of news items from a different town daily; "Life in the Piedmont Daily Chronicle," up-country news items; and "Spice of Variety," a column of Columbia chitchat which ran the gamut of news, jokes, poems, and proverbs. The delicate term "a nameless crime" was still used instead of "rape," but the writers overworked the indelicate phrase "his body mashed to jelly" in such news stories of violence as some in 1902 under such charming heads as "The Engine Plowed Through the Coach," "Shooting and Cutting All Around

[111] N. G. Gonzales was one of the active pallbearers.
[112] *The State,* July 7, 8, 9, 1902.

Converse," "A Gruesome Find," and "His Body Cut in
Twain." Other headlines demonstrated less violence and
more tantalizing originality: "Frisky Foreigner's Flimsy Fab-
rication," "Mouth Menders Give Up to Mind Moulders" (a
teachers' convention following a dentists' convention at a
hotel) , and "The Cup Defender Shows Her Bottom" (a boat
race) .

Ambrose Gonzales' business department showed no startling outward changes, but the growth of circulation was
steady: 1896, 3,090; 1901, 4,542; 1905, 8,164. In that last year,
The State claimed to be the biggest paper in South Carolina.[113] The advertising in the paper did not vary greatly,
however. At least half a page daily consisted of schedules of
all railroads in the state. Most glorified of the railroad ads
were those featuring the "vestibuled trains." Steam laundries
were flourishing, with two in Columbia and Laurens solic-
iting work from all over the state with delivery by mail. In
1901 the numerous Columbia livery stables which advertised
their services met a new rival, an agency for the Locomobile.
The American Dental Parlors, lavish advertisers ("painless
extracting, 50¢; artificial plates, $8.00") , vied for space with
Mrs. A. Ruppert's Face Bleach, but nobody could vie with
Lydia Pinkham's pills and the scores of other patent medi-
cines for all the ills that beset the human race.

Gradually the Gonzales brothers revealed a mania that was
to be reflected in the paper as long as they controlled it: an
interest in South Carolina history. They devoted much of
their newspaper space to this topic and also promoted it in
other ways. This was particularly a pet interest of Ambrose
Gonzales. By 1900 Professor R. Means Davis and other college

[113] By 1915, The State had doubled the circulation of its nearest competitor in the state. It maintained the lead until 1928 when the Greenville News
overtook it, but by 1949 The State regained the lead with a circulation of
62,694. Ayer's American Newspaper Annual, passim. It has continued to
have the largest circulation of any paper in South Carolina.

people contributed an increasing number of historical feature articles. Always, there was a surplus of items on the glories of the Confederacy, and to that they added new productions on Reconstruction. Several series on the latter, written by non-academicians and not exactly objective, first appeared in the newspaper and later were reprinted as books: John S. Reynolds, *Reconstruction in South Carolina;* Alfred B. Williams, *Hampton and His Red Shirts;* and E. L. Wells, *Hampton and Reconstruction.* James H. Rice, Jr., did a series of biographical sketches entitled "Paladins of South Carolina." Under Ambrose Gonzales' influence, The State Company published at least twenty-two books on South Carolina topics by the early 1920s.[114] He also had founded a Columbia Book Company by 1900, typical of his ceaseless labor of love which never proved financially rewarding to him.[115]

With the success and fame that was coming to the paper by the end of the decade of the Gay Nineties, the Gonzales life was less tempestuous, with their paper noting in 1899, "There seems to be now a better feeling than ever before between the newspapers of the State."[116] Until 1899, the Gonzaleses rarely attended the annual meetings of the State Press Association, but thereafter they became regular fixtures there. These sessions were usually gay affairs, followed by long and luxurious trips largely provided by the railroads, towns, or hotels catering to the power of the press; if one of the perennial regional "expositions" was being held, it was sure to be the destination of the special Pullmans of the press party. In 1899 N. G. Gonzales arranged a trip to Cuba for the editors, and in 1900 Ambrose Gonzales made a speech

114 Listed in an advertisement in Snowden Papers. Snowden and Gonzales were close friends and consulted on these topics.
115 Receipt signed by Gonzales as president of the book company, dated May 9, 1900, in Kohn Papers, South Caroliniana Library.
116 *The State*, July 24, 1899.

typical of these gatherings: "Advantages of Type-setting Machines in a Country Office."[117] Most of the time was spent in livelier activity; for example, on the trip to the Nashville Centennial Exposition (1897), according to N. G., "Champagne and a special Pullman had a very exalting effect on the editors, so that they did not need to climb Lookout Mountain to feel up in the world."[118]

The success and stability which had come to the paper by 1903 did not permit relaxation, but the brothers Gonzales did begin to earn some of the rewards of their hard work. Although by no means rich, they could foresee some security and possibly personal prosperity in the future. Ambrose Gonzales was recognized as one of the prominent and influential men in Columbia business circles, and N. G. Gonzales continued as one of the more famous and most controversial figures in the state. Even he did not conduct the fervent editorial page with the pen lashings that once had been almost a daily ritual, and on occasion his long, philosophical leaders read very much like something from the "Old Lady of Broad Street." Described by his secretary as "one of the most self-centered yet absolutely the most unselfish man" he had ever known,[119] N. G. showed some signs of mellowing, and his close friends were aware that he was generally a mild person who really did not welcome controversy. Yet his convictions were so strong and so tenaciously held, and he never sought to evade issues. The man had weaknesses and he made

[117] S. C. State Press Association *Proceedings* (1899), pp. 38–39. He and his sister, Harriett, accompanied the party. See *The State*, February 27; March 1, 7, 14, 26, 27, 1900. For the flavor of these larks, see the scrapbooks in the Kohn Papers, and Clark, *Southern Country Editor*, pp. 327–28. *The State*, September 9, 1900. According to *ibid.*, May 27, 1895, N. G. was to speak in 1895 on "Relations of the Daily to the Country Press," but the writer has been unable to locate any account of it, and the *Proceedings* of that year do not even list him among those present.

[118] *The State*, May 29, 1897.

[119] Robert Lathan, "Men Who Have Made Newspaper History in South Carolina," in S. C. State Press Association *Proceedings* (1911), p. 36.

mistakes, but he nevertheless was accurate in 1901 when he wrote that *The State* had finally achieved success simply because it had striven sincerely and conscientiously to adhere to its original mission

to be helpful in good works and good causes; to broaden as far as may be done the public mind; to advance material and social developments; to heighten the sense of the responsibilities of citizenship and of office; to stand for the weak who are oppressed and to curb the arrogance of the strong; to teach . . . the duties of obedience to law, to the dictates of humanity, and to the obligations of public and private honor.[120]

[120] *The State,* February 17, 1901.

CHAPTER VIII

Jim Tillmanism

O N JANUARY 15, 1903, N. G. GONZALES WAS SHOT TO DEATH by the lieutenant-governor of the state. The shooting, which occurred on the northeast corner of Main and Gervais Streets, almost in the shadow of the State Capitol, shocked South Carolina as perhaps no other single crime in its history has done. The deed was a direct outgrowth of animosities and a bitter feud that accompanied what can best be called "Jim Tillmanism."

As has been seen, "Tillmania" had died down before 1903, with Ben Tillman by then showing signs of conservatism and Gonzales giving evidences of restraint. In general, the state government was then run by some of the more responsible and moderate Reformers, and some of the earlier ruling classes were also successfully reentering politics. Into this scene at the State Capitol, Jim Tillman crashed, and his character, words, and actions caused N. G. Gonzales again to dip his pen into gall and to open a new Tillman-Gonzales hostility. To all appearances, it all ended with a Gonzales

286

victory in early September 1902, and no more was said about it. But the hatred rankled and festered in the soul of Jim Tillman for five months, and the explosive sequel came at the corner of Main and Gervais. James H. Tillman, son of George D. and nephew of Benjamin R. Tillman, "represented the Tillmans and Tillmanism at its worst."[1] He had many of the qualities that added up to political success in the Palmetto State of his day. Feverish black eyes, a strong face, long raven hair—all of these contributed to a striking appearance. "Reckless but affable," he was popular with the roughest elements of Tillmanism, and in the political world he was quite willing to capitalize on his uncle's name. By bragging of his fistfights, by making frequent and loud threats of personal conflicts, he appealed to the worst element among South Carolinians. In political life, he outdid his uncle as a master of demagoguery—particularly in arousing bitter anti-Negro prejudices.

But, as Ben Tillman said, Jim Tillman "could not control his passions."[2] He was a gambler, a drunkard, a rascal, and a free spender of his own and other people's money. Once he was arrested in Augusta for gambling, and he was frequently reported as attending cockfights. His unpleasant personal life was well known, but he seemed to prefer being known as a flamboyant figure rather than not being known at all. The reputation of being "one hell of a fellow" flattered rather than displeased him. The publicity of the "scrapes" in which he managed to get involved did not seem to embarrass him, and in 1895 several "cards" were passed over his most serious affair to date, a well-publicized personal clash with Bernard B. Evans, brother of John Gary Evans, in the law offices of S. M. Simkins in Edgefield.[3]

[1] Simkins, *Tillman*, p. 380. For an excellent sketch of Jim Tillman, which is the basis for the condensation above, see pp. 380–384.
[2] *Ibid.*, p. 381.
[3] *The State*, January 16, 1895.

Despite his shortcomings—or, perhaps with a certain element, because of them—Jim Tillman enjoyed some political success. Prominence in the militia during the Spanish-American War helped him, for he was a colonel commanding one of the two South Carolina regiments in that 1898 episode.[4] Even in that military capacity, he managed to become implicated in unpleasantness and notoriety because of his insulting a superior officer and for ordering three Negro boys whipped for stealing a pistol.[5] In 1900 he was elected lieutenant-governor by "championing the Dispensary, parading his services for his uncle, and appealing to the anti-Negro prejudices of the cotton mill operatives."[6]

A man of such principles in political life was fair game for Gonzales, and when Jim Tillman sought the governorship in 1902, *The State* was unsparing in its castigation. But the feud went much farther back than that, all the way to 1890.

In that year the Winnsboro *News and Herald* had contained an anonymous letter which made an abusive attack on N. G. Gonzales, calling him, among other things, "a treacherous Spaniard," who in the *News and Courier* had misrepresented a speech made by Ben Tillman.[7] Although the editor of the Winnsboro paper refused to divulge the name of the letter writer, N. G. learned that James H. Tillman, then editing a small Tillman "organette" in Winnsboro, was the author.

When a political candidate years later, Jim Tillman bragged, "But this Cuban pony knows me. He has not forgotten a certain circumstance in 1890, when because Senator Tillman's hands were tied I extended to him a cordial in-

---

[4] Floyd, *Historical Roster and Itinerary*, p. 53.
[5] *The State*, October 6, 8, 12, 15, 16, 26, 1898; Simkins, *Tillman*, p. 381.
[6] Simkins, *Tillman*, p. 382.
[7] Letter in Winnsboro *Tri-Weekly News and Herald*, April 26, 1890, reprinted in *The State*, October 10, 1903. N. G. G. replied in *News and Herald*, May 7, 1890.

vitation to go to Georgia with me. The invitation was declined with thanks."[8] This "invitation to Georgia" (where duels were sometimes fought, especially on islands between the two states) stemmed from the sequel to the Winnsboro letter and centered around a prominent club in Columbia in which N. G. Gonzales was instrumental in blocking Jim Tillman's becoming a member.[9] Hearing that the name of Jim Tillman was to be presented for membership, Gonzales told his friends of the anonymous letter incident in which Tillman had made "a false and scurrilous attack on a gentleman" and was therefore not fit to associate with gentlemen. Although N. G. threatened to blackball him, he never had to do so since his name was withdrawn. Hearing of this action, Tillman sent word to Gonzales by George Legare that he understood that Gonzales was going to blackball him in the club and further that Gonzales had been saying that he had tried to obtain "satisfaction" for the Winnsboro incident and that he (Tillman) had refused. N. G. denied the latter, but accepted responsibility for developments in the club. Tillman thereupon sent Legare to ask if Gonzales would accept a challenge to a duel if one were sent, but the journalist notified him that he would have to send one to find out. Since a challenge was illegal, Tillman tried the unspecific "invitation to Georgia," which Gonzales declined. Both sides then retired from the field accusing each other of having prevented the issue from coming properly to a head. N. G. ended

[8] *The State*, July 31, 1902, citing the Yorkville *Enquirer*, July 30, 1902.

[9] It is not clear whether this was the Columbia Club or the South Carolina Club. N. G. contradicted himself in his accounts of the incident; in his card in the *News and Courier*, January 9, 1891, he said the Columbia Club; in *The State*, July 31, 1902, he identified it as the South Carolina Club. Simkins (*Tillman*, p. 382) says the "club which gave the State Ball"; this was the South Carolina Club. Most secondary accounts say the Columbia Club, but it would have been strange indeed that a Tillman would have wanted membership in a group so frequently condemned by Ben Tillman. Ambrose Gonzales said it was the South Carolina Club (in *The State*, September 3, 1903), and he was probably correct.

his published account of the affair at the time with, "I regret having made so long a statement about so contemptible an object as this callow braggart."[10]

Although this new Tillman became Columbia correspondent for the *Atlanta Constitution* in 1892, no friction occurred between the two until 1893.[11] In March of that year, Gonzales went to Washington in the interest of his candidacy for a consular post. Although Wade Hampton took him to see President Grover Cleveland and he was endorsed by Secretary of State Walter Q. Gresham, his nomination promised to encounter political difficulties since Tillmanite Senator John L. M. Irby said he would oppose Gonzales for any diplomatic post whatsoever—unless America could somehow establish diplomatic relations with hell in which case he personally would nominate him as minister plenipotentiary and envoy extraordinary.[12] As if to prove he was no sycophant for his candidacy, N. G.'s editorials in *The State* seemed to be baiting the South Carolina congressional delegation even more than usual; but Jim Tillman, then a newsman in Washington, reported in the *Evening Journal* that Gonzales had asked the president not to nominate him until after Senate adjournment because of Irby's opposition.[13] Hampton joined in "giving the lie" to Tillman,[14] and Gonzales called him a liar to his face. In reply to this dangerous duel-causing charge, Tillman said that he had merely printed that "it was reported," but now that the matter had been brought up, he insisted that the charge was true, whereupon Gonzales "gave him the infernal lie." Matters became tense, but Jim sent

---

[10] N. G. Gonzales' "card of explanation," in the *Columbia Record*, January 8, 1891, reprinted in *News and Courier*, January 9, 1891; also, retold in the famous editorial, "Partly Personal, Partly Public," in *The State*, July 31, 1902.

[11] *The State*, April 21, 1892.

[12] *Ibid.*, March 25, 1893, citing the Columbia *Evening Journal*, March 24, 1893.

[13] *The State*, April 12, 1893, citing the Columbia *Evening Journal*, n.d.

[14] *The State*, April 16, 1893.

no challenge, and on their next meeting in a Washington hotel, Tillman offered the editor a cigar and failed to mention the affair.[15]

After a friendly letter from Jim Tillman to Gonzales, matters flowed rather smoothly. In 1898 *The State* gave much attention to the charges of military misconduct against Colonel Tillman but added no special implications of its own. During his 1900 race for the lieutenant-governorship, *The State* said little about him. At the end of the campaign, the editor observed that the trouble with South Carolina was that it did not know Jim Tillman, but he himself would not begrudge Jim the job if there were no chance that the governor would die.[16] After his victory, Gonzales wrote, "Well, we can stand it if the senate can."[17] It did report, however, that according to the *Florence Times* "our nominee for lieutenant governor was 'pulled in an Augusta dive' for gambling and was 'tried next morning under an assumed name.' . . . We made our little protest, but we accept the inerrancy of the majority."[18]

Three climactic crises marked the feud in its last year, 1902. In February 1902, President Theodore Roosevelt was scheduled to attend the South Carolina Interstate and West Indian Exposition at Charleston.[19] Colonel Tillman had raised funds to buy a sword for Major Micah Jenkins, a famed South Carolina "Rough Rider" hero, and the president had agreed to present the sword during his visit. After the fistfight on the floor of the U.S. Senate between South Carolina's Senators John L. McLaurin and Ben R. Tillman,

---

[15] *Ibid.*, April 12, 14, 16, 1893; July 31, 1902.

[16] *The State*, August 30, 1900.

[17] *Ibid.*, September 12, 1900. The lieutenant-governor presides over the Senate.

[18] *Ibid.*, October 17, 1900.

[19] George B. Cortelyou (secretary to Roosevelt) to J. C. Hemphill, November 8, 1901, in Hemphill Papers.

however, Roosevelt had canceled a dinner invitation previously sent to Ben; two days later, Colonel James Tillman
withdrew the invitation to the president to present the sword
at Charleston. The insulted president of the United States
then threatened not to visit South Carolina. *The State* notified the world that Jim Tillman "cannot represent any reputable element in South Carolina" and that "South Carolina is
not responsible for this act of boorishness" by "Tillman the
Little," "a chronic notoriety-seeker."[20] Later it added that
"this particular Tillman is unworthy of being Ben Tillman's
nephew."[21] Several papers, including *The State,* raised funds
to get another sword, and Willie Gonzales persuaded the
president to make the presentation of this new sword "given
by another class of people."[22] *The State* boasted that it raised
$100 for the fund in one day whereas it had taken Jim Till-
man three years to collect $65.[23] Without the help of the
lieutenant-governor, President Roosevelt presented the
sword to Jenkins on April 9.[24]

Jim Tillman's bad manners apparently determined Gonzales now to expose him fully. Within a month, amid as
blaring publicity as he could give to it, the editor proved
with a series of telling documents that the lieutenant-governor, acting officially, had lied to the state Senate. Presiding
over that body, he had ruled that a certain motion was not
debatable; when issue was taken with him, he wired Senator
W. P. Frye, speaker pro-tem of the U.S. Senate, and Speaker
D. B. Henderson of the U.S. House of Representatives, concerning his ruling. Both of these authorities reversed his de-

[20] *The State,* March 28, 1902.
[21] *Ibid.,* March 21, 1902.
[22] W. E. Gonzales to J. C. Hemphill, September 30, 1902, in Hemphill
Papers.
[23] *The State,* March 8, 1902.
[24] J. C. Hemphill, "A Short Story of the South Carolina Interstate and West
Indian Exposition," in *Charleston Year Book* (1902) , pp. 163–64.

cision, but he deliberately announced and had entered in the Senate *Journal* that they had sustained him. N. G. Gonzales then communicated with Frye and Henderson, who gave him copies of their replies to Tillman. *The State* published all of the contradictory documents together.[25] To Gonzales' credit, it can be said that he repeatedly warned his readers that his old Tillmania was not involved, that Ben himself was not involved or responsible, and that in comparison with Jim, Ben was "a gentleman and a patriot."[26]

Three months later James H. Tillman entered the 1902 race for governor. In the first campaign meeting he explained the parliamentary basis of his disputed senate ruling but made no explanation of his misstatement of the opinion of other parliamentarians. He did refer to his exposer: "This man Gonzales is actuated by malice and spite. He is a modern Ishmaelite, whose hand is against every man. . . . The only explanation I can offer for his enmity toward me is that I bear the name that I do."[27] In reply, Gonzales said his attacks were not personal and that he "never had anything against 'Jim' Tillman except that he was a man without character and therefore unfit for public office and both disgraceful and dangerous in it."[28] N. G. further wrote that he was still devoted to his old friend, George D. Tillman, father of Jim, who was "unworthy of the father and even of the uncle." Two days later, this friendship was denied by the candidate. On that score, Gonzales definitely was accurate since he and George Tillman had been close friends in the early 1880s when N. G. was a young Washington correspond-

[25] *The State*, March 24, 1902. Also summarized in detail, *ibid.*, June 16, 1902. A lengthy, detailed statement tracing the whole controversy and signed by Paul M. Brice is in the Gonzales Mss., South Caroliniana Library. Many newspaper clippings on the controversy are filed in the Hoyt Papers in the South Caroliniana Library.

[26] *The State*, April 11, 1902.

[27] *Ibid.*, June 16, 1902, citing the *News and Courier*, June 15, 1902.

[28] *The State*, June 16, 1902.

ent; their friendship had even weathered "Tillmania," with George having written N. G. in 1895, "I have always liked you & like you Still in Spite of your unpleasantness with Some of my family." The editor thus labeled the lieutenant-governor as "a disgrace to his uncle, and a double disgrace to his father, George D. Tillman, whose brave and manly soul deserved no such punishment as the character of his son inflicted upon it."[29]

South Carolina tradition is that Gonzales conducted an unmitigated and unjustifiably bitter editorial campaign against Tillman. He did say harsh things, but none harsher than he had said in the past. Other editors said the same things—and much more—but their words have been forgotten since they did not get shot. Actually, the chief difference between N. G.'s 1892 and 1902 political campaigns was that there was no humor whatsoever in his 1902 words—there was no "Zerrachaboam" to lampoon a man whose character offered no grounds for jest. Different from many other papers, *The State* left Tillman's private life and activities largely alone, except by such innuendoes as, "we held our hand, for not being a clean person, he was an unpleasant one to handle."[30] But his character was not his private life, and before the campaign Gonzales had said that a man's right to have a base private character exempt from exposure by the press was forfeited when he held office: "his character becomes most legitimately a subject for public consideration and it is the duty of the press to contribute to a true understanding of it."[31]

[29] *The State,* July 31, 1902. George Tillman's letter, February 6, 1895, in the Gonzales Mss.

[30] *The State,* August 9, 1902.

[31] *Ibid.,* March 24, 1902. Earlier, N. G. had written: "When confident of my own rectitude of intention I have never cared, and never will care, what the public choose to think of me or my acts." N. G. Gonzales to R. Means Davis, March 30, 1888, in Davis Papers.

During the long summer campaign Gonzales frequently attacked Tillman, and on the stump his target spent much time vilifying the editor. Referring to "the case of the fraud upon the Senate," *The State* said: "It is a serious reflection upon Satan, a really strong point against Satan, to call him the father of lies."[32] Under such headlines as "A BRANDED ANANIAS CONTINUES TO PARADE," the paper constantly needled the increasingly irritable Tillman, who, according to the paper, was "the worst and most indefensible man who ever sought the Democratic nomination" and who had "literally lied his way into secondary office."[33] The editor also said he had "disgraced himself by his conduct while in command of the first regiment."[34]

All of the major papers in the state—except the ostrichlike *News and Courier*—loudly assailed Tillman. The most severe phrases attributed to Gonzales actually were not his own but those of small papers which he kept reprinting. For example, *The State* republished the following from the Anderson *Daily Mail:*

. . . [H]is notoriously bad and unsavory repuation . . . ranks alongside that of Scott and Moses [worst of the Reconstruction governors]. . . . He is the one candidate in the race about whose character nothing good is ever said. . . .

A GOOD AND VIRTUOUS MAN MIGHT BE PERSE-CUTED BUT A VILE AND WICKED MAN, NEVER. . . .

HE IS A PROVEN LIAR, DEFAULTER, GAMBLER AND DRUNKARD.[35]

Edited by E. H. DeCamp, alumnus of the early *State,* the *Gaffney Ledger* supplied plenty of ammunition for use

32 *The State,* August 19, 1902.
33 *Ibid.,* August 25, 1902.
34 *Ibid.,* July 31, 1902.
35 *Ibid.,* August 23, 1902, citing the Anderson *Daily Mail,* n.d. *The State* summarized the censure of Tillman by other papers on August 8, 9, 11, 14, 20, 21, 22, 23, 25, 1902.

against the "gambler, liar, and drunkard." After telling of Jim's notorious drunkenness, the *Ledger* said:

He attended the Keeley institute in Columbia . . . , was arrested in Augusta, Ga., for gambling and drinking, and we have it on the best authority that he misappropriated funds belonging to the Ladies Monument association of Edgefield . . . and failed to turn over to a North Carolina firm money collected from J. A. Attaway, Saluda, S.C.[36]

When the campaign party reached Gaffney, DeCamp took the stand in person, accused Tillman to his face of being a "gambler, liar, and a drunkard," and proved his lie charge with documents. Although "the ladies left precipitately," no fireworks followed—proof sufficient to Jim's enemies that the charges were true and that he lacked courage.[37]

During the course of the campaign both the staff of *The State,* his friends, and even Ambrose and Willie Gonzales warned N. G. Gonzales that his vigorous course was a dangerous one. In his paper he acknowledged the warnings and said they were as numerous as those he received in 1896 when during the senatorial campaign he had attacked John Gary Evans' record; pointedly, he noted that Evans had been de-

[36] *The State,* July 24, 1902; and August 4, 1902, citing the *Gaffney Ledger,* n.d. *The State* later confirmed and proved the charges concerning the Monument Association funds after Tillman had made some misleading and incomplete explanations. Although Gonzales did not make the most severe charges against Tillman but simply stressed that he was repeating what others said, DeCamp was corresponding with Gonzales and asking, "Can't you assist me in getting several affidavits from people in Columbia regarding Jim's character, especially his drinking and gambling. I want them. . . . I shall certainly not violate any confidence imposed in me." DeCamp to Gonzales, July 25, 1902, in Gonzales Mss. DeCamp called Tillman "the d—— coward" without "a spark of manhood in [his] dirty carcass."

[37] *The State,* July 24, 1902. Unique sidelight: The Tillman opponents liked to stress in their criticism his participation in cockfighting, but the "documents" DeCamp used to prove his charges were correspondence and bills from *Grit and Steel,* a cockfighting magazine published by DeCamp.

feated, whereas *The State* had remained silent in 1900 and Tillman had been elected.[38] Privately he told a friend that nothing could induce him "to notice J. H. Tillman personally," and that if the latter were going to shoot him he would already have done so. He added that it was "nauseating . . . to touch him, even metaphorically with his pen."[39] To the editor of the *Baptist Courier* he said virtually the same thing, assuring him that he felt it an editor's duty to create public sentiment in favor of the good and the right, and that he was justified in enlightening the public about their officials. In this long, reserved conversation, Gonzales insisted that personal animosity did not animate him, that he had no apprehension of a personal encounter, and that he never went armed.[40]

Apparently the public was enlightened and aroused by the exposure, for Tillman ran fourth in the first primary.[41] The day following his defeat, Tillman, in a circular letter, said: "But for the brutal, false and malicious newspaper attacks headed by N. G. Gonzales, I believe I would have been elected."[42] On September 3, 1902, the editor through his paper replied to an offer made by the lieutenant-governor to resign

if the editor will go to him and call him a "liar and a blackguard or a coward." The editor of The State is not playing in a melo-

---

[38] *The State,* August 13, 1902. The statement that the other Gonzales brothers did not fully approve N. G.'s course is based on the later reminiscences of one of his newspaper associates. See James A. Hoyt, Jr., to W. W. Ball, December 14, 1938, in Hoyt Papers.

[39] Wade H. Gibbs in *The State,* November 8, 1903.

[40] A. J. S. Thomas, account of Gonzales-Thomas conversation held in July 1902 in *The State,* November 1, 1903. In the Tillman trial, it was brought out that Gonzales had ceased to carry a pistol many years before this.

[41] *The State,* August 28, 1902. Eventual winner was D. C. Heyward, close friend of the Gonzales family.

[42] J. H. Tillman's circular letter of August 29, 1902, reprinted in *The State,* September 1, 1902.

drama. . . . In his paper he has called Jim Tillman what he was, and what, in public interest, it was necessary to call him.

If any grievance exists it is not on the part of Mr. Gonzales, who proudly admits the election has given him full satisfaction. Therefore it would be quite superfluous as well as stale and cheap to do the DeCamp act over again after the curtain had been rung down.[43]

With that, N. G. had his last word on Jim Tillman. Quiet reigned—for five months.

But Jim Tillman had the last word. About 1:45 on the afternoon of January 15, 1903, N. G. left *The State* office and started to his home on Henderson Street for dinner. As always, he walked down Main Street toward the Capitol, less than a block away, where he always turned east to continue down Gervais. It was a cold day, and both of his hands were rammed into his overcoat pockets, a habit characteristic of all three Gonzales brothers. At the same time, the lieutenant-governor left the Senate over which he had been presiding and with four of his friends started toward Main Street. Two of them walked in front, and two—including his close friend and later a famed governor, Cole L. Blease—walked with him. Gonzales and Tillman had met frequently on the street and always passed without speaking. As the editor met the group this day, he cut across the sidewalk to the inside to make his turn at the corner on the inside against the building and thus avoid brushing against Tillman, who was on the outside as his group approached the corner. When Gonzales came almost abreast of them at the corner, Tillman whipped out a pistol and fired one bullet which went all the way through Gonzales' body. Lying against the building, the unarmed victim glared at his enemy and said, "Shoot again, you coward!" Tillman said nothing. In testimony later, there was

43 *The State*, September 3, 1902.

much controversy as to whether before the shooting he had said, "I got your message, Mr. Gonzales," or words to that effect. He turned from the scene and surrendered to a policeman nearby, who found that he was carrying another pistol besides the one he had used. Leaning on others, the suffering editor trudged back to his office. There, lying on the floor amid tearful co-workers, he dictated a statement in which he swore that he had no premonition of new trouble and had not heard his antagonist utter a word. After the shot, he believed that Tillman had said, "I took your advice," or such words, which he swore had no special connotation to him. Taken to the hospital, he became the focal point of South Carolinians' interest.[44]

Although the bullet had gone through Gonzales' intestines, there was hope at the Columbia Hospital that he might survive. An operation was performed, and many doctors were in attendance. All of Columbia seemed to be solicitous for him: even Mrs. J. H. Tillman sent expressions of regret and hopes of recovery to Mrs. Gonzales;[45] and prayers for the wounded editor were said in Columbia churches on Sunday, January 18, and also in the city schools. A friend who visited the dying man said that he never once expressed any vindictive feeling.[46] But peritonitis was too much for the medicine of the day, and on January 19, N. G. Gonzales died.

Public reaction to the event varied. Despite a freezing rain and a bitterly cold day, 2,000 people attended the Gonzales funeral, which save for Wade Hampton's was the largest as-

[44] This account has been reconstructed from the *News and Courier*, *The State*, and Raleigh *News and Observer*, all of January 16, 1903; and clippings of other papers concerning the attack and legal testimony of the subsequent trial, in the Gonzales Scrapbooks. The latter voluminous collection seems to have everything ever printed by the press on the whole episode.

[45] *Savannah Press*, January 19, 1903, a clipping from the Gonzales Scrapbooks. Mrs. J. H. Tillman was a very different and better kind of person than her husband and was muchly respected. She did not die until 1962.

[46] The Reverend Samuel M. Smith in *The State*, January 19, 1904.

semblage of mourners in state history.[47] Despite the genuine grief which seemed to grip the state, mixed feelings were understandably widespread. To many people, the only surprise was not that Gonzales had been shot but that he had not been shot five or six months earlier when he was making—and reprinting—the journalistic assaults on Tillman. Some were not eager for prosecution because they considered it "persecution" to expose an infamous character and the killing of the "persecutor" justifiable.[48] The most partisan Tillmanites openly rejoiced and loudly demanded an immediate acquittal.[49] Robert R. Hemphill's was probably typical of much apathetic or fatalistic thinking: "Many people expected Gonzales to be killed some day and I don't suppose anything will ever be done to Tillman."[50] Others were reconciled to such an outcome, as in a sample opinion: "If a man insists upon playing with live wires—electrocution generally results—nevertheless it is a great pity."[51] Editor J. C. Hemphill was circumspect in a letter which he wrote to August Kohn to learn Columbia reactions and what opinions he had heard expressed about the course of the *News and Courier*.[52]

Kohn could well have told Hemphill not to believe everything he read in the papers. Editors everywhere expressed maudlin rage and grief, and within days they had made Gonzales a martyr for the freedom of the press. Despite their uninhibited denunciations, renewed analyses of Tillman's character, and reports that feeling in Columbia was intense, bitter, and deep-seated, editors almost universally predicted

[47] Raleigh *News and Observer*, January 22, 1903.
[48] Wallace, *History of S. C.*, 111, 412, 414.
[49] For example, see George S. McCravy (politico-postmaster of Laurens) to B. R. Tillman, April 13, 1903, in Simkins Notes.
[50] R. R. Hemphill to J. C. Hemphill, January 31, 1903, in Hemphill Papers.
[51] Ella C. Cromer to R. R. Hemphill, January 16, 1903, in Hemphill Papers.
[52] J. C. Hemphill to August Kohn, January 26, 1903, in Letterbook, 1900–1903, of Hemphill Papers.

at first that the assailant would be exonerated.[53] Although a rumor was spread by the New York *Daily News* that a lynching mob was in the streets, various rumors of impending violence were quickly squelched by calmer papers.[54]

The New York paper reported the Gonzales family was making threats against Tillman—a story quite different from the facts. Despite their customary impetuous and emotional reactions, the only feelings they now demonstrated were grief and calmness. Upset members of *The State* staff asked "Mr. Ambrose" how the family had refrained from vengeance; very quietly he replied, "Had we done so, all the righteousness and law and order which The State has stood for would have been brought to naught."[55] The day after N. G.'s death, Ambrose concluded a signed editorial: "With heavy hearts his work is taken over by those who loved him well, and in his name The State is pledged anew to the principles for which he gave his life."[56]

To avoid charges of prejudice, *The State* did not print anything on the event written by members of its own staff. Although other papers praised its restrained policy, some question might be raised about the objectivity of the four "outsiders" it employed to cover the story: August Kohn, Thomas R. Waring, Howard A. Banks, and William Watts Ball, all of whom were at one time or another close to the Gonzaleses. The attitude of other papers was also interesting. Generally state papers were unrestrainedly bitter against Tillman (ten of the eleven dailies in the state having acidly opposed his candidacy for governor) and agreed that Gon-

[53] Based on a study of scores of clippings in the Gonzales Scrapbooks.

[54] "There is no real excitement about the shooting as the papers say," wrote R. R. Hemphill to R. S. Hemphill, January 16, 1903, in Hemphill Papers; for rumors and denials, see Gonzales Scrapbooks.

[55] Reminiscences of W. W. Watson in *The State*, February 18, 1931. This attitude was substantiated in an A.P. story by T. R. Waring in *The State*, January 19, 1903.

[56] *The State*, January 30, 1903.

zales, however tactless and blunt, had shown the man in his
true light. Scores of papers condemned the deed—from the
New York Times to the *Wateree Messenger,* the *Springfield
Republican* to the *Pee Dee Advocate,* the Philadelphia *Public
Ledger* to the *Barnwell People.* All, including editors friendly
to Ben Tillman, deplored the tragedy as a disgrace to state
politics and demanded a fair trial. The strongest of the pro-
Gonzales papers hinted strongly that a fair trial could end
only in conviction and that acquittal would prove that Gonzales had failed in his campaign to bring law and order to
violence-ridden South Carolina.

During this renewed examination of his character, Jim
Tillman sat in jail. Chief Justice Young J. Pope refused him
bail,[57] but the accused was hardly incommoded as hundreds
of his supporters called on him at his cell which they out-
fitted with a suite of furniture, books, magazines, and flowers.
Most of the time, Judge O. W. Buchanan, a brother-in-law,
remained with him. Occasionally the prisoner issued statements in which he complained bitterly that the press was
still persecuting him.

And some of the press did injure its own cause. Two days
after Gonzales' death, the New York *World* sent to all newspapers a circular letter to solicit funds for hiring "the best
lawyers in the South" to prosecute the perpetrator of a crime
that "involves the liberty of the press and its freedom to comment freely and fearlessly on the conduct of politicians and
parties, answerable only to the law and to public opinion."[58]
The well-intended move backfired, for the Southern press
was almost unanimous in rejecting such a scheme which
would have evoked loud cries of "Yankee interference."[59]

Both sides brought a formidable array of legal talent into

[57] *Ibid.,* February 20, 1903. Tillman's term of office expired a few days
following the shooting.
[58] New York *World* to the editor of the *News and Courier* (a circular letter) , January 21, 1903, in the Hemphill Papers.
[59] Gonzales Scrapbooks.

the case of the *State* versus *Tillman*. To help Solicitor William Thurmond prosecute the prisoner, the Gonzales family retained G. Duncan Bellinger, Andrew Crawford, William Elliott, Jr. (a kinsman from Columbia), I. L. Asbill, and L. T. Sturkie. To defend Tillman, the following were retained: George W. Croft, Patrick H. Nelson, Osmund W. Buchanan, Cole L. Blease, George Johnstone, W. T. Sharpe, G. T. Graham, George R. Rembert, and Efird & Dreher.[60]

The first move of the defense was to get a change of venue. In April hearings on this request were postponed until June 1903, when lengthy testimony was presented. The counsel for defense introduced 356 affidavits to prove that Tillman could not get a fair trial in Columbia, where he was denounced as an assassin, where Gonzales was hailed as a martyr, and where a monument was being planned to honor the dead editor. Over four hundred affidavits were introduced to say just the opposite thing for the state, and prosecuting lawyers observed that *The State*, lambasted by the defense as having aroused public passions so that a fair trial was impossible, actually had been "abstaining from any criticism of the said Tillman except the signed editorial [by James A. Hoyt] which appeared . . . the day after the homicide."[61] This same comment was made by many admiring papers which insisted that Tillman did not want justice or the fair trial that he talked about so much;[62] but the court agreed that the trial should be moved as requested to neutral Lexington County, which —not coincidentally, perhaps—had always shown a larger proportionate vote in support of Ben Tillman than any other county in the state.[63]

The trial finally began—more than eight months after

[60] *The State*, September 29, 1903. William Thurmond was father of J. Strom Thurmond, later governor and senator. On his later career and involvement with Ben Tillman and patronage, see Simkins, *Tillman*, pp. 531–34.

[61] *The State*, June 23, 1903.

[62] Press opinion summaries in *ibid.*, July 2, 1903.

[63] *News and Courier*, October 16, 1903.

Gonzales had died. The important story received full coverage in *The State,* which hired a young court stenographer, James F. Byrnes, to record verbatim all the testimony for its columns. Daily, W. W. Ball wrote an introductory account of these proceedings—a report that was highly biased, especially when compared with the objectivity of August Kohn and John Marshall in the *News and Courier.* For example, in one story after praising the eloquence of the prosecution, Ball wrote, "The painful laboring of the speakers for the defense was all too evident." He also told of "the tattered theory of self-defense" and the "sickly sentimentality with which the defense has persistently and incessantly sought to becloud the position in which the prisoner at the bar of justice stands."[64] Ball also was close to Ambrose Gonzales during the trial and convinced him of the ability and reliability of his old college mate, William Thurmond, the state solicitor.

Much legal maneuvering and skirmishing took place, the record of which would fill a book.[65] The defense arranged to get Judge Frank B. Gary, "closely allied by ties of friendship and politics to the Tillmans," assigned to preside.[66] The defense likewise thwarted the state's hope to get the case tried during the first week of the court term in "neutral Lexington" but managed to have it held the second week when a new panel of jurors would be available. Among the strongest assets for the defense were the influence and presence of the prisoner's uncle, Senator Tillman. Ben never approved of Jim and never sanctioned his killing Gonzales, but "Jim Till-

[64] *The State,* October 13, 14, 1903. His resumé of the case (October 2, 1903) is an excellent condensation, but it sounds like a speech by an attorney for the prosecution. Nevertheless, the paper received lavish praise for its objectivity. See *The State,* June 23; July 6, 9, 1903.

[65] The writer has had difficulty in making even this brief condensation when confronted with the volume of material available. James A. Hoyt, Jr., an assistant to N. G. Gonzales, left a copious collection of clippings in his papers and also wrote a number of articles about the affair.

[66] *The State,* September 26, 1903.

man was my nephew and blood is thicker than water."[67] He spent money, used his influence to hire lawyers and help get the trial moved to Lexington, and answered the lawyers' request to "come down and mix with the boys."[68] But because of the illness of his wife, he actually spent only one day at the trial which ran three weeks, though he was "constant in his advice and suggestions."[69]

The strategy of the defense, in brief, was to show that Tillman saw Gonzales' hands in his pockets, thought that one of them moved in a menacing way, and shot him in self-defense. The lawyers also introduced witnesses who had been at the State Capitol earlier on the fatal day and implied that Gonzales had been there seemingly testing Tillman to see if his presence would precipitate an attack. A doorkeeper and a custodian of a committee room swore that N. G. had said something about having made Tillman "show the white feather" once and would make him do it again. More influential was the defense strategy of introducing editorials from *The State* as evidence that homicide was justified by such inflammatory attacks.

The state met each of these defenses as follows: Tillman had met Gonzales frequently before without danger, and he could have ascertained that the editor never went armed; sarcastically, it was noted that wriggling a thumb could hardly justify murder. The testimony of the witnesses from the Capitol was shown to be weak and contradictory, and reputable persons swore that they would not believe those witnesses even under oath. The parts of *The State* which had

[67] B. R. Tillman to A. W. Williams, October 11, 1916, in Simkins Notes. Also, see B. R. Tillman to Lehman Johnson, August 21, 28, 1914, in Simkins Notes.

[68] G. W. Croft to B. R. Tillman, June 9, 24, August 1, September 2, 16, 1903; P. H. Nelson to B. R. Tillman, June 24, 1903; J. S. Johnson to B. R. Tillman, April 30, 1903; B. L. Caughman to B. R. Tillman, July 11, 1903, all in Simkins Notes.

[69] *News and Courier*, October 16, 1903.

been introduced were shown to have been quotations from other papers which were even more unrestrained than was the dead editor's. The prisoner himself also admitted that he had assailed Gonzales on every stump in South Carolina. At that point, it seemed perhaps that the plea of self-defense had failed.

Crux of the case then became the effort of the defense to convince the jury that Tillman had been justified in his action because, with the facts at his disposal, he had reason to fear the editor. The prosecution, however, claimed that Gonzales had never made spoken or implied threats against Tillman—Ambrose Gonzales even swearing that he had never heard N. G. verbally denounce or threaten anyone in his life[70]—and showed that Tillman had never even contemplated the possibility of a lawsuit against the editor for the attacks which his lawyers claimed were so provocative and libelous. The attorneys for the state also introduced witnesses who swore that several times in 1902 Jim Tillman had said that he ought to murder N. G. Gonzales, and E. J. Watson had even once declined to carry such a threat from Tillman to Gonzales. Witnesses of the crime also swore that the victim had shown no evident signs of anticipating an attack.[71]

To offset this, the defense lawyers introduced witnesses— who were accused by the prosecution of not being shining lights of virtue and character—who related how various people had informed Tillman that Gonzales was threatening to kill him and was spreading rumors of his cowardice. Although the prosecution showed these witnesses to be weak, the informants unreliable, and the information (relayed to Tillman) erroneous and illogical, the testimony carried weight in the effort to indicate that Tillman could possibly

[70] *The State*, September 30, 1903.
[71] *News and Courier*, October 3, 7, 1903.

have built up in his own mind the idea that Gonzales had designs on his blood. Even conceding that obsession and persecution complex, the state asked why the lieutenant-governor had not resorted to legal methods to silence Gonzales or his editorials, or to thwart any plot or crime. William Elliott closed his peroration to the jury by saying a verdict of "not guilty" would sanction the shooting of public-spirited editors and would end the freedom of the press and by noting that Tillman had "but slain the prosecuting witness, and added a crime to his record which far exceeds anything charged against him by the dead editor. James H. Tillman's motive was revenge, and he is a murderer."[72]

The jury, however, saw the shooting as self-defense—or, perhaps more aptly put, as justifiable. *The State* headlined the verdict: "THE FARCE IS ENDED. . . . THE CARDS WERE STACKED." There is an undocumented tradition that the defense before the trial had sent Ben Covar, an Edgefield Tillmanite posing as a photographer, to call on the members of the jury panel; while demonstrating samples of his workmanship, he observed the jurors' reactions on viewing pictures of Gonzales and the Tillmans that were among his samples, thereby learning which jurors to reject.[73] One of the defense counsel wrote to Senator Tillman: "We canvassed through the jurors of both weeks [of the term of court] and many of the jurors have been sounded & we determined if possible to postpone the case so as it will be tried on the second week."[74] Both Wallace and Simkins have called the self-defense plea "farcical," and the latter adds: "The assassin . . . went legally unpunished; but the Gonzales family

---

[72] William Elliott, Jr., *Speech of William Elliott against James Tillman during the Trial of Tillman for the Shooting of N. G. Gonzales* (a pamphlet, n.p., n.d.; in South Caroliniana Library), p. 15.

[73] Simkins, *Tillman*, p. 383. In interviews with the author, both W. W. Ball and J. A. Hoyt insisted that the story is true.

[74] G. W. Croft to B. R. Tillman, September 2, 1903, in Simkins Notes.

experienced a ghastly vengeance. The ghost of the dead man pursued Jim Tillman the rest of his unhappy days."[75]

With the acquittal, *The State* at once ended its widely acclaimed neutrality and restraint by publishing editorials entitled "The Crime of Lexington," "A Nauseating Spectacle," and "The Testimony of Perjurers."[76] James A. Hoyt wrote a long statement to seek to refute the truth and the logic of the witnesses for the defense. Both pulpit and press roundly condemned the verdict as a travesty of justice and a frustration of law,[77] and *The State* repeatedly took it as a text for its demands for a stronger public conscience in order to effect jury reforms and law enforcement.

The week following Gonzales' death, various citizens, led by W. A. Clark and J. J. McMahan, began a fund to erect a monument to the editor; $600 was raised the first day.[78] Temporarily suspended lest it "jeopardize justice," the campaign was resumed later. On December 12, 1905, a monument at the corner of Sumter and Senate streets was dedicated before a large crowd. The main oration was delivered by the Reverend Samuel M. Smith. Editors everywhere took the occasion to laud their departed colleague. Said Josephus Daniels in his Raleigh *News and Observer*: "He was simply an editor in a small Southern capital, who made a great newspaper simply through his ability and his pluck. . . . The people of South Carolina erected a monument to that editor because he fought their battle and because he was the foe to public men who do not have the high conception of public office as a sacred trust."[79]

[75] Simkins, *Tillman*, p. 383. J. H. Tillman died April 1, 1911.

[76] *The State*, October 16, 1903.

[77] For quotations of these condemnations, see *ibid.*, October 19–24, 28; November 1, 2, 5, 12, 1903. Also, see Gonzales Scrapbooks.

[78] *The State*, January 29, 1903.

[79] *Ibid.*, January 2, 1906, citing the Raleigh *News and Observer*, n.d. On the monument, see *The State*, January 29, 1903; March 28, 1905; and December 13, 1905.

No lengthy summary evaluation of the stormy petrel editor is needed since appraisals have appeared frequently in the pages above. In political history, N. G. G. ranks as a foremost opponent—perhaps *the* foremost—to that form of America's "Agrarian Revolt" known as Tillmanism. Nevertheless, he should not be classed as the foremost defender of its rival political force, Carolina Conservatism or the Bourbon Regime, although certainly he was a spokesman for its better aspects and an advocate of coupling compassion to conservatism and of making government both progressive and efficient. Certainly he helped to make South Carolinians aware of political life, although they may already have been overly aware without journalistic inducement.

He left behind a monument to himself in a newspaper, one which represented the "personal journalism" still so prevalent and one which did much to further the economic growth of Columbia and the state. Most South Carolinians were keenly aware of the existence of this newspaper, and most had very strong feelings about it. After his departure, it became less strident and less controversial as his brothers continued it, and by the 1920s *The State* truly was as much "a state institution" as it was a business enterprise, with W. E. Gonzales serving as editor until his death in 1937.

Although N. G. G. had given the paper a note of flamboyance and during "Tillmania" had made it a major issue in political controversy, it was "Mr. Ambrose" who made it "a state institution" and who to a large degree determined its character. Many of his contemporaries—both journalists and others—felt strongly that Ambrose Elliott Gonzales not only was the real power of the paper but also was one of the greatest South Carolinians produced since 1865.

N. G. Gonzales' shortcomings hopefully have been apparent in this study. He himself acknowledged them, and Dawson was correct in calling him "bad-tempered and querulous" just as Ambrose had described him when both were still boys on the plantation. As a person, he was the opposite of vicious, but when he was stirred into "righteous indignation," his indignant prose could fairly crackle on the printed page. After "much close association with him," the author can only conclude that he was utterly sincere and conscientious in his strongly held convictions. Through it all, he was independent—nobody's man, not even Wade Hampton's. In his editorial wrath, no matter how vigorous and stinging his words, he was convinced that he was following the proper course, for, after all, as George D. Tillman had told N. G. G. when he was only twenty-four, "And damne! you're independent as hell!"

Most perspicacious was South Carolina's leading historian, D. D. Wallace, who characterized the founder of *The State* by pointing to both sides of his character:

With the ideal of unflinching public service, he repeatedly risked his life. In controversy he was often overbearing and relentlessly pursued an antagonist, rubbing salt in the wounds which his shafts had opened. His faults were virtues carried to excess. His strength lay in his dauntless courage and his sun-clear integrity.[80]

[80] Wallace, *History of S. C.*, III, 414.

APPENDIX

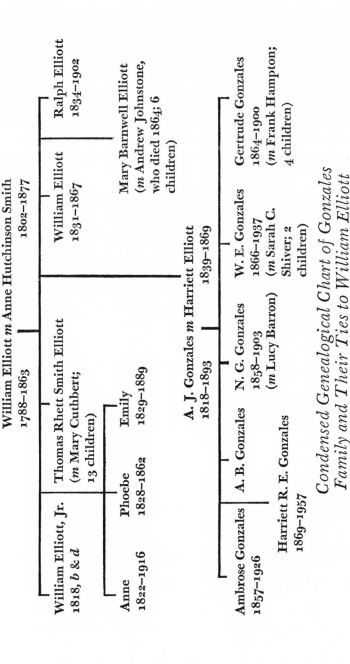

Condensed Genealogical Chart of Gonzales Family and Their Ties to William Elliott

William Elliott *m* Anne Hutchinson Smith
1788–1863   1802–1877

William Elliott, Jr.
1818, *b & d*

Thomas Rhett Smith Elliott
(*m* Mary Cuthbert)
13 children)

William Elliott
1831–1867

Ralph Elliott
1834–1902

Anne
1822–1916

Phoebe
1828–1862

Emily
1829–1889

Mary Barnwell Elliott
(*m* Andrew Johnstone,
who died 1864; 6
children)

A. J. Gonzales *m* Harriett Elliott
1818–1893   1839–1869

Ambrose Gonzales
1857–1926

A. B. Gonzales

N. G. Gonzales
1858–1903
(*m* Lucy Barron)

W. E. Gonzales
1866–1937
(*m* Sarah C.
Shiver; 2
children)

Gertrude Gonzales
1864–1900
(*m* Frank Hampton;
4 children)

Harriett R. E. Gonzales
1869–1957

BIBLIOGRAPHY

BIBLIOGRAPHY

A. Manuscript Collections

1. William Watts Ball Papers, in Duke University Library. A tremendous collection of great value for history of South Carolina journalism, but most of it dealing with the Gonzales family and *The State* comes after the death of N. G. Gonzales.

2. James Conner Papers, in South Carolina Historical Society, Charleston.

3. William A. Courtenay Papers, in South Caroliniana Library, University of South Carolina, Columbia.

4. R. Means Davis Papers, in South Caroliniana Library. Davis was a history professor at the University of South Carolina, was close to the Gonzales brothers, and did some writing for their newspaper.

5. Francis W. Dawson Papers, in Duke University Library. This exceedingly valuable collection contains much of the business correspondence—both incoming and outgoing—of the *News and Courier* office. While not complete, it is of tremendous significance to scholars interested in such persons as Dawson, Gonzales, J. C. Hemphill, and B. R. Tillman.

6. Thomas Rhett Smith Elliott Papers, in Duke University Library. A small collection of family correspondence, largely of the 1860s. Contains interesting (and not always pleasant) aspects of one of William Elliott's sons.

7. John Gary Evans Papers, in South Caroliniana Library. Not

much on Gonzales in this collection of papers of Tillman's successor as governor.

8. Elliott-Gonzales Papers, in Southern Historical Collection, University of North Carolina. By far the most valuable source (4,000 items, 25 volumes) for the student interested in the family and personal life of William Elliott and his family. Covering the period from the late seventeenth century to about 1895, these papers are a remarkably entertaining collection for the person seeking an understanding of plantation life. Most of the letters were written in the lifetime of William Elliott (1788–1863), but there are also scores written later by the ladies of the family and the younger Gonzaleses.

9. Gonzales Manuscripts, in South Caroliniana Library. Although not extensive (50 items), this collection contains some valuable letters of Gen. A. J. Gonzales and his three sons and ranges over a wide span of years. There is no extensive collection of correspondence after 1895 that can properly be labeled "the Gonzales papers." Prof. R. L. Meriwether once told the writer that Mr. W. E. Gonzales had informed him personally that he had burned all of the family correspondence.

10. Wade Hampton Papers, in Southern Historical Collection, University of North Carolina. Small, mainly personal, and not very important.

11. Hemphill Family Papers, in Duke University Library. A titanic collection (12,371 items, and 28 volumes), much of it centering around J. C. Hemphill, which does much to offset the absence of extensive Gonzales correspondence for the period after 1895.

12. James A. Hoyt Papers, in South Caroliniana Library. Hoyt, a newspaperman at one time, was once associated with the Gonzales brothers. He collected and kept most of his correspondence and preserved hundreds of clippings from many newspapers, well organized in scrapbooks.

13. August Kohn Papers, in South Caroliniana Library. Since Kohn was a newspaperman in Columbia, his large file of

outgoing mail contains many observations on *The State* and its owners.

14. John P. Richardson Letter Books, in South Carolina Department of Archives and History. Official correspondence; of some help since W. E. Gonzales was private secretary to Governor Richardson.

15. Yates Snowden Papers, in South Caroliniana Library. Like the Hemphill and Kohn Papers, this collection helps to offset the destruction of the latter-day Gonzales papers. Snowden was a close personal friend of Ambrose Gonzales, and these letters show some of the humor and sparkle which marked both men. Snowden started as a Charleston journalist and ended as a history teacher ("professor of Confederocracy") at the University of South Carolina for many years.

16. Simkins Notes, in Southern Historical Collection, University of North Carolina. These are the voluminous verbatim transcriptions which Prof. Francis B. Simkins made from large portions of the letters in the B. R. Tillman Papers, in the Clemson University Library. At the time that the research for this study (itself a portion of much longer dissertation) was being undertaken, the Tillman Papers were not available and open to scholars. Much of the material derived from this source never appeared in Simkins' book on Tillman.

17. Tillman Manuscripts, in Duke University Library. Very small collection of no great help or significance.

B. Newspapers

1. Athens *Banner-Herald,* August 31, 1931.
2. *Charleston Courier,* May 1850; May 1851; February 1–5, 1863.
3. Charleston *Journal of Commerce,* January–March 1877.
4. Charleston *News and Courier,* August 1, 1880–January 31, 1891; also, May 20–June 3, 1876; March 15–April 17, 1893; September 10–October 15, 1903; and January 13, 1938.
5. *Columbia Journal,* June 28, 1893; September 22, 1894.
6. *Columbia Daily Register,* 1885–1896.

7. Columbia *State,* February 18, 1891–November 15, 1937.
8. *Greenville News,* September 25, 1949.
9. *Greenville Piedmont,* August 30, 1931.
10. *Patria,* December 31, 1892. A Spanish-language newspaper published 1892–1898 [?] in New York by Cuban refugees.

C. Scrapbook Collections and Pamphlet Collections

1. *Pamphlets By and About Hon. B. R. Tillman and Tillmania in South Carolina, 1890–1918.* This volume contains nineteen pamphlets bound together in the South Caroliniana Library.
2. South Carolina State Press Association. *Proceedings of the 15th, 16th, 17th, 18th, 19th Annual Meetings of the South Carolina State Press Association. Reprinted from the News & Courier.* Newberry, S. C.: Elbert H. Aull Company, 1907. (A collection in one pamphlet.)
3. South Carolina State Press Association. *Proceedings of the Seventeenth Annual Meeting of the South Carolina State Press Association, Held at Georgetown, S. C.* Greenville: Keys and Thomas, 1892.
4. South Carolina State Press Association. *Proceedings of the Eighteenth Annual Meeting of the South Carolina State Press Association, Held at Anderson, S. C., July 6–8, 1892.* Abbeville: Hugh Wilson, Printer, 1892.
5. South Carolina State Press Association. *Proceedings,* 1889–1893; 1895–1896; 1898–1900; 1909; 1910; 1911–1915; 1921. (This entry is a compilation of the Proceedings used by the author as they are bound together in the Duke and South Caroliniana Libraries; the preceding three entries refer to separate pamphlets which have also been located.)
6. Scrapbooks of Newspaper Clippings concerning the Murder of N. G. Gonzales and the Trial of James H. Tillman, 3 vols., in South Caroliniana Library. Cited in this work as Gonzales Scrapbooks.
7. Scrapbook of Press Association Clippings, prepared by August Kohn, and in South Caroliniana Library.

8. T. Larry Gantt Scrapbook, in possession of Mr. Robert J. Gantt, Spartanburg, S. C. (Since the writer used this, Mr. Robert J. Gantt, son of T. Larry Gantt, has died.)
9. In the Hoyt Papers in South Caroliniana Library are a number of scrapbooks and collections of clippings used for this study.

D. Miscellaneous Primary Sources

1. Aull, Elbert H. "Newspapermen I Have Known Since I Have Been President of the Association," in South Carolina State Press Association *Proceedings* (1910), pp. 54–62.
2. Barnwell, Joseph W. "Life and Recollections of Joseph W. Barnwell." Unpublished manuscript of memoirs, 1929, in South Carolina Historical Society, Charleston.
3. Chesnut, Mary. *Diary from Dixie,* edited by Ben Ames Williams. Boston: Houghton Mifflin Company, 1949.
4. Elliott, William. *Speech of William Elliott against James Tillman during the Trial of Tillman for the Shooting of N. G. Gonzales.* N.p., n.d. A copy of this pamphlet is in the South Caroliniana Library; at the time of the trial, it appeared in the press.
5. *Journal of the Constitutional Convention of South Carolina, 1895.*
6. *Rowell's American Newspaper Directory,* 40 vols. New York: George P. Rowell and Company, 1869–1908.

E. Interviews

The author was fortunate in being able to talk to a number of people once associated with the Gonzales brothers. Most of these interviews took place when the writer was first interested in this topic, and nearly all of these people have since died. In some cases, he had many informal chats with them on visits in addition to the "formal interview" cited here—especially in the cases of Miss Harriet R. E. Gonzales (sister of the Gonzales newspapermen) and Mr. W. W. Ball, then editor of the *News and Courier.*

1. Mr. W. W. Ball, September 8, 1948. Long associated with the Gonzales brothers and once (1913–1923) editor of *The State*. The author had known Mr. Ball for a number of years.

2. Mrs. Clarendon Barron, January 22, 1950. Sister-in-law of Mrs. N. G. Gonzales, who lived with her.

3. Dr. William R. Barron, August 31, 1949; December 21, 1950; January 20, 1951, and several other occasions. Brother of Mrs. N. G. Gonzales and physician of Ambrose E. Gonzales.

4. Mrs. Lucy Hampton Bostick, January 25, 1951. Daughter of Mrs. Frank Hampton (née Gertrude Gonzales).

5. Judge and Mrs. R. A. Cooper, June 11, 1951. Longtime friends of the author and also friends of the Gonzaleses. Judge Cooper was elected governor in 1916.

6. Professor Henry C. Davis, January 24, 1951. The son of Professor R. Means Davis, who was prominent when *The State* was founded by his friend N. G. Gonzales.

7. Miss Emmie Fielding, January 29, 1951. Friend of the W. E. Gonzales family, who lived in the home with them. Miss Fielding is one of the people who have assured the author that all the family papers were burned about 1936.

8. Mr. Robert J. Gantt, January 27, 1951. Son of T. Larry Gantt.

9. Miss Harriett R. E. Gonzales, September 8, 1948, and September 4, 1949. Miss Gonzales was as perfectly cooperative as any writer could wish. Not only did she give the Elliott-Gonzales Papers to the Southern Historical Collection, but she also has provided the author with every possible fact and assistance that she could. Incidentally, she herself could write a letter which rivaled the charm of those written by other members of her family.

10. Mr. Frank Hampton, February 2, 1951. A son of Gertrude Gonzales.

11. Mr. Charles O. Hearon, January 27, 1951. Associate editor of the *Spartanburg Herald*. Long in charge of Ambrose Gonzales' newspaper property in Spartanburg.

12. Mrs. Helen Kohn Hennig, December 22, 1950. Daughter of

August Kohn and long an able writer on South Carolina topics.

13. Mr. R. Beverly Herbert, June 6, 1951. A Columbia lawyer who was once active in the Chamber of Commerce and a close friend of Ambrose Gonzales. His vivid memory and honest frankness were a great help to the author.

14. Mr. James A. Hoyt, April 7, 1951. Associate editor of *The State* under N. G. Gonzales and in South Carolina newspaper work until 1912.

15. Mrs. Legare Inglesby, January 23 and 25, 1951. A friend of the W. E. Gonzales family.

16. Mr. Sam L. Latimer, December 22, 1950, and on other occasions while the author was using files of the paper in *The State* office. Editor of *The State*, 1941–1961.

17. Mr. Joe B. S. Lyles, June 6, 1951. Son of W. H. Lyles, an associate of the Gonzaleses; also, lawyer for Ambrose Gonzales.

18. Mrs. Fitz Hugh McMaster, January 25, 1951. Mrs. McMaster's husband was long associated with *The State* and the Gonzales brothers.

19. Miss Louise McMaster, February 1, 1951. A friend of the Gonzaleses and a relative of Major R. K. McMaster.

20. Mrs. Robert W. Moore, January 18, 1951. Née Lillie McLaughlin, she was secretary to Ambrose Gonzales in the early 1920s.

21. Mr. Edward G. Siebels, June 12, 1951. A prominent Columbia businessman who was a close friend of Ambrose and William Gonzales, and acquainted with N. G. Gonzales. As kindly helpful to the author as Mr. R. B. Herbert.

II. Secondary Materials Cited

Ball, William Watts. *An Episode in South Carolina Politics.* In Tillman Pamphlets, no. 13, in South Caroliniana Library.

———. *The State That Forgot.* Indianapolis: Bobbs-Merrill Company, 1932.

Caldwell, Robert J. *López Expeditions to Cuba, 1848–1851.* Princeton: Princeton University Press, 1915.

Cash, Wilbur J. *Mind of the South.* New York: Alfred A. Knopf, 1941.

Christensen, Niels, Jr. "State Dispensaries in South Carolina," in *Annals of the Academy of Political and Social Science,* XXXII (1908), 545–55.

Clark, Thomas D. *Southern Country Editor.* Indianapolis: Bobbs-Merrill Company, 1948.

Cooper, William J., Jr. *Conservative Regime: South Carolina, 1877–1890.* Baltimore: The Johns Hopkins University Press, 1968.

Dabney, Virginius. *Liberalism in the South.* Chapel Hill: University of North Carolina Press, 1932.

Davidson, Elizabeth H. *Child Labor Legislation in the Southern Textile States.* Chapel Hill: University of North Carolina Press, 1939.

Elliott, William. *Carolina Sports, by Land and Water.* Charleston: Burges and James, 1846. Later editions: New York, 1859; London, 1867; Columbia, 1918. Available in 1973 from Abercrombie & Fitch Library, New York.

Eubanks, John E. *Ben Tillman's Baby: The Dispensary System in South Carolina.* Augusta, Ga.: published by the author, 1950.

Ezell, John S. *The South Since 1865.* New York: The Macmillan Company, 1963.

Ezell, William C. "Tillman and Blease as 'Popular' Leaders in South Carolina." M. A. thesis, University of North Carolina, 1931.

Floyd, Joseph W. *Historical Roster and Itinerary of South Carolina Volunteer Troops Who Served in the Late War between the United States and Spain, 1898, Coupled with Brief Sketches of their Movements from the Beginning to the Ending of the Conflict.* Columbia: R. L. Bryan Company, 1901.

Gonzales, N. G. *In Darkest Cuba.* Columbia: The State Company, 1922.

Grantham, Dewey W. *The Democratic South.* Athens: University of Georgia Press, 1963.

Green, Fletcher M. "Some Aspects of the Convict Lease System in the Southern States." In *Essays in Southern History,* edited by Fletcher M. Green. Chapel Hill: University of North Carolina Press, 1947.

Hemphill, James Calvin. "A Short History of the South Carolina Inter-State and West Indian Expedition." In *Charleston Year Book* (1902).

Hendrick, Carlanna L. "John Gary Evans, a Political Biography." Ph.D. diss., University of South Carolina, 1966.

Hendricks, Ellen A. "South Carolina Dispensary System," in *North Carolina Historical Review,* XXII (1945), 176–97, and 320–49.

Hennig, Helen Kohn. *August Kohn: Versatile South Carolinian.* Columbia: Vogue Press, 1950.

———, ed. *Columbia, Capital City of South Carolina, 1786–1936.* Columbia, S. C.: Columbia Sesquicentennial Commission, 1936.

———. *Great South Carolinians of a Later Date.* Chapel Hill: University of North Carolina Press, 1949.

Jones, Lewis P. "Ambrosio José Gonzales, a Cuban Patriot in Carolina." *South Carolina Historical Magazine,* LVI (April 1955), 67–76.

———. "Carolinians and Cubans: The Elliotts and Gonzales, Their Work and Their Writings." Ph.D. diss., University of North Carolina, 1952.

———. "James Calvin Hemphill." In Herbert Ravenel Sass, *Outspoken: 150 Years of the* News and Courier. Columbia: University of South Carolina Press, 1953.

———. "William Elliott, South Carolina Nonconformist," in *Journal of Southern History,* XVIII (August 1951), 361–81.

Kohn, August. "How To Get the News," in South Carolina State Press Association *Proceedings* (1899).

Logan, S. Frank. "Francis W. Dawson, 1840–89: South Carolina Editor." M. A. thesis, Duke University, 1947.

Logan, S. Frank. "Francis Warrington Dawson, 1840–1889." South Carolina Historical Association *Proceedings* (1952), pp. 13–28.

Mabry, William A. "Ben Tillman Disfranchised the Negro." *South Atlantic Quarterly*, XXXVII (1938), 170–83.

McGhee, Zach. "Tillman, Smasher of Traditions." *World's Work*, XIII (September 1906), 8013–20.

Neuffer, Irene L. "J. Gordon Coogler: The Bard of the Congaree," *South Carolina History Illustrated*, I (August 1970), 29–32.

Patton, James W. "Republican Party in South Carolina, 1876–1910." In *Essays in Southern History*, edited by Fletcher M. Green. Chapel Hill: University of North Carolina Press, 1947.

Portell Vilá, Herminio. *Narciso López y su Época*. 3 vols. Habana: Cultural, S. A., 1930–1958.

———. *Vidas de la Unidad Americana*. Habana: Editorial Minerva, 1944.

Rice, John A. *I Came Out of the Eighteenth Century*. New York: Harper and Brothers, 1942.

Santovenia, Emeterio S. *Huellas de Gloria: Frases Historicas Cubanas*. 2nd ed. Habana: Editorial Tropico, 1944.

Sass, Herbert Ravenel. *Outspoken: 150 Years of the News and Courier*. Columbia: University of South Carolina Press, 1953.

Simkins, Francis B. *Pitchfork Ben Tillman*. Baton Rouge: Louisiana State University Press, 1944.

———. *Tillman Movement in South Carolina*. Durham: Duke University Press, 1926.

Stark, John D. *Damned Upcountryman: William Watts Ball*. Durham: Duke University Press, 1968.

Tindall, George B. "South Carolina Constitutional Convention of 1895." M. A. thesis, University of North Carolina, 1948.

———. *South Carolina Negroes, 1877–1900*. Columbia: University of South Carolina Press, 1952.

Wallace, David Duncan. *History of South Carolina*. 4 vols. New York: American Historical Society, 1934.

Wauchope, George A. *Writers of South Carolina*. Columbia: The State Company, 1910.

Woodward, Comer Vann. *Origins of the New South, 1877–1913*. Baton Rouge: Louisiana State University Press, 1951.

———. *Strange Career of Jim Crow*. New York: Oxford University Press, 1955.

Woody, Robert W. *Republican Newspapers in South Carolina*. Charlottesville: Historical Publishing Company, 1936.

Work, Monroe N., ed. *Negro Year Book: An Annual Encyclopedia of the Negro* (1925–1926). Tuskeegee Institute, Alabama: Negro Year Book Publishing Company, 1926.

INDEX

post, 135; engages in real estate
business, 137, 149; joins *The
State*, 149; writes features for the
early *State*, 163; depicts Harris
Springs, 171–72; Columbia home
of, 181; personality of, 184–85; as
political reporter, 225–26, 228;
becomes news editor (1901), 271;
serves in militia in Spanish-
American War, 277–78; sends
articles from Cuba for *The State*,
278; gets Theodore Roosevelt to
award sword to Maj. Micah Jenkins, 292; warns N. G. Gonzales
to temper attacks on J. H. Tillman, 296; becomes editor, 309
Grahamville, S.C., 42–44, 139
Gray, J. Walter, 152
Green Pond, S.C., 48–49
Greenville *Enterprise and Moun-*.
taineer, 151
Greenville Mountaineer, 271
Greenville News, 59, 66, 142, 151,
154–55, 194, 203, 206, 236, 259
Greenwood *Index*, 195, 249
Guiteau, Charles J., 79
Gullah: dialect stories of A. E. Gon-
zales, 110–11, 170

Hagood, Johnson, 194
Hamilton, Mrs. C. A., 31–32, 37, 38
Hampton, Frank, 180
Hampton, Wade, 59, 61, 62, 65, 77–
78, 117–18, 132, 165, 199, 206, 208,
214, 281, 290, 299
Harris Springs, 171–72
Haskell, Alexander C., 130, 131,
133, 137, 138, 149, 230
Haskell, John C., 132, 137, 178
Haskellites, 205. *See also* Straight-
outs
Hawaii: *The State* on revolt of
(1893), 257
Hearst newspapers, 273
Hemphill, J. C., 199, 208, 212, 218,
220, 221, 232, 235, 236, 237, 274,
300; serves on *News and Courier*
(early 1880s), 86–87; receives
major post (1884), 94; policy of,

toward Tillman (1888), 122–23;
heads *News and Courier*, 124; relations of, with N. G. Gonzales,
124–25; N. G. Gonzales criticizes
policy of, 133; influence on
Southern Railway by, 156–57; role
of, in Associated Press row, 158;
continues opposition to Tillman,
188
Hemphill, Robert R., 300
Henderson, Sen. D. B., 292–93
Herndon, Va., 37, 40
Heyward, D. C., 233
Hobbes, John F., 72
Hoyt, James A., 129, 151, 233
Hoyt, James A., Jr., 160, 181, 271,
303, 308

Imperialism, 269
In Darkest Cuba, 276
Irby, John L. M., 108, 120, 125, 126,
129, 133, 199–201, 214, 220, 223,
228, 229, 240, 290

Jacksonborough, S.C., 20
Jenkins, Maj. Micah, 291–92
Jeter, H. M., 53
Jim Crow laws, 260
Johnston, David S. S., 37–39, 41
Johnstone, Mrs. Mary Elliott, 28, 29,
55
Jones, Sam, 92–93
Jones, Col. Wylie, 278

Keeley Institute, 170
Key West, 179
Koester, George R., 154, 190, 243
Kohn, August, 125, 134, 146, 147,
151, 159, 188, 199, 207, 219, 245,
300, 301, 304

Labor unions, 252–53
Lancaster, S.C., 128
Lathan, Robert, 246, 271, 284 n
Laurens Advertiser, 146
Laurens County, 104, 108–9
Lee, Robert E., 26
Legare, George, 289

62, 118; launches his movement (1885), 114–15; personal background of, 117–18; conducts campaign of 1890, 125–33; begins his administration, 135; comments on the first *State*, 141; speaks at national Democratic convention (1896), 161; program and accomplishments of first administration of, 187–88; plagued by Gonzales' attacks, 189; seeks a newspaper voice, 190; reacts to attacks of N. G. Gonzales in 1892 campaign, 198; second administration of (1892–94), 199–214; prohibition views of, 201; endorses Dispensary idea, 201; accuses editors of being responsible for "Whiskey Rebellion," 206, 207-8; runs for Senate (1894), 212–13; supports John Gary Evans, 213–16; becomes less harsh toward his political opponents, 229–30; attacks Gonzales and Hemphill, 232; gets into fight with John L. McLaurin, 234–35; relations with Hemphill, 236; personal attitude of, toward Gonzales, 240–41; attitude of, on lynching, 262–64; comments on nephew James H. ("Jim") Tillman, 287–88; indirectly involved in Jim Tillman's snub of Theodore Roosevelt (1902), 292; defended by N. G. Gonzales as not responsible for Jim Tillman, 293; Jim Tillman a disgrace to, according to Gonzales, 294; conduct and attitude of, during trial of J. H. Tillman, 304–5
Tillman, George D., 80, 83, 114, 213, 223, 231, 232, 287, 293–94, 310
Tillman, James ("Jim") H.: sketch of, including pre-1900 background, 287; has first clash with N. G. Gonzales (1890), 288–90; has second clash with N. G. Gonzales (1893), 290–91; criticized by *The State*, 291; elected lieutenant-governor (1900), 291; involved

with incident with Theodore Roosevelt because of earlier snub of his uncle by president, 291–92; accused by N. G. Gonzales of falsifying documents, 292–93; enters 1901 race for governor, 293; blames Gonzales' opposition to him on "anti-Tillmanism," 293; drunkenness and other shortcomings of, reported by many papers, 295–96; blames his defeat on N. G. Gonzales, 297; offers to resign as lieutenant-governor with veiled hint of duel, 297–98; meets Gonzales on street and shoots him, 298–99; summary of attitude of press toward candidacy of, 301–2; in jail, 302; trial of, 303–8; legal counsel (both sides) in trial of, 303; pressure for changing location of trial of, 303; strategy of defense counsel of, 305–7; basic defense, 306; acquittal of, 307; jury probably composed of Tillmanites friendly to, 307
Tillman, Mrs. James H., 299, 299 n
Tillmanism, 1–2, 113; summary of background of, and issues involved in, 114–18, 120; analysis of victory over Bourbonism by, 131–32; unceasingly criticized by Gonzales, 186 *passim*

United Press, 140, 157
University of South Carolina (South Carolina College), 105, 115, 125, 173, 175, 187, 256

Valdosta, Ga., 51–55, 58
Varnville, S.C., 44, 45, *passim*
Violence and lawlessness, 72, 104, 143, 167–68, 204–9, 234–35, 261–65, 281–82

Wagener, F. W., 94
Wagener, John A., 95
Walterboro, S.C., 197
Waring, Thomas R., 301
Washington, D.C.: Gonzales as

Stormy Petrel

Composition, letterpress printing, and binding by Kingsport Press, Inc., Kingsport, Tennessee. The typeface is Linotype Baskerville, and the paper Warren's University Text watermarked with the emblem of the University of South Carolina Press.